THE CHALLENGE OF THE GREEK

THE JERASH HEAD

(*By courtesy of the Liverpool Institute of Archaeology and of* The Times)

The

Challenge of the Greek

and other Essays

BY

T. R. GLOVER

CAMBRIDGE
AT THE UNIVERSITY PRESS
NEW YORK: THE MACMILLAN COMPANY
1942

913.38
B51C

Copyright 1942, *by*
THE MACMILLAN COMPANY

REPRINTED FEBRUARY 1943

23952
Feb. '48

PRINTED IN THE UNITED STATES OF AMERICA

ALMAE MATRI CANADENSI
CENTUM JAM ANNOS FLORENTI
AMICORUM
MEMOR
REGIODUNENSIUM

Ego mente laeta
Regium nomen referamque laudes
Urbis amicae

CONTENTS

PREFACE

MOST of the essays in this book are printed here for the first time, but a few have appeared before. *The Challenge of the Greek* was delivered as a National Lecture in December 1935 under the auspices of the B.B.C., to whom I am indebted for permission to reprint it. I am similarly indebted to the Classical Association for leave to reprint the Presidential Address of 1938 on *Purpose in Classical Studies*. The theme of each of these two papers is, in essence, the same, but the reader will perceive a difference in treatment; the one audience was to consist of classical scholars who, I was told, would not be a majority in the other. They were not, as I found; but it was a pleasure to hear from a Cambridge bus-conductor and a bookbinder of their interest in my "talk". The pages on Virgil appeared in the American *Classical Journal*; the article on Erasmus in *The Times*; and that on Iced Water in *The Cambridge Review*. My thanks are due to all three. Here and there something or other has been relevant to more than one of the subjects treated; but, as this is a book of essays and not a consecutive treatise, it seemed needless to multiply cross-references and simpler to let the fact stand where it seemed wanted. The proofs have been read by Mr R.J. Getty of St John's College and I am grateful to him.

Varro, in his book on Country Life, tells his readers that the approach of his eightieth year hints to him to "truss up his fardels". I am not quite so old yet; but it is forty years since the Cambridge University Press published my first book, which I wrote when I was young *audaxque juventa* in Canada. It is pleasant to have the same imprint on my *extremum hunc Arethusa*.

A last paragraph, but for my friends alone. From time to time of late it has been suggested to me that I should write an autobiography. I have been reluctant to do this; I cannot think the subject of it very interesting; and who wants a story without episode? But I have a confession to make. As I read the proofs of this book, it came to me that the autobiography, without set design or conscious purpose, is written in these pages. Here are the things that have made the life—the great Classics, the great lake and river by which I lived, the Dominion; interwoven are memories of friends and colleagues, outlooks, fancies, impressions, and impulses of deeper birth.

T. R. G.

January 1942

THE CHALLENGE OF THE GREEK[1]

It was perhaps between 600 and 700 B.C. that the Greeks began to have any real acquaintance with Egypt; and it surprised them. The country itself was unlike any other known to man. Eight hundred miles long and some thirty across, it consisted of a river and a delta. It was the strangest river in the world; for every river the Greeks knew would dry up in summer and become a torrent in winter; but the Nile overflowed in summer, and the prosperity of the land depended on its overflowing. Why it should do so the Greeks wondered; they guessed, and guessed again; and it was some centuries before elephant hunters in Abyssinia discovered the true cause in the monsoon rains. The things in the river were not less strange. Lizards in Greece seemed obvious and natural; the lizard of Egypt grew to be a nightmare twenty feet long—a quite impossible creature. The hippopotamus was another surprise; and we still call it by the name the first Greeks gave it—the horse of the river. The people in their way were quite as curious; they did everything the wrong way round. Men did women's work. When they were in mourning they let their hair grow instead of cutting it off. They handled their boats differently. They had caste rules and purification laws of their own; and "no Egyptian would kiss a Greek or use a Greek's knife"—as if the Greeks were unclean in some way, like Europeans in India to-day. Egyptian religion was a thing apart. No people was more religious; none spent more money or labour on temples; and yet—it became a Greek proverb, "Like an Egyptian temple, all splendour outside, and inside a priest singing a hymn to a cat or a crocodile." For the cat was an Egyptian beast, new to the Greeks, and not needed in Europe, for the rat had not yet come from India. A strange land altogether Egypt was—a contradiction and a challenge to all received ideas.

1 The B.B.C. National Lecture, 19 December 1934.

Egyptian Challenge to Greek Instincts

You might say that Egypt and Egyptian life were in a sense upside-down; yet you could not say they were wrong. Everything seemed to fit in with everything else, and some things were done better than in Greece. The Egyptian calendar, for instance, was intelligible; and it was based on real astronomy. Egyptian religion had an immensely long history, and it was impressive, in spite of the worship of animals; perhaps even that meant something mysterious or true; it might. For Egyptians were the first men to teach the immortality of the soul; and the pyramids seemed to say that they believed in it. The pyramids—what other land had anything to show like them, structures immense and ageless, greater than anything man had ever devised? Yes, in the arts, too, Egypt astonished the Greeks. Egyptian civilization had thus reached a very high level; it implied a thought-out life, a philosophy of life; but one thing after another in it contradicted something taken as natural by the Greeks, and challenged Greek instincts. Of course the Greek thought the Greek way of life was right; then the Egyptian must be wrong. But it was right, warranted by history, art, and religion; then opposite ways of life may be right—how can you explain that? Egypt set the Greeks wondering, putting new questions to life, to tradition, and to themselves. "Wonder", said Aristotle, "is the beginning of philosophy."

Mexican Challenge to Europe

So much for prelude. Now let us look at our own story for a moment. About the end of the middle ages two things happened which put a similar challenge to Europe. Columbus found the Americans, and a generation later Cortes found the Mexicans; and the Mexicans had reached a very high stage of civilization. A people still using stone tools achieved surprising effects in art, working upon stone and gold. Their discoveries in astronomy in remote ages were as wonderful— and quite beyond the soldiers of Cortes to understand. Yet these people and the Peruvians knew nothing of Europe; nothing of the Orient which Marco Polo had revealed and which Vasco da Gama was making known anew; nothing of Latin, Greek, or the Christian church; it was a new way of life altogether, and not obviously a bad one. Rather earlier, Europe had discovered ancient Greece with immense surprise and much self-questioning. Here was yet another way of life—poetry beyond anything known in Europe for a thousand years, a great philosophy, amazing triumphs of art, and endless experiment in politics. Every medieval idea, monarchical, political, ecclesiastical, was challenged at once—no Emperor, no Pope, no priests (worth talking about), no nobles, no Turks: but commonwealths of thinkers, artists, and poets. They were free men, those ancient Greeks, men who did their own thinking, governed themselves, uncramped by empire or church; and they achieved intellectual and artistic triumphs, which men felt to be utterly out of reach of medieval Europe, saddled as it was with kings and nobles and priests. And new thoughts rose very naturally; might not that freedom for the human mind be recovered? Some people may not sympathize with these men and their feelings; then let me say "So much the better." You learn more from people who contradict you and challenge your ideas, than from people who echo what you say. "What is the good", asked a great man, "of reading a book, when you agree with all of it?"

Now please understand what I take my task to be here. I have been told to explain why the classical discipline is of value; and, to put it in a sentence, I would say, "Because it offers to us the same challenge that Egypt made to the ancient Greeks, and that the ancient Greeks and new-found Mexicans did to the Renaissance world." The object of my talk is to challenge, and perhaps even to annoy. Do you remember how Socrates said that the Athenian public was rather like a great and noble horse inclined to be lazy and lethargic, and that he himself was a sort of gadfly that came and stung it and made it wake up? If now I undertake his task, I don't forget what befell him. Lord Macaulay, you will remember, said he was not surprised that Socrates was condemned to drink hemlock.

The Limitations of the Greeks

The Greek view of life is a challenge to us in all sorts of ways. We accept one another's ideas to-day, almost without examination; and the Greek held that "the unexamined life is not liveable, for a human being". We live the unexamined life very generally; we go to the cinema, listen to the wireless, believe in peace, slum-clearance, disarmament, all sorts of splendid things, without thinking about them or what they may involve—and the ancient Greek didn't care about any of them. Just look for a moment at the way in which he organized life in outward things—or (if you prefer) didn't organize it—left it alone and took chances, seeming quite unconscious of what we think so all-important. To begin then—he spent next to nothing on paving or cleaning his city; he had no compulsory schools; he neglected the children's teeth; he didn't trouble even to have drains. (A clever man once pointed out the contrast; it was the Roman who was celebrated for his Drains, the Greek for his Brains.) There was no League of Nations, no Geneva; nothing like an Empire; nothing like a united Great Britain, and no Parliament in London. Greece consisted of dozens and dozens of cities which were independent states, with bits of land about them smaller than English counties. Imagine Bristol going to war with Bath in order to annex Keynsham, while Taunton joins in to support Bristol, and Cardiff of course supports Bath and sends a fleet across, if possible, to burn Avonmouth and starve Bristol into surrender. It would not be unlike what you find over and over in Greek history. In the city state itself a large part of the work was done by slaves; most things manufactured were slave-made; the clerks in the bank were slaves (and very clever ones); the housemaid was a woman-slave from Thrace; the very police were state slaves from Russia. A slave, they said, was a tool come to life. There were no official inspectors of factories or of anything else. Private persons, who meddled with such things, were called "sycophants"—the Greek for "nosy Parkers", and not a term of respect. Women had no votes and were expected to stay at home and not meddle. The freemen governed themselves; a mass meeting made the laws; two hundred or five hundred, picked by lot, made the lawcourt, without Mr Justice This or Mr That, K.C. If there was a change of government, it was sometimes much safer for the defeated party to hurry abroad, as in modern times the United Empire Loyalists left their old homes in the "United States", and went to Canada.

What was Valued in Ancient Greece

Think next of the ideas of the Greeks and what a challenge they are to us. Some of the very best of them valued birth; they admired wealth and physical beauty; they despised tradesmen (for niggling, stooping, cheating lives, they said, make men bad citizens); and they thought that Nature perhaps meant barbarians to be slaves. The life of the average Englishman they would have counted uncivilized, half a life. No! Not half a life; a man who lets Parliament and the Town Council, the Trade Union and the policeman, control him at every point—you could not possibly, the Greek would say, call such a fraction of a creature a man. (You wanted, my dear Sir, to hear what the Greek thought of you and me; and I am telling you; he is not complimentary to either of us.) He was not much interested in Heaven—there might be Islands of the Blessed, as the poets said; but for himself he was intensely interested in this world, in Nature and her ways. (Would you call Nature's ways *laws*? You might, he said, by and by.) He was interested in the ways of man, in human life, in the ironies of life, in human suffering, in the triumphs of the human brain, of the human mind, of the human soul. He loved beautiful things, in a way that we English do not. His jar, his cup, his chair, his temple, should be beautiful. His amusements were on a higher plane than ours; he was not "flick-minded"; he preferred Tragedy and Comedy; he knew a good actor from a bad one; a good voice from a bad one; he hated clumsiness and clownishness; he loved grace; and the plays that he preferred to see—well, they remain the foundation of drama and poetry for ever. And in one way and another, however shocked you may be at his limitations, the Greek had great qualities which shaped human life for ever. You can feel, I hope, what a series of contrasts Greece offers to us wonderful moderns. How did the Greeks come to do so much, then? I will suggest four things, or five perhaps, outstanding in Greek life, which I think deserve our reflection.

First, then, the Greek was young-minded. "Ah! Solon, Solon!" said the old Egyptian priest to the Greek visitor, "you Greeks are always children; there is not an old man among you. You are all young in your souls." So they were; they kept the freshness and curiosity of the child which the English public school so successfully eliminates from the nice English boy. They must meddle with things; they can't let them alone; they keep asking questions. "A question?" says one of them, "Why, isn't a question a sort of education?" Of course they are right. If all I can do is to *tell* you a lot of things, you might as well listen to a modern politician or statistician; but if I can rouse you with a question, I have done something; you will do the rest, and you will never be the same again. The wisest professor I ever knew (he was a Scotsman, of course) said that the object of a university education was to break up a man's dogmatism and put him at a universal point of view. That was thoroughly Greek. The Greek in the best days went travelling among foreigners "because he wanted to know"; to know what? To know what they ate, how they governed themselves, what they thought of the gods, the stories they told, the wonders their lands produced. And then, when he knew *what*, he wanted to know *why*. "It is not *what* happens that matters," wrote a Greek historian, "but *why* it happens." If I may coin a new English word to translate a much nicer old Greek word, "wanting-to-know-it-ness" was their characteristic; wonder, as we saw, was the mother of their philosophy. The Greek comic poet made fun of his countrymen for always saying: "Now what do you *mean* by that?" If you say this is essentially like the modern scientific spirit, you will not be far wrong; only it is *not* modern but Greek. A Greek taught that the earth went round the sun—sixteen centuries before Copernicus thought of it. A Greek said that if you sailed out of Spain and stuck to one latitude you would come at last to the Indies—seventeen hundred years before Columbus did it. A Greek was the pioneer in zoology. Darwin once said, "Linnaeus and Cuvier have been my two gods; but they were mere schoolboys compared to old Aristotle."

A Voice—and not an Echo

My next point it takes some courage to put before you. The Greek was a thorough-going individualist. You can see it in the names. I wonder how many John Smiths are listening to me; probably dozens, and there ought to be dozens more, if their mothers had not fancied Michael or Martin; and half the Romans must have been Marcus; and one John Smith and one Marcus is very much like all the rest. There is no typical Greek name; I can only suggest Alcibiades, and there was only one of him, and it was quite enough. The Greek was very much himself; plenty of Greeks were stupid, no doubt; but he was apt to be a voice and not an echo. "What is born in' a man, that is the real thing", says their poet. "Every work belongs to him who found it." That is sheer individualism. A man is born with a brain—thank God! That is the Greek attitude. A brain: and society to-day thinks it progress to treat that brain like a Chinese woman's feet in the bad days—tie it here, bind it there, fetter it, and get it into a conventional shape. Not so the Greek. In his city a craftsman did a whole job—made the whole of a thing, not a minute bit to fit into a thousand other little bits made by a thousand other men; he had to think of the whole thing at once, and to think of the whole thing all the time. That probably gives us the clue to the amazing feeling the Greek had for proportion, balance, symmetry, measure. You remember how Touchstone describes some one as "like an ill-roasted egg, all on one side", and says abruptly that that is the same as being "damned". How much of our modern thinking and doing Touchstone here touches off! The Greek did better, and did it with fewer aids. The closer the study one gives to the history of Greek arts (I use the plural, arts), the more amazed one is at the immense range of discovery, ingenuity, and invention, implied in ancient arts and crafts; no chemistry, no state scholarships; but they went to Nature, and they wrung her secrets from her; and Nature is not apt to vouchsafe ideas to committees. The Greek poet is as intensely individual as the craftsman; he, more than all men, does his own thinking, "sees life steadily and whole", as Matthew Arnold put it. In politics you find the same individualism. The Greek wants as little interference with himself from other states, or his own, as he can manage. He wishes to be "autopolitan", as he calls it—a citizen of *this* city, unmeddled with by the next or by any league; he wishes further to live as he himself, he the individual, pleases, whatever the police or the laws or the philosophers say. "Yes," said Plato, "and when everybody pleases himself, when everybody's mind is a whole bazaar of fancies, impulses, and contradictions; when no two men will pull the same way, nor the same man for two days, it is an end to democracy, and the next thing is the autocrat." Some of us thought that was ancient history. So the Greek was an individual—and he also saw what individualism run wild brings in its train.

Freedom for Individual Development

The Greek believed in the individual, while we believe in committees and government offices. But it is only in the individual that you get enterprise and creation. The Council of War, we read in military history, is always less inspired than the soldier of genius, and more timid, too. Alexander the Great did his own thinking, his own strategy; and there at least Caesar and Napoleon were as Greek as he. The most fruitful legislation in Greece was in Athens, where first Solon and then the "tyrant" Pisistratus untied the hands of the individual, and told him to get to work. Older Greeks, like some modern reformers, would not let a man make his last will and testament as he would wish; so and so must inherit. "Nonsense!" said Solon, "bequeath your goods as you will." He would allow no fixing of the rate of interest. He meant to encourage individual enterprise, and he did. He called to settle in Athens men who wanted to be let alone, to work and live in peace. There they should ply their arts and crafts, pottery, shipbuilding, trading, seafaring—"go to it!" They took him at his word; and in Athens, a state disentangled from traditions of the clan and of the past and not yet enslaved to inspectors and educationists, there came to be the nidus which gave the world its eternal models in art, poetry, letters, history, and philosophy; and when Athens lost her freedom to Bumbles and Emperors, genius died with it.

Why Greek Art Still Lives

For, lastly, I come to two great gifts of the Greeks, not unconnected with those features we have already found in them. We have noted their young-mindedness, the passion to be oneself, and the freedom of enterprise. The two gifts I mean are Interpretation, the eye that "sees life steadily and sees it whole", and Creation. "There is an ancient quarrel", says Plato, "between Philosophy and Poetry"—one works by reason, the other by intuition and emotion. As we look at the great poets and thinkers, Euripides, Shakespeare, Plato, we see that this old battle was fought out anew in the soul of every one of them. A pity for him in whose soul there is no consciousness of this battle! But the Greek knew it well. He knew also of another war, familiar to every great artist—the ancient quarrel between Law and Freedom. Is Art to be ruled by the past, to know nothing but the "oiled and curled Assyrian bull"? Can it be Art, if it knows nothing but an unchartered freedom, the horrid "bazaar" that Plato describes of impulse, freak, and fancy? The Greek understood both law and freedom, loved both poetry and philosophy; and this double capacity gave him the joy and the sense of power, the guidance of Nature's laws and the freedom of the human spirit, that enabled him to create. Socrates speaks of the statues of Daedalus; "What about them?" says his friend. "Wonderfully beautiful," says Socrates, "only they will get down from the pedestal and walk off." That is the glory of Greek art; the thing is alive. The Venus di Milo is as lovely, as womanly, as living, to-day as in the second century B.C., and she makes you believe in women. The *Odyssey* is as good a tale as three thousand years ago, and it makes you believe in men and in life. Plato still stirs the soul, and Socrates still plays at being gadfly to this day. And certain other books there are, of the first century A.D., in which the greatest story of the world is told in mankind's most beautiful language—living to this hour, with a great transforming power. It was the Renaissance of Greek studies that revealed to Europe the beauty of the Gospels, their greatness and their significance in the lives of men.

Now, to conclude. I have not told you the whole story; I have emphasized one phase of it. Egypt was a challenge to the Greeks; Greece was a challenge to Renaissance Europe; and in each case the benefit derived from the challenge was very great. I ask, do we not need some intellectual challenge to-day? Look where you will in Europe or America, and you see a growing standardization. Russia (I speak from a distance) seems intent on producing citizens of a single type; Italy and Germany (we are told) do not encourage the multiplication of independent types. In America, I am informed by a shrewd observer, the object of education is to turn the human mind into a card-index; but perhaps he is something of a satirist. Yet look at our own education: we go to schools of one type; we read newspapers of one type; as for books we read best-sellers or none; we listen to the same gramophone records; go to the same films; and the wireless (if I dare say it) is correcting the peculiarities of our accents. Every fresh government inspector makes his schools, his factories, his drains, or whatever it is, a little more like the standard required by his department. The Roman Empire fell at last, sick unto death and beyond recovery, as we now see, from over-administration. Yes, you rejoin, and Greece fell, too. She did, but not till she had made an imperishable contribution to the human spirit which never dies—no, it does not die, but it gives life to any people who will take it. Chemistry, I suppose, matters enormously to-day, but I cannot see much scope for individuality or character in its teaching; there is no getting away from H_2SO_4; it is the "quantitative thinking" desired by some men of science. But no two teachers ever said or could say the same thing about Aeschylus' play *Agamemnon*, or an ode of Pindar; the poets speak to the man who reads them, or they do not speak at all; Homer makes the reader's heart beat, as geometry never does; the Venus di Milo says nothing, but she makes life beautiful. That is the freedom we need—freedom of mind and heart, freedom to be the men and women God meant us to be, not the lead toys in a box that standardization produces so successfully; and of all disciplines to set the mind free and to set it growing, there is none known to me (nor, I think, known to anybody else) like living with the great souls of Greece.

PURPOSE IN CLASSICAL STUDIES[1]

Do Classical studies hold their own in Britain? When I tell my friends that there are still such and such numbers studying Classics in Cambridge, not so very far (I plead) below the numbers in my youth, a terrible question is put. Are not the numbers in the university greatly larger than in those days— are not the numbers of boys and girls in every conceivable school still larger—and does not that mean that your figure which stands the same (if it *does* stand the same) is really a smaller fraction and proves a decline?

I

The causes? There are all sorts of causes, educational, spiritual, political, economic. I must not fatigue you by discussing things too painful and familiar already, but you may be patient enough to endure a short enumeration by way of reminder.

The study of Natural Science has for three generations been promising a new heaven and a new earth; and the amazing discoveries made in every field of science seem to some people to have redeemed the promise, though aeroplanes do not always mean heaven. Yet scientific study appears to achieve its end by concentrating on some section, some fraction of the knowable, on the part as against the whole; and I wish at once to become controversial by suggesting that a whole view is the real essence of education, and that it is very rarely that Natural Science gives its votaries anything more than a fractional universe, a diminished life. Half-men are hardly to be called educated—"like an ill-roasted egg, all on one side"; you do not educate a man by halving his universe and his mind. To be a man one must "contemplate all time and all existence".

In the next place it is familiar how this change in common education—inevitably, for the sudden demand for Science

[1] The Presidential Address, Classical Association, 1938.

teachers has flooded the schools with people, earnest if strident, many of whom seem never to have given much thought to anything beyond the material world and hardly to realize that there are problems outside the laboratory—this change in curriculum and emphasis, and in the mental habits of teachers, has produced a weakening of spiritual ideals. I do not propose to discuss religion with you, though I hope you will keep it in mind. Failing religion, a great many people have had to cast about for new standards of life; they have lost traditional outlooks; and, when children arrive in the family circle, they are at a loss what to do with them. Hence a great deal of loose and vague theorizing—about teaching them, or leaving them alone to the mercy of impulse and nursemaids and accidents generally—from the American heresy of omitting the alphabet to the sixty-six "essential subjects" of professed "educationists". But "educationists" are a sad lot, living in the grey atmosphere of theory, impressionists (one fears) trying by dint of dogmatism to look scientific. The more you hear of them, the less you will wish to have children. One hardly wonders that the California legislature, perhaps in revolt against this medley of nostrums, some years ago enacted that "American ideals" must be a part of every curriculum—vague enough, but implying a feeling for something constructive and unitive, a realization that citizens were being trained.

Thirdly, education has come into the range of common politics. Regius Professorships remind us that the bearing of education on politics and on parties is no new thing. But years of observation in Canada and America may raise the doubt in any man's mind whether democratic control is good for education. The minister in charge of schools has to reckon with voters; and good practical mothers, a very dangerous class, have votes nowadays; at all costs he must remember the next election. It may be—I think it is—desirable for the young, who will so soon be driving powerful cars, to be brought up with some accurate knowledge about alcohol and its effect on body and mind; but when the minister of education yields to pressure from people of my habit, and orders a "period" a week on Temperance in every school, I feel a doubt whether the gain in sobriety may not be over-balanced by a loss in education. Other people with worse theories may follow our example too successfully. Even if England is not Ontario, still dread of the voter has already influenced educational policy here.

Politics in our day fall more and more under the influence of economic theory; and trade school ideals, cloaked in the decent obscurity of a dead language, find great acceptance as "vocational training". Perhaps England is not as yet so devoted to Domestic Science as America; in a land of no servants, if home is to be domestic, every woman must know, if not how to cook, at least how to put purchased ice-cream on a plate.

Finally, we are all becoming standardized, intimidated more and more by common opinion. The B.B.C. gives us all the same tastes in music, quite obviously the best (I dare hint nothing else), doubtfully in letters, certainly not in humour. The Book of the Month Clubs and other such enterprises carry on the standardization. If we are all reaching higher levels, it is like people in aeroplanes who develop no individual wings. But we grow to be oppressively alike. A new-comer to Cambridge tells me he finds an amazing uniformity among us there. Lord Bryce remarked long ago the great likeness of one American town to another, over hundreds of miles. But is a man educated who only knows the best things because people say so? Ought he not to find them out for himself, to have the gift for finding them? Read Wordsworth's sonnet, about Flamininus proclaiming the Liberty of Greece—

> A gift of that which is not to be given
> By all the blended powers of Earth and Heaven;

and tell me whether it is not relevant. Does not Socrates too say something about virtue unconscious of its reason? And are not individuals rather more interesting than standard products?

But, at this point, I want to pay a tribute to two schools, to neither of which I belong. As I contemplate American education, I realize the immense debt of the British Empire to Eton and Winchester. It was to their standards that the revived and the new Public Schools were graded, and the revived Grammar Schools and Secondary Schools after them. The standards were set high, and the uneducated voter was not asked to fix them. It is a staggering discovery to find how much America pays for education, and how little she really gets for her money. American education to-day appears to be designed for people who will read newspapers and not books. Indeed it is hardly flippant to suggest that the American school seems one of the great grounds of hope for the British Empire. "Education", writes an American historian of President McKinley, "had not closed his mind" —a very ambiguous sentence.

The effect of all these tendencies of three generations is to be seen everywhere in the decline of culture—that is to say in the wild tastes of our day in literature, art and architecture, in the unconsciousness of background (and in art background and some kind of a grandfather are essential), in still wilder theories of education, and in the loss of happiness that is the nemesis of narrowed outlook, distracted taste and loss of belief. If, as some people say, civilization itself is in danger of perishing (whatever that means), I believe the menace to lie not so much in war, as in the thoughts and policies of those who may control our education, who will shape our spiritual ideals. I doubt if war ever ends a civilization, unless there is something very wrong inside that civilization.

II

But, while we look out upon changes in society and new habits of mind, I recall a Latin poet, who suggested that we should look at home and see whether anything was missing in the furniture.

To begin then, is there some lack of distinctness in our conception of the purpose of Classical studies, and of the

work and opportunity of the Classical teacher? Do we
know what we are aiming at? Or might we come under
that criticism levelled by Socrates at virtue unconscious of
its reason and purpose? (I assume virtue in a student of
the Classics.) Or is it possible that, intent upon the means,
we forget the end? and that our pupils, unaware of what
we forget to tell them, assume that the means are all? Very
much as if our colleague of the vocational side spent years
in teaching his students the use of hammer and brace and
saw, yet never suggested any real application of carpentry
to domestic or other purposes, but maintained that to realize
the difference between the tools, and to know how to hold
them, was enough in itself. You will see my direction and
begin to disagree with me, or, at least, like all educated
people, to make reservations. Is it not among the English
the hall-mark of an educated person never to make up his
mind about anything of first importance, but in the meantime to suggest qualification of any affirmative statement?

Taking my life in my hand—and I am fortunately so old
that the risk by now is a small one—I suggest that we have
laid too much emphasis on Grammar. I shall qualify this
later on, and (I hope) regain something of your goodwill.
But I look back to hours of *Amnis axis callis collis*, of *Cum quo
concordat gerundivus*, and so forth, while in French and German
it was the same or worse—"The dative with *entgegen, sammt*"
and lists of French nouns that took -*x* or some equivalent
letter in the plural, with hardly a hint that either language
had a literature.

Later on, at college, we had to pretend to learn something
of Philology, a science perhaps relevant to the study of
Anthropology, but only very remotely related to the study
of literature. So heavy was the emphasis on the linguistic.
It was not for the young to criticize, or to ask what Cicero
or Homer thought of Grimm's Law. The scholars of those
days knew much more grammar than Homer ever knew;
and they saw values in grammar and Philology. They were
real values, perhaps; but, one dares to say now, they obscured

values profounder and more universal. Think how they taught us to hate Virgil—most lovable of poets lost in his own datives!

To this day we are overshadowed by examinations—inevitably, I suppose. They are a medieval invention; but democracy a century ago hailed them as a safeguard against aristocracy and family compacts. India was long to be governed by the Competition Wallah. Perhaps it says something for our race that, notwithstanding, India has been so well governed. At Cambridge we seem to believe more intensely in examinations than Oxford does. We tend to lay the stress on what J. B. Bury called "brute learning", and do not quite understand Oxford's belief in the essay; it is too subjective for us. But neither do we quite understand the passion of Oxford for set books.

But whatever differences there are in our methods, surely it is true that emphasis on examinations leads to the worship of merely secondary matters. The development of our students and the appeal of the Classics are sacrificed to the convenience of examiners. For literature is surely a subject on which it is almost impossible to examine; and an examiner has to examine. He can do it most easily by side-stepping his task, by concentrating on language, grammar, Philology, or on manuscripts and their corruption and transmission. It is what, I understand, men of science would call putting Morphology before Biology. Among ourselves Morphology has of late been acquiring German aliases—*Quellenkritik* and *Formlehre*, and so on. The morphologist, however, has the advantage of handling bones instead of conjectures.

III

At this point you will wish to pull me up; there are things of which you will remind me; and (though you may not think it) I recognize them. First of all, the blunter among you will tell me that this is not a University Extension meeting; the kinder will put it more generally, and politely hint that smattering doesn't educate anybody; that value is lost in literary study if the reader has a habit of inexactness. I agree at once, but would urge in self-defence that the sort of literary and historical study for which I plead is not really easier but more difficult than the things which stir my protest.

That grammar has a signal value as a mere discipline of mind, anyone knows who has stood over his son translating into Latin: "He came to Rome in order that he might surround the head of the boy with a garland." It may, I admit, be the most valuable thing he does at school; for, at least in my experience, the riddles about taps filling baths of such a capacity with an escape of given dimensions do little to equip you for life; they so rarely reveal the 'phone number of the plumber.

Everybody can see that place has to be kept for the discipline and development that must precede advanced study, and for the equipment of people who are to pursue research. I am grateful for having been subjected to that discipline.

Again, it is notorious that British scholarship has rested, since Roger Ascham and his "making of Latins", on ever-rising standards of ease and grace in Greek and Latin composition. All the "reformers" are against us here, particularly where verse is concerned; and, at the risk of being told I have one foot in sea and one on shore, I can only give my experience, my own and that of my pupils, that there is great delight in it, and therefore education. Even so the case is not closed.

All these things are good and praiseworthy—composition, grammar, even Philology, but none of them is the best; they are all means to an end; and often they seem to stand between us and that end.

IV

So I pass on to matters of more significance, and ask once more the fundamental question: Do we conceive aright of our aim and purpose in advocating the study of the Classics, and in presenting them to the young? How do we think of the great literature and of the great history which we have to handle?

Looking back over the years, I recall the inaugural lectures of two famous professors in Cambridge. Three decades ago J. B. Bury came to us from Dublin, and told us with emphasis that History must discard the old companions with whom she had trailed about too long, viz. Literature and Moral Philosophy; History was a science, nothing more and nothing less.

My first comment shall be a story about Lord Acton whom Bury succeeded. Cecil Rhodes, we are told, once met Lord Acton, and asked him bluntly: "Why doesn't Theodore Bent say straight out that those ruins of his in Mashonaland are Phoenician?" "I suppose", said Lord Acton, "that he is not quite sure that they are Phoenician." "Ah!" said Rhodes, "that's not the way Empires are built." You may think this story irrelevant, but it gives me great comfort; it is so dislocated. But it is right; I have had in one land and another some acquaintance with professors, but I have also lived for years in a great Dominion which was not built by professors; and I crave of the historian some sense of how Empires are built. Few studies are more fascinating, if you can get at the heart of the men who build Empires, and watch them at work—fur-traders, diamond-seekers, sailors, farmers and proconsuls; few more tiresome if you don't. But, as a rule, it is not in universities that one looks for interest in Empires—they are too big, too living, too ill-defined; subjunctives and Samnites are more within compass, there are books about them, and they make no heart beat; they are dead enough to admit of dogmatism.

Bury's own book on St Patrick in a way illustrates my point; it is crammed with learning; the author is interested in everything conceivable about Patrick—excepting his character, which he touches off in a paragraph, adding that "subtle analysis might disclose other traits". It is the life of a saint, written by a man who was frankly not interested in saints and did not conceal a certain contempt for their central thoughts. Yet it is precisely because Patrick was a saint, and was a character, that he matters to the historian—matters because the character, so cavalierly treated, touched the imagination of a race. History is made by imagination and emotion, factors very difficult to get into documents; and, unless you have some response in you to imagination and emotion, it will not be History that you write. It is made by the characters of men, which are not amenable to the quantitative methods of science any more than their emotions. Those of you who are interested in a kindred branch of study will perhaps think of another creative figure, whose force and lineaments and significance are obscured by *Quellenkritik*. "In war", said Napoleon, "*men* are nothing; it is a *man* who is everything." Yes, and in other things than war; and the "other traits" are often those that count—so irrelevant and so potent. After Dean Swift's death there was found among his papers an envelope on which he had written: "Only a woman's hair."

I once heard an ex-Minister of State telling how Oxford impressed him on his return to it from a larger world. The character of "Greats", he said, was changed; the interest of students of ancient history was directed to minute research of the German sort, while the larger horizons (if I understood him aright) were of less account; the sense of proportion was lost. It often is lost. One recalls the question raised by a sentence of Thucydides—as to who really ruled Athens in those older days, whether the *prytanies* of the *naukraries* or the nine archons. How much time, too, has been spent by moderns on actions and reactions in Athenian politics in the ten years before Marathon! And how slight the basis there for any conjecture! And then what is to be said of a university course in ancient history which deliberately excluded Alexander and ignored the Hellenistic period? Dr Johnson laid it down that "the spirit of history is contrary to minute exactness". "There are some facts", writes Sir John Squire, "which are worth neglecting"; to which one may add the saying of a brilliant German: "Du sollst Quisquilien als Quisquilien betrachten."

I would go further, and ask this question: Even if we take a rather larger view, and deal with a decade, a war or a reign, can we call it History, if we do not look before and after? Is History (in Aristotle's dreadful phrase) merely "what happened to Alcibiades"? Or ought we, with Polybius, to think less of what happens in our chosen decade and more of what is going to happen—of what, in short, shapes the next age—of the forces and factors, personal and other, that *make* history—saints, emotions, inventions and Empires included?

Some years after J. B. Bury's inaugural we listened to that of A. E. Housman, when he explained his view of his new Cambridge duties. He conceived his function to be to teach Latin, and not to lecture on literature or to train taste. He was very explicit upon this. It is familiar to us all how he laboured to restore the texts of certain Classical poets—*in usum editorum*. The real interest in Housman comes from something else. But why should he, of all men, have limited himself in this way? We may well ask this, we who are faced with a student-world, and a still larger world, which refuses to be interested in the restoration of texts. Of course texts have to be restored—even the texts of Manilius and Lucan; but one thinks of Carlyle's picture of the French Revolution in full swing while we are "perfecting our theory of irregular verbs".

A man of genius may do as he will. But why should we so limit ourselves? why be so tongue-tied about the vital things? May not the young need some training in the art of reading, as the young prospector in the North needs hints from the old as to what to look for, before he goes out to make his own discoveries—a few words, perhaps, on methods of distinguishing iron pyrites from gold? The young seem to love iron pyrites.

Too much of our Classical work is open to the reproach that we sacrifice end to means, and that, in our colleges, forgetful of man and citizen, oblivious of life, we devote ourselves to training specialists, who restore texts and pursue minutiae, and forget to read the great literature.

V

It is a poor literature that is not a better training for a man than the acquisition of the means of reading it. I still hold to Matthew Arnold's view that literature is a criticism of life, an interpretation of life. Of course, like all real definitions, this one, as Pindar would say, "hath voice for them that understand, but for the many an interpreter is needed". For, if life has asked you no questions, you will naturally not think in this way of literature. If there is literature which is not criticism of life, I cannot believe that it could be of value in any real training of the mind, or the making of men and citizens.

If our Classical teaching has no philosophy—I don't mean lists of philosophers' names, dates and dogmas; if it has no general outlook; if it is all minute research, paper-work with books and data, isolated chapters as it were, without realization all along of life lived and life judged by our ancient writers; if it lacks sense of the world; then, I say, the modern theorists are right in their assertion that our work has no great value for a living age. There is such a thing, quite apart from Theology, as gaining the whole world and losing one's own soul. What *can* be the value of Greek history or Greek literature, if we add fact to fact and lose life? There are more ways than one, as St Augustine said, of sacrificing to the angels that fell. You can sacrifice too much to the cyclopaedia. Read the first chapter of Polybius again, with its challenge to us as well as to the Greeks; recall his repeated emphasis that it is not *what* happens that matters so much as *why* it happens. If he is right in saying that Rome's empire was the natural outcome of character and sense, what was that character? I believe more and more that Greek and Roman are the great pioneers in human life, and are worth everything to us if we understand them, and little enough if we don't. Some of you will see that I am almost quoting the added verse which the Codex Bezae gives us in St Luke.

But I will abruptly change my tactics and risk being called a hedonist, or belletristic, or worse names, and ask you a different sort of question. If you don't *enjoy* literature, is it any good? The soul, wrote Longinus, takes wings at the sight of the "sublime"—he means the real thing—and soars aloft in glad exultation, as happy as if it had itself created what it has read. Is this the common effect of Classical education? If it is not, why study the Classics? Oh! I know —discipline and so on, information and so forth. What was it Aristophanes used to say? *Babaiax!*

Aristophanes, since I have mentioned him, though in some quarters treated as a historian and an authority on Greek dialect, was a comic poet and a wit. He seems also to have had a sense of humour and to have been able to laugh at himself and his heroes and his ideas. In a spirit of burlesque he makes Aeschylus himself propound the conventional view that poets are teachers—and teachers of such subjects!—

And gat not Homer his glory divine
By singing of valour and honour and right, and the sheen of
    the battle-extended line,
The ranging of troops and the arming of men?

When I suggest that the great value of the Classics is their contribution to the making of men and citizens, it is not in the spirit which Aristophanes is laughing at; Homer has more than an O.T.C. value. Nor do I do it in Plutarch's vein, with promise of useful maxims and moral lessons, analogies and parallels. The suggestion of Horace takes us to a higher plane; he finds Homer's poem

Better than all the logic of the sage,
Than Crantor's precepts or Chrysippus' page.

Horace comes nearer to the true account; what he says here squares with his general outlook; right and wrong are learnt, as he learnt them, from life; and Homer is life. It is life that really teaches us; and it does not consist of minutiae, dates, various readings, grammatical rules and Grimm's Law. If you want an answer to the question of Pindar and the psalmist "What is man?" the dissecting room will never give you the real answer; Homer will do it better. The father of Niceratus had a sound instinct; the boy would be all right, if he once got Homer into him; and, if you doubt it, there is Alexander the Great to prove it. But, as W. P. Ker said about Chaucer, you will only know Homer by knowing the whole of him; and a great deal of him is not in print, but only comes to you when you have shut the book. A ha'p'orth of Homer is not Homer. Then, if the Classics are a discipline for life, what has Homer to say about life? Nothing very much; he leaves that to Plutarch and King Solomon. He doesn't talk about life; he shows you life, takes you into the thick of it, makes you believe in it, makes you live it. Remember what Fra Lippo in Browning says of painting.

Here let me quote favourite passages from two men to whom I owe much. "Always", writes A. C. Bradley, "we get most from the *genius* in a man of genius and not from the rest of him." And Thomas Carlyle (on Novalis)—"the most profitable employment any book can give them is to study honestly some earnest, deep-minded, truth-loving Man, to work their way into his manner of thought, till they see the world with his eyes, feel as he felt and judge as he judged, neither believing nor denying, till they can in some measure so feel and judge".

The curious thing is that some readers, with very slight hold upon grammar—or with none, like John Keats—can achieve this, while the grammarian very often comes, in Plato's phrase, to the doors of the Muses and goes away empty, though, by a kind dispensation of Providence, he doesn't know he is empty. What I urge is that those of us who are teachers have more to do than to construe and to teach grammar. We have to be inspired and to believe in life; and then our authors will be alive and will themselves start talking to our students; and when a man is on such terms with Homer and Virgil, his education is indeed begun and is not likely to end. It is the man that matters; Carlyle is right.

Let me go back forty years and more. When Sir Richard Jebb returned from Glasgow to Cambridge as Regius Professor of Greek in 1889, we were all sent to his lectures; and his theme was Sophocles—no, it wasn't; it was a play of Sophocles. He gave us a skeleton analysis of the different plots that the dramatists constructed out of the theme; and then he fell to translating and commenting, line by line, almost word by word. I never forgot the criticism made at the time by H. D. Darbishire, shrewdest of B.A.'s, and afterwards Fellow of my College, too early lost; the ideal of college lecturing he called it, but not quite what a professor should do. Years later I knew intimately a very able Scot, who had gone to those lectures of Jebb's in Glasgow for a whole session, and at the end (though no doubt he had learnt some Greek) he said he felt he had gained no clear idea of Sophocles. Another colleague, a brilliant Highlander, said roundly that this was due to stupidity. Perhaps; but it was my experience too. To this day most people who talk about Sophocles seem to me to think he was a book.

One is tempted sometimes to say that Classical scholars prefer language to literature, that they hardly care for literature. But let me speak of one lecture on Euripides' *Trojan Women*, given many years ago in Cambridge by Gilbert Murray—an experience I can never forget, and an illumination I never lose; and of many lectures to which I have listened from the Provost of King's, who seems unable to speak of Homer without making you feel that Homer is a man and a poet, and that Homer handles real life with a deep sense of what life is.

Perhaps the trouble with Jebb was that he was afraid of giving himself away, of betraying real feeling; Cambridge men often are. So he never did give himself away, never challenged his class to face anything big, and never faced the class himself, but looked at us only out of the corners of his eyes. I have heard he did the same in Parliament. But you

will never win disciples if you only look at them sideways.
This is not to deny a real value to Jebb's work, but you and
I are living in another world, where the supreme value of
the Classics is not taken for granted, and we have to give a
reason for our faith.

One constant feature of real life is reaction to background,
to conditions we cannot change, to the ideas of those around
us, and of those who went before us. So we have a large
field of work, if we are to place the men we study in the world
that they knew. An earlier generation read more widely than
we in general dare suggest; and they realized (and were
happy in realizing) how human are Xenophon, and Plutarch,
and Arrian, and what a world of interest—"God's plenty"—
they give you. They went further afield still, some of them,
and explored Strabo and Pausanias. Who has time nowadays
for all that? The answer is: *We* have, if we dare take the time.

Let me digress: Do you ever, now you are grown up, read
Robinson Crusoe? The *Odyssey*, of course, has been called "*die
älteste Robinsonade*"; and the books have this in common: you
always realize the situation of the hero, Odysseus or Crusoe,
and see what he is grappling with, his practical problem and
how he handles it;—and it fascinates. Our Greeks then lived
in and about the Aegaean and neighbouring seas—seas with
winds and currents, headlands, islands, and strange varieties
of soil and climate. Can we, like Defoe and Homer, help our
students to live that life over again, and to realize at least
some of the problems which men who wish to live find in
such things as food, mines, forest, winter, ship-building,
road-making, and so forth? Are not all these as significant
to human life as the subjunctive? Real men, at any rate, think
more about them. But there are problems more universal
than the currents and winds of the Aegaean and the influence
of forests, fascinating as these are.

I quoted Pindar just now. In my youth I had to struggle
to translate him; in my old age I have to struggle to make
others translate him. Sometimes when the passage is more
or less translated, I ask them what it all means, what it is

about, why a man speaks in that way, what thought or what experience is in his mind behind the words. And, like my pupils, I find that, hard as it is to translate a strophe, it is easier than to interpret Pindar himself. But, since I realized that Pindar is to be interpreted, and that he has something to say to me about life and the things that matter—beauty of youth, colour of the world, high renown and *lacrimae rerum*—how much he has added to my outlook—now and then, as Carlyle put it, "operating changes in my ways of thought"! I won't tell you what I think about him, or what he tells me; I will only say that, since we took to consorting, I find him to be a great poet, in the high sense of the word poet.

"Creatures of a day! what are we, and what not? A dream of a shadow is man." Is that his last word? I turn to another great poet who occupied my youth.

"Dust and ashes!" So you creak it, and I want the heart to
    scold.
Dear dead women, with such hair, too—what's become of all
    the gold
Used to hang and brush their bosoms?

No, they are not gone; nor has Jason ceased to stand in the market-place, making trial of his high-hearted youth; and I like to watch him; life means more when one does. The flowers still drench the tender body of Iamos with their colours, Greece is still alive—and her athletes, as Pindar said they would be; and her legends sometimes hint high things beyond the range of chemists and grammarians. "Nevertheless, when a glory from God hath shined upon them, a clear light abideth upon men, and life serene."

I wonder how many of you talked with James Adam about Plato, or (better still) let him talk to you about Plato. Here is what he once wrote to me: "I am now deep in Plato. Of course he knocks all the others into cocked hats: there is no one like him, none. It is tremendous how he searches the depths of one's whole being. You really must devote a year or two to the exclusive study of his works if you mean to do

anything useful for the interpretation of religious thought."
It is the same conception—it is the man that matters, a man
with a character framed of imponderables, "other traits",
divine elements, who has lived and interprets life, and gives
us life. Plato, Pindar, Homer—the *man* is far more even than
the best he gives us.

I have talked long enough; and, if I have so far failed
to make my drift clear, let me try again, doing it this
time without qualification, bluntly, roughly, controversially.
I suggest then that the Classics have been losing their place
in education because we have forgotten the real aim and
purpose of Classical study, and the real significance of the
Classics; because we have tried to be efficient and precise
and scientific, and like those who have such ambitions have
counted the part above the whole; because we have found
our centre in details, side-issues, intricacies; because we have
believed in examinations and lived for them; because we have
forgotten that we are training men and citizens; because we
have not believed enough in the Classics, nor loved them
enough, nor been made over by them. No literature can
defend itself, if you stop people reading it; it can only defend
itself as literature. History is nothing, if you study it without
Plato's contemplation of all time and all existence. The
Classics will live if we let people get at them in earnest. As
with all great causes, the advocates of this cause must be
converts, not traditionalists, they must have got at the heart
of the matter, they must know life and realize its questions.

THE GREEK AND THE FOREST

I

IT is difficult for a modern Englishman to realize very readily how large a part the forest once had in the life of man compared with what it has to-day. It is more than two centuries since John Evelyn wrote his *Sylva* to warn his countrymen what the loss of the forests would involve; and in the eighteenth century England (so the historians tell us) found his warning true. But everything is changed to-day; coal or its products have replaced wood in the kitchen, the parlour and the factory. Ships are built of steel and are driven by steam generated by oil furnaces. Population has covered England; the forests have disappeared; copses remain and shade-trees in park and street; wood for doors and window-frames and flooring is imported, but not altogether from its old sources. When I was young and lived on the shore of Lake Ontario, rafts of immense size, 120 feet broad and 1000 to 1400 feet long, were built at an island that faced our city—rafts that covered a bigger spread of water than the *Queen Mary*—to go down the St Lawrence to Quebec, where the timber was taken aboard ships for Britain. It had been collected over an almost incredible range of country, to be gathered at the raft-building station; and it is happy for Britain that steel, coal and oil are available as the forest fails in the New World as it did in this island. The newspaper, as we shall see, is a danger to what woodlands are left. No doubt there is forest still in the New World, but it owes its safety to its inaccessibility, its distance from waterways.

The Greek scene of to-day is not that of ancient times. Already Plato speaks of deforestation. As our ship skirts the coasts and threads its way among the Greek islands, it is bare rocks and gaunt hillsides that we chiefly notice. The magic line of Virgil that haunted R. L. Stevenson through life[1] and

1 Sidney Colvin, *Memories and Notes*, p. 138.

was, one might say, a sort of *sors Vergiliana* forecasting Samoa, speaks of a distant past—

Jam medio apparet fluctu nemorosa Zacynthus.[1]

Henry Holland, in 1815, says Zante is no longer *nemorosa* save for olives and other fruit trees.[2] The woods of Olympus were being felled in 1869 for a contract of £330 a year.[3] Places once named from trees may keep their names, but the trees are gone.[4] Other trees, chiefly fruit trees, have been introduced from other lands—the peach from Persia after Alexander's conquest, the cherry after the campaigns of Lucullus,[5] apricot, date-palm and pomegranate; and in more modern times oranges and lemons in many a place, grape fruit on Naxos.[6] Cotton is a gift from India if mediated from Egypt; and from the New World the lowlier but delectable tomato and tobacco (where would the Régie be but for it?) have been introduced; maize too, whose stalks serve as fuel. From the Antipodes the eucalyptus has been brought. It is a story like our own; quite apart from fruit trees, the larch is an eighteenth-century addition to the English scene. Spruce is an immigrant, and some assure us that we owe the elm to the Romans. One recalls the tradition of a queer half-insane philanthropist in Ohio a century and a half ago, whose mission was to scatter apple-seeds (from cider mills in the Atlantic states) on beaver meadows or any likely spot he saw as he travelled year by year on his raft down the Ohio river. He earned a name that deserves its place in New World history, Johnny Appleseed.

Ancient Greece must have been like early Eastern Canada in being very largely forest-clad, but unlike Canada for it is a land of slight streams though of many springs. The roads were mere trails through the woodland. The climate was not that of Canada, and the forest would seem never to have been

1 Virgil, *Aeneid*, iii, 270.   2 H. Holland, *Ionian Isles* (1815), p. 17.
3 H. F. Tozer, *Highlands of Turkey*, ii, 8–11.
4 H. F. Tozer, *ib.* ii, 107–8.
5 Peach, Pliny, *N.H.* xv, 45; cherry, *ib.* xv, 102.
6 J. T. Bent, *Cyclades*, p. 306.

as dense as that of Canada or of Germany, and therefore to
have been easier for early man to deal with—in fact, too easy
a prey for axe and fire.[1] But we have pictures in some of our
writers of what the ancient forest was. Polybius dilates on
the huge herds of swine that fattened on the acorns of the
great oak forests of the Po region, and their responsiveness
to the horn of the swineherd, and, as a sort of consequence,
the cheap rate of living in the inns of that countryside, where
the traveller paid so much a day, "on the American plan".[2]
Pliny emphasizes the delight that the swine offers—fifty
different *sapores*, while other creatures can only provide one
each;[3] and we recall the sign of the very fertile sow that meets
Aeneas at the Tiber mouth, though there seems to be a doubt
whether he and his men ate it, as an antiquary speaks of the
carcase being preserved in brine and exhibited by the priests,
apparently at Alba.[4] Theophrastus confirms Virgil as to the
forests of early Latium.[5] Pausanias, in the second century A.D.,
tells us of the famous oak woods of Arcadia, the home of
bear and boar;[6] and Sir William Gell, a caustic traveller,
opines that the Muses of Yorkshire might delight in the
scenery.[7] Strabo tells of oak forests lining the Spanish shore
and the tunnies gathering to feed on the acorns that fall into
the water.[8] The ancients were aware of the fact, which
modern anthropologists confirm, that primitive man himself
lived a good deal on acorns, supplemented (being a con-
stipative food) by arbutus and mulberry.[9] Herodotus (i, 66)
gives us the epithet "acorn-eating" as applied to the
Arcadians. "Man", says White of Selborne, "in his true
state of nature, seems to be subsisted by spontaneous
vegetation."

1 Cf. M. R. Shackleton, *Europe, a regional survey*, p. 43; and M. I. New-
biggin, *Balkans*, p. 153.
2 Polybius, xii, 4.   3 Pliny, *N.H.* viii, 77.
4 Varro, *de Re Rustica*, ii, 4, 18.   5 Theophrastus, *Plants*, v, 8.
6 Pausanias, viii, 11, 1–5; 23, 9.
7 Sir W. Gell, *Journey in the Morea* (1823), p. 126.
8 Strabo, iii, C. 145.
9 Varro, *de Re Rustica*, ii, 1, 4. Cf. Lucretius, v, 939.

II

It was not primitive man, but man as he began to be civilized, that was the enemy of the forest; it was inevitable. Progress in the arts demanded wood; agriculture required open land; food became a more and more clamant need which the forest could not meet; wild life has not been so plentiful in the forest as outside it. South Africa was not a land of forests, but it abounded with wild animals, as the treeless prairies of North America did with buffalo. The earliest men, of whom we have knowledge, kept in the main out of the forest; the open was perhaps less dangerous or suggested fewer supernatural terrors; and better game was to be found on the plains. It can be urged too that primitive man had not the tools to deal with the forest; but the evidence of New Zealand raises a doubt; the Maori with stone tools felled the forest and did amazing wood-carving, as the Maya of Central America, also without metal tools, carved stone with wonderful skill and intricate designs. But races differ in their rate of progress and decline. The edges of the forest, however, soon revealed their value. Agriculture does better in a forest area, the humus is helpful, the water supply is better (as a beautiful passage of Lucretius suggests—v, 948, the rivulets from the haunts of the nymphs), and of course the trees would not be growing there, if there were not virtue of some sort in the soil. It has been the way in various countries and at various times to fell the forest and burn over the fallen trees for agricultural purposes; it yields a rich field for a season or two, but it is essentially wasteful in its destruction of the humus. The Greeks pastured their domestic animals in the forest—disastrously, as we shall see. But in any case agriculture meant the attack on the forest. When French Canada was first settled, land grants were made conditionally on the clearing of the forest; the land would be forfeited if not cleared; and cleared it has been, too efficiently, but in those early days the oaks were reserved for the French king's navy.[1]

> Nor is that soil inept, whence husbandmen
> Have, all impatient, cleared the trees, and hewed
> The longtime cumbering groves, and, root and branch,
> Despoiled the ancient homestead of the birds,
> Who from their nests forlorn speed to high heaven,
> What time the field, once their's and nature's, gleams
> Burnished by ardent shares.

So Lord Burghclere renders a passage in Virgil's *Georgics* (ii, 207 f.), on which, in passing, it may be permitted to remark that the poet's father was, amongst other things, what Canada calls a lumberman; he made money by acquiring forest limits and felling the trees in that Po region which Polybius described, where to-day maize and not timber is the crop; and it is hardly digression to note the future poet watching the process, with a sympathetic eye for the birds. As a later poet wrote: "the blackbird is fled to another retreat". In our own country there was another reason for felling the forest, to which I do not find an allusion in antiquity, though doubtless it did not escape attention. In Scotland, we read, the forest was the refuge of "caterans"[2]—"he needs must walk in wood that may not walk in town" is quoted by Mr H. S. Bennett in dealing with the Pastons' England;[3] Robin Hood is associated with Sherwood Forest; Henry Holland has the same story about the extensive forests on the mountains near Janina—"they were destroyed as being the resort of bands of robbers who infested the tranquillity of the city".[4]

Homer, who cannot have been as blind as legend says—at least not always as blind—(and even the colour-blindness, which some moderns thought they detected in him, is given up)—Homer turned an interested eye and ear to the work of the forest. Sarpedon, most sympathetic of heroes, falls suddenly, "falls as an oak, or a silver poplar, or a slim pine

1 Wilfrid Bovey, *Canadien*, pp. 66, 68.
2 Ritchie, *Animal Life in Scotland*, p. 318.
3 H. S. Bennett, *The Pastons*, p. 139.   4 H. Holland, *Ionian Isles*, p. 131.

tree, that on the hills the shipwrights fell with whetted axes, to be timber for shipbuilding" (*Iliad*, xvi, 482). He uses the same simile at the fall of Asios (xiii, 389). Yet another hero falls "like an ash that on the crest of a far-seen hill is smitten with the axe of bronze, and brings its delicate foliage to the ground" (xiii, 180). When the pyre is being built for the burning of Patroclus, we are told once again that the trees are felled with a bronze axe—"with long-edged bronze" (xxiii, 118), and are reminded of the crashing of the trees as they fall. Elsewhere the noise of the axes plied by the wood-cutters is suggested by the din of battle (xvi, 633). But perhaps his most revealing simile is that of the mules, "that throw their great strength into the draught, and drag out of the mountain down a rugged track some beam or huge ship-timber, and their hearts are spent with toil and sweat" (xvii, 742). That work in British Columbia was done by a donkey engine; and there also it was on a mountain side. Homer does not tell us what Mr M. A. Grainger does in his *Woodsmen of the West*, that the huge ship-timber has to be stripped of branch, twig and bark before it starts on this rough course down the hillside; but at a later point we may conclude more decisively that he knew more about lumbering than some of his commentators and translators, that he had seen it and knew what it meant and involved.

III

So the long war of civilization against the forest had begun, a truceless war. There was little sentiment among primitive man and practical colonist, as little perhaps as the speculative builder of to-day feels for the trees. In the new country the tree is almost a weed; fields and roads have to be made, and fuel is a constant necessity. As with Lausus in the *Aeneid*, it is not till the enemy has fallen that pity for him is apt to begin. Three quarters of the forests of New Zealand were destroyed in seventy-five years by the British settlers;[1] and Canada and

---

1 Cf. Pember Reeves, *Ao Tea Roa*, one of the most attractive books yet written on any British dominion.

the States have a similar tale to tell—no leisure for *Wald-zauber* in a battle for food. The Greek again was very little of a hunter, though Polybius, an Arcadian from a land of forest and wild animals, hunted in Italy with the Seleucid prince Demetrius;[1] the Macedonian hunted, which, Mahaffy suggested, might be a contributory cause to his victory over a nation of athletes. Yet the poets show, as one might expect, a sensitiveness to the beauty of woodland which the lumberman did not know. The poet-son in North Italy, for instance:

> *Juvat arva videre*
> *Non rastris, hominum non ulli obnoxia curae.*[2]

Gardens are described by Homer, the gardens of Alcinous and Laertes, gardens of fruit trees;[3] and the god pauses to note wild trees, haunted by birds, about the cave dwelling of Calypso, alder and poplar and cypress[4]—the last perhaps an immigrant tree, a favourite with the Turks, the poplar introduced (Pausanias tells us, in his matter-of-fact way) by Herakles.[5] Pindar informs us that Olympia was barren of trees till Herakles went North of the Danube, saw and was fain to plant them in the ground that was to be famous.[6] Theophrastus[7] tells us about the North country that the silver fir of Macedon is best, and that generally the wild wood of the mountains is more abundant and more beautiful in the northerly regions than in those towards the South. So Euripides found, if we may judge from the lines in the *Bacchae*, written (we are told) in Macedon:

> In the elm wood and the oaken
>   There where Orpheus harped of old.
> And the trees awoke and knew him,
> And the wild things gathered to him,
> As he sang amid the broken
>   Glens his music manifold—
> Blessed land of Pierie![8]

---

1 Polybius, xxxi, 22.   2 Virgil, *Georgics*, ii, 438.
3 Mr Pickard-Cambridge suggests that the Homeric epithets applied to trees show feeling.   4 Homer, *Odyssey*, v, 63.   5 Pausanias, v, 77.
6 Pindar, *Olympian*, 3, 25 ff.   7 Theophrastus, *Plants*, i, 9, 2.
8 Euripides, *Bacchae*, 560 f. (version of Gilbert Murray).

We may believe him, though Strabo long after hints that poets touch things up, "and call all sacred places *groves*, even if they are bare".[1] Later still, the elder Pliny notes that the ancient sanctuaries were in simple country places, where to his day they count any notable tree the property of a god; and he thinks this right; the groves are better than images of gold and ivory, "and in them we worship the very silence itself".[2]

Ancient Greece and modern Greece alike associate big trees with the nymphs.[3] Modern travellers, Lord Rennell, Theodore Bent, J. C. Lawson, have much to say of the survival of ancient beliefs about trees. But we can go further back for a pleasant picture in the Homeric *Hymn to Aphrodite*— a poem of a later day than Homer; and if we put beside it a passage from the poet Hesiod, who may be two centuries later than Homer, we shall have a contrast of outlook in poets perhaps nearly contemporary, which may suggest much. Here then is what we read in the *Hymn*:

The deep-breasted mountain Nymphs that dwell on this great and holy mountain [Ida] shall nourish him [viz. Aeneas, the child that Aphrodite is to bear to Anchises]. They rank neither with mortals nor with immortals; long indeed do they live, and eat immortal food, and tread the lovely dance with the immortals. With them the Seilenoi and the quick-eyed slayer of Argos [Hermes] mate in love, deep in the pleasant caves. At their birth pines or high-towering oaks spring up with them upon the fruitful earth; beautiful and flourishing trees on the high mountains they stand, sun-trodden; and men call them the holy places of the immortals. These trees no mortal fells with iron; but when the fate of death is near, first the fair trees wither upon the earth, the bark shrivels away about them, the twigs fall from them; and at last the soul of the tree and the soul of the nymph leave the light of the sun together.[4]

And now Hesiod, who also had dealings with nymphs, for they set him singing, but he is here severely practical; and

---

1 Strabo, ix, C. 412.   2 Pliny, *N.H.* xii, 3.
3 Cf. p. 114.   4 Homeric *Hymn to Aphrodite*, 256 ff.

it will be noted that he, like the poet of the *Hymn* and unlike Homer, thinks of an iron axe:

When the mighty Sun abates his heat, when Zeus sends the autumn rains, and men's flesh comes to feel lighter... then the wood you cut with iron suffers least from worm; then remember to hew your timber—work that fits the season.[1]

It is a different outlook; he is thinking of the sap ceasing to run, perhaps; and other hints are given us in similar vein. Athenaeus (vii, 276e) tells us, for instance, that timber cut by moonlight rots more easily. Pliny reports the suggestion that trees and plants, felled or reaped, are better so dealt with when the moon is waning.[2]

IV

We have now to attempt a brief survey of the uses to which the Greeks put the timber when they felled it. First comes the house, as we saw when we watched the mules struggling downhill with the lumber; in more modern times the work has been done by oxen, and, says Mr Tozer,[3] considering how narrow and winding the mountain paths are, the process can be no easy one. Theophrastus tells us that of trees the silver fir is more generally useful for all purposes, especially for ships and house-building, but many woods are used for houses; any, in fact, that is strong enough.[4] Till a century ago the wooden house was to be seen in Asia Minor; Fellows[5] has a story of a Turkish governor forbidding some owners to build a house of stone, after two considerable fires, on the ground that it would mean loss to forest-owners and to builders. (Little thought has been given to the profits of

---

1 *Works and Days*, 415.
2 Pliny, *N.H.* xviii, 321. Cf. J. G. Frazer, *Adonis, Attis and Osiris*, p. 298f., who gives a number of ancient references, p. 301. Modern men of science are not impressed by these suggestions, for they are scarcely more.
3 H. F. Tozer, *Islands of Aegean*, p. 304.
4 Theophrastus, *Plants*, v, 7, 4; and iv, 1, 2. Cf. Vitruvius, ii, 9, on building timbers generally, with an interesting section at the end on larch.
5 C. Fellows, *Asia Minor* (1839), p. 77.

British builders from successful German air-raids; the Turk was perhaps more considerate.)

Reserving ships, an obvious use for timber, till a later point, we pass to tools, and especially farm tools and appliances. Here Hesiod has guidance for us;[1] of course, the plough is to be wooden, of holm oak preferably; and I learn from a modern expert that on clay land, when wet, the wooden plough is still used, as the soil there slips off wood and sticks to steel. So that the wooden plough is not always and necessarily a sign of unprogressive farming. Then there is the waggon, about which Hesiod says bluntly that there is a foolish or innocent type of person who does not know that it takes a hundred pieces of wood to make a waggon. We meet the waggon-builder in the *Iliad*,[2] who for some reason has an iron axe (αἴθωνι σιδήρῳ), the date of which I must leave others to conjecture. When Odysseus built his raft on Calypso's island, his tool was brass.[3] We hear a little about indoor furniture; a springy bedstead would be of ash or beech (μελία and ὀξύη),[4] and we are told that modern man uses ash in his aeroplane. Of casks I cannot speak; probably it was always a clay jar that was used.

We come next to charcoal manufacture, in ancient and modern times alike a most important and wasteful industry. England,[5] Scotland,[6] Southern France, the Po Valley,[7] have seen their forests disappear, and, despite the modern use of coal, half the timber felled in Poland to-day is used for fuel.[8] Much will be found on the subject in Mr T. A. Rickard's most interesting volumes, *Man and Metals*, and notably comment on the inevitable conflict between those for whom

1 Hesiod, *Works and Days*, 422, plough; 456, waggon.
2 *Iliad*, iv, 485.   3 *Odyssey*, v, 234f.
4 Theophrastus, *Plants*, v, 6, 4.
5 G. M. Trevelyan, *History of England*, p. 528, on the fuel famine of eighteenth-century England, the danger to the iron industry, and domestic discomfort.
6 Tansley, *The British Islands and their Vegetation*, p. 188f., on the destruction of Highland forests, repaired in measure by the planting of millions of trees in the eighteenth century. Cf. H. G. Graham, *Social Life in Scotland*, i, 218.
7 Deecke, *Italy* (tr.), pp. 187–9, on charcoal burners of Italy.
8 Dyboski, *Poland*, p. 208.

charcoal comes first and those concerned with the ship-building industry. Bricks were generally sun-dried (ὦμαί) and not burnt (ὀπταί); and salt-making perhaps generally, especially in Illyria, depended on the sun.[1] There was, it would seem, some lignite in Elis and in Liguria, but the main fuel of antiquity was charcoal; and how seriously the industry took itself, we read in Aristophanes' *Acharnians*—"I shall know pretty quickly which of you has charcoal at heart", and we recall how the kidnapping of a basket of charcoal secures a truce. The modern expert points out the wastefulness of the ancient method resulting in the loss of all by-products, creosote, wood-alcohol, acetic acid.[2] Mining and metallurgy obviously were dependent on the forest. Theophrastus tells us that the best charcoal comes from the hardest wood, oak, holm oak, arbutus; so it is used by the silver miners for the first smelting; the ordinary smith may use a poor charcoal useless for other work, but he prefers charcoal of fir even to oak.[3] A fan or bellows was needed when charcoal was used; hence the point of the oracle that gave his clue to Lichas, "where two winds blow from stout necessity", and he guessed he had come to the right place in the forge.[4] Strabo (C. 303) even preserves the name of the alleged inventor of bellows—Anacharsis.

As in modern Greece, little if anything was expended on charcoal to heat the house; the climate as a rule saves the Greek that item of expense. But of course cookery largely depended on charcoal. A portable little stove and a fan were needed; and one wonders how far, as in the English house with the coal fire and open grate, waste balanced use. Probably the Englishwoman, with her sad climate and her fancy for a blazing fire, is the more wasteful. But coal or charcoal, either, as we saw, means loss of by-products. For baking bread, the field oven was used, as till recent times in Cambridgeshire, and in France in the 1914 war; it was, and

1 Strabo, C. 317.
2 C. R. Van Hise, *Conservation of Natural Resources in U.S.A.*, p. 233.
3 Theophrastus, *Plants*, v, 8, 9; and iii, 8, 7.
4 Herodotus, i, 67.

is to-day in Greece, heated with brushwood, which again involved waste, as we shall see.

Other industries depended on the forest. Tanning required galls and valonia—the latter a considerable industry to-day (or yesterday), for the vast oak park of the Troad and other regions in Asia Minor and the islands supplied Britain, at any rate, with some part of its requirements.[1] But the demand for resin was more ruinous. The oak sheds its valonia itself; the pine trees were gashed by man for the resin. Theophrastus held that it did not hurt the tree; Sir Thomas Wyse speaks of a half mile of trees, pine and fir, gashed and killed in reckless waste, the tree sacrificed for eight drachmas worth of resin. Incidentally a modern parallel—the French explorer in North America used the Indian canoe, a light structure of birch-bark for which resin was essential; and when he left the region of pine and birch, he was in difficulties, as in early days in the lower reaches of the Mississippi. Picturesque as Spanish moss is, it will not make a canoe. One modern industry was not there in the ancient world; there was no wholesale destruction of trees to produce cheap newspapers. It would be an interesting study to consider how far the lack of news-print and a steam-driven printing press, by limiting output and securing reflexion and relevance, determined the superiority of Greek style to English and American.

V

So far, in outline, the uses of the forest; it remains to look at the abuse of it. A first question might be as to the ownership of the forest in one and another of the many small states that made Greece. What the largest number share, the fewest care for; is a suggestion of Aristotle's. If the forest was the property of the state, as it would seem *a priori* likely, and as the appointment of "wood-wardens" ($\dot{v}\lambda\omega\rho o\acute{\iota}$) seems to

---

1 See J. I. Manatt, *Aegean Days*, pp. 256, 236, 245; H. F. Tozer, *Turkey*, i, p. 9 and Sir W. Gell, *Morea*, p. 222. Theophrastus, *Plants*, iii, 8, 6, galls. I have sailed on a tramp steamer from Smyrna, part of whose cargo was valonia.

imply, it would surprise no one that private persons used and abused, when wish and chance availed, what was common property. In modern Greece, a united kingdom as it is, protection of forest has been inadequate, as the passage quoted from Sir Thomas Wyse shows; and much other evidence supports it. Wyse quotes Pliny's sneer at the forests of Euboea and Parnassus.[1] We do not read of national attempts at re-forestation, and the geographer of to-day roundly asserts that woods cannot be properly managed if divided up into small plots.[2] In Poland we hear of exploitation of private forest, in the years before the present war, for fear of nationalization.[3] What happens if care of the forest is no man's business, or at best of petty officials without expert knowledge and amenable as small officials in Greece (and greater ones, as Polybius laments) were to private considerations? Japan, which is not a democracy, has been, especially since 1901, steadily planting and repairing its forests.[4]

Apart from deliberate human abuse, theft and depredation, three main factors combined to ruin the Greek forest and induce the loss and disaster with which Nature avenges it. These were the forest fire, the torrent and the goat.

Forest fires are the result of folly and carelessness, sometimes of sheer accident, sometimes of natural causes which man cannot altogether control. We are told that lightning may cause the fire, and that it may spring from the wind rubbing dry boughs together; neither seems very probable in a damp climate like our own, but we are assured that both are possible.[5] Whatever the causes, forest fires were very familiar; Thucydides speaks of a fire "bigger than man's kindling but not like a forest fire".[6] Homer has several similes taken from forest fires,[7] which, as already suggested,

1 Sir Thomas Wyse, *Impressions of Greece*, p. 110; Pliny, *N.H.* xvi, 197.
2 M. I. Newbigin, *Balkans*, p. 200.   3 Dyboski, *Poland*, p. 208.
4 R. P. Porter, *Japan*, ch. xv, p. 279.
5 Van Hise, *Conservation*, p. 236, says that in 1907 lightning caused 458 fires in the Rocky Mountains. It rivals locomotives and campers as the great danger. Pausanias, iii, 26, 6, adds sparks carried by wind.
6 Thucydides, ii, 77, 4.
7 Homer, *Iliad*, xiv, 396; xx, 490; and xi, 155 (ἄξυλος).

seem to imply personal knowledge. First, the noise of the fire—"not so loud is the crackling of flaming fire in the mountain glens when the woods are burning"; next, a hint at the factors—"as when fire rages through the glens of a summer-dried mountain, and the deep forest burns, and the wind driving it whirls the flame to and fro, so raged" the warrior; and finally a peculiarly interesting passage which raises one or two questions—a question of the meaning of Greek, and one as to Homer's knowledge of the most dangerous cause of forest fire—what does ἄξυλος mean? Here is the passage with the doubtful word untranslated: "As when devastating fire falls upon a wood ἄξυλος, and the swirling wind carries it all abroad, and the bushes fall in a heap before the onrush of the headlong fire." Ἄξυλος— holzreich, says the German; dense, say the English translators, or unthinned. The word seems only to occur here; it should be a negative, and the commentators want to make it highly positive, perhaps forgetting what ξύλα are, and perhaps ignoring the experience of lumbering regions in the new world. When we watched the mules sweating down the mountainside with the balks of timber, we noted that the lumber had to be trimmed before they started; a tree, as it is when felled, would never get downhill; and Canadian experience suggests that it is in the dried "slashings" that the fire starts—twigs, leaves, bark, neglected and left to dry, admirable tinder. Suppose, then, we assume that Homer knows what he is talking about, knows where and how the fire starts, and we translate ἄξυλος, "whence the timber has been cut"—? That would be true to experience. Everyone who crosses Canada by train must know the printed and pictured appeal hung in the railroad carriage—a cigarette end, a forest afire, and the bilingual appeal "Conservons nos forêts", "Prevent forest fires". Even postage stamps are at times cancelled with the words "Help prevent forest fires"; and to throw away a cigarette end is punishable by fine, very properly.

Virgil in his turn has a picture of a forest fire in

the *Georgics* (ii, 303) which Lord Burghclere has rendered:

> Some heedless husbandman lets fall a spark,
> Which by the oily rind at first concealed
> Seizes the solid trunk, and shoots aloft
> Amongst the leafage, waking with a roar
> The skyward air; then, wending on its way,
> Lords it o'er branch and utmost bough supreme,
> Wraps all the boskage (*nemus*) with a cloak of fire,
> And, close compacted in a murky reek,
> Belches black clouds to heaven. Most dire its rage
> When from on high storms sweep upon the woods,
> And the gale fresh'ning hurries flame on flame.[1]

Charles R. Van Hise, in the valuable book that I have already quoted once or twice, sums up what the forest fire does—it destroys acres of forest; even when the tree is not reduced to ashes or left a charred pole, it destroys the bark and the tree is doomed; it burns up the humus, and leaves the soil exposed to being washed off by rain. He writes of America: travellers tell the same stories of Greece—loss of

1 Compare Pindar, *Pythian*, 3, 36, πολλὰν δ᾽ ὄρει πῦρ ἐξ ἑνὸς σπέρματος ἐνθορὸν ἀΐστωσεν ὕλαν.

moisture in the soil, soil washed away, floods, and so forth. So we read in Lord Carnarvon, Rennell Rodd, William Miller, Theodore Bent, Sir Thomas Wyse—the last blaming shepherds also who burn over the surface to promote grass, as on British moors the heather is burnt for the same purpose.

The torrent comes next. Forest and undergrowth naturally hold rain and snow. It has been calculated that (at least in North America) of a rainfall half goes back to the air, one-sixth is absorbed for the time by plants, a third goes to streams and rivers.[1] If there is no forest, no undergrowth, no grass, to hold the rain, it will obviously run off the hillside. Empty a can of water into a bath, and it runs out in a few seconds; but let a sponge or two be lying in the bath, and some will be saved; it is exactly so with forest and the deforested hillside from which the earth is washed away. But rivers, especially in alluvial regions, are constantly washing away bits of their banks, and with the bank the trees on it, which are swept away untrimmed, and may not travel far, but are caught and block the stream, catch silt and form islands, sometimes swamps and alternatively floods. Mark Twain's fascinating chapters in his book *Life on the Mississippi* tell this tale. The Mediterranean is a tideless sea and will do nothing to help the blocked river. Homer lets us see the thing again here[2]—"as when two winter torrents flow down the mountains to a watersmeet and join their furious flood within the deep ravine from their great springs, and the shepherd hears the roaring from afar among the hills"; and again, with fuller consequences, "as when a brimming river comes down upon the plain, in winter flood from the hills, swollen by the rain of Zeus, and many dry oaks and many a pine it sucks in, and much soil it casts into the sea". Irving Manatt has the same story of modern Greece; and Sir Thomas Wyse follows up his account of the abuse of the forest with the words:[3] "The rains are not provoked, nor the

1 Van Hise, *Conservation*, p. 107, quoting McGee.
2 *Iliad*, iv, 452; xi, 492.
3 Sir Thomas Wyse, *Impressions of Greece*, p. 232.

streams collected and usefully distributed, nor the soil nourished, nor the temperature moderated." (To this we shall
have to return. He continues:) "A fierce storm carries away
all the soil, substitutes torrents and devastation for rivers and
irrigation, burns up crops, and plants irremediable fever." [1]

Last comes the goat. The sheep in the modern world
sometimes proves to be the enemy of trees. So notably is the
rabbit in time of snow, gnawing away the bark round the
tree on the level of the snow. But so far, the rabbit was a
denizen of Spain, [2] not yet in England or Australia; and
Majorca, where it became a plague, is not Greece. Insects,
as modern science recognizes, can be a curse to forest tree
and fruit tree; a quarter of our fruit is destroyed by wasps
and other unpleasant creatures and the spores of fungi; gypsy
moths have devastated elms in New England—not native
insects but fugitive immigrants from a laboratory; chestnuts
in New England suffered terribly about 1910 from another
pest, and Poland lost in a few years 175,000 acres of pine. [3]
I do not know of any wide observation as to such pests by
the Greeks, but the goat sufficed. The country people would
keep goats, for goats would keep themselves if turned out
on to the hills and into the woods. Grass is not too abundant
in Mediterranean lands, and cattle like leaf-feeding; the
frondator, the leaf-gatherer, has a regular role in old Italian
farming. The beasts thrive on the leaves, but are said to give
less milk. Old Cato recommended planting elm and poplar
for cattle-feed. [4] But the goat looked after itself; and a few
lines from a "goat chorus" of the comic poet Eupolis will
suffice. [5] A rough translation may save labour with Liddell
and Scott, without much loss of poetry. One verb suffices

1 Parallel instances are given by Van Hise, *Conservation*, p. 247, viz.: Po
  Valley floods from the deforestation of the Apennines; the desert of
  Rajputana traceable to abuse of forests.
2 The rabbits in Strabo, C. 144 and 168; Polybius, xii. 3.
3 Dyboski, *Poland*, p. 208.
4 Varro, *de Re Rustica*, i, 24.
5 Eupolis, quoted by Macrobius, *Saturnalia*, vii, 5, 9. Add Virgil, *Georgics*, ii,
  196 and 378-80.

the catalogue in the Greek, but English rhyme asked
more.

> Every kind of tree must render
> Tribute in its shoots so tender;
> Oak and fir and arbutus
> All are eatable for us;
> Spurge, laburnum, fragrant sage
> Must our goatish greed assuage;
> Smilax, olive, mastich, ash—
> All their hopes of growth we dash;
> Sea-oak, ivy, heather, pine,
> All is one when goats will dine;
> Buckthorn, mullein, asphodel,
> Rock-rose, ilex—but why tell
> One by one, when twig and prickle,
> Leaf and flower, our throats must tickle.

Seedlings and new growth they ruined, as red deer re-
introduced into Epping Forest did.

The consequences of all this abuse of forest by man and
beast is given us by Plato:[1]

All the richer and softer parts of the soil have fallen away
and the mere skeleton of the land is left. But in former days
and in the primitive state of the country, what are now
mountains were only regarded as high hills; and the plains
as they are termed by us of the Phelleus were full of rich
earth, and there was abundance of wood in the mountains.
Of this last the traces yet remain; for, although some of the
mountains now only afford sustenance to bees, not so long
ago there were to be seen roofs of timber cut from trees
growing there, which were of a size sufficient to cover the
largest houses; and there were many other high trees, bearing
fruit and abundance of food for cattle. Moreover the land
enjoyed rain from heaven year by year, not as now the water
which flows off the bare earth into the sea....The fact is,
a single night of excessive rain washed away the earth and
laid bare the rock.

If one may slightly misapply Theocritus, it is "no more in
the dells, no more in the groves, no more in the woodlands!
Farewell, Arethusa! farewell, ye rivers!"[2]

---

1 Plato, *Critias*, 111.   2 Theocritus, 1, 117.

From another and more modern source we learn much the same things that Plato teaches us. "In the mouth of two witnesses...."

When the forest is gone, the great reservoir of moisture stored up in its vegetable mould is evaporated, and returns only in deluges of rain to wash away the parched dust into which that mould has been converted. The well-wooded and humid hills are turned to ridges of dry rock, which encumbers the low grounds and chokes the watercourses with its débris, and—except in countries favoured with an equable distribution of rain through the seasons, and a moderate and regular inclination of surface—the whole earth, unless rescued by human art from the physical degradation to which it tends, becomes an assemblage of bald mountains, of barren turfless hills, and of swampy and malarious plains.

This is written of the forests of North America; and the Forestry Department of the Government of India and the experience of Scotland and many other regions confirm it.[1] No one who knows the history of ancient Greece, with its many divisions of territory, the instability of its governments, its poverty and its want of science, would expect "human art" to make or sustain any such endeavour.

VI

No great reflexion is required to recognize how physical changes of this kind will affect the conditions of human life, beginning with the climate itself. Warde Fowler long ago put a question about Virgil, who, he said, spoke of birds breeding in North Italy, which do not breed there; did it mean ignorance of the birds and general want of observation in the poet? (Poets are not always precise in reference to birds, as L'Allegro's lark reminds us, which would not naturally visit a window but can only be kept from doing so by great grammatical efforts.) Or is there another explanation? He answered his question by stressing the disappearance of the forest and the resultant rise in average temperature; and the birds want a cooler air and go North to find it. There has

1 Ritchie, *Animal Life in Scotland*, pp. 327–8, quoting Professor G. P. Marsh.

been much speculation as to the effect of forest destruction on rainfall. In the tropics, Alfred Russel Wallace tells us, the rock once bared tends to accumulate heat; the air above it is warmed, and ascending currents of warm air prevent condensation, which is greatly influenced by hills and forests.[1] The botanists supplement this with data which the non-scientific would hardly expect as to the contribution of forest to humidity. An oak in England, we are told, draws from the soil and gives off two hundred times its own weight of water in a year. An acre of forest, writes Van Hise, thinking at any rate of America, gives off through its leaves in the growing season 1000 to 20,000 pounds of water per day.[2] Long ago White of Selborne made a similar observation:[3] "In heavy fogs, on elevated situations, trees are perfect alembics.... Trees perspire freely, condense largely, and check evaporation so much that woods are always moist." A natural circulation of moisture is suggested, held by trees, given out by trees, returned to trees. Since the woods in North America were grubbed and cleared, White adds, all bodies of water are much diminished. A *caveat* must be entered about the five great lakes, and particularly Lake Ontario, where the recorded levels of the water have varied up and down in a very remarkable but as yet unexplained way for more than a century; but White's general conclusion seems valid.

It will be quickly realized how such changes of climate, quite apart from the alternating of casual spells of flood and drought which we have considered, will bear upon agriculture. Flood, drought, deposit of silt and débris, fire and the destruction of humus—such factors mean declining returns from agriculture, lessened or lost crops, and increase in the cost of living. There are, of course, political and other factors to be considered; no single group of causes can be supposed responsible for everything; but those named are not

1 A. R. Wallace, *Tropical Nature*, pp. 16, 19.
2 Van Hise, *Conservation*, p. 110.
3 White, letter to Daines Barrington, no. 29.

to be lost from the reckoning. In particular, water supply has to be considered. Human life depends a great deal on the underground accumulation of water, and deforestation is blamed for the lowering of the water table or the level of saturation; springs fail, and Greece is a land that depends on springs. The water table in California, I am told, has been lowered six feet; for man wastes water as well as wood; and, all the time, it is computed that a man weighing 150 lb. wants 264 gallons of water to drink *per annum*;[1] and he has other uses for water. One thing that militates against water supply in Greece is the fact that the limestone, which abounds, "drinks up the rain and leaves the land thirsty".[2] If further glimpses of the obvious are desired, Aristotle emphasizes the importance to a city of water supply—springs or rain cisterns;[3] and Xenophon pungently observes that the value of a water supply is better recognized by those who lack it.[4] It is significant, too, that the historians tell us of work done by the famous tyrants of Athens and Samos to secure ready and abundant water for their citizens; and the pollution of the small river was one factor in the discontent that made Theagenes tyrant of Megara.

A smaller loss to a countryside, it would seem, but a real one, was the disappearance of small plants with the washing away of the soil or the raging of hillside fires. Plato spoke of nothing being left but sustenance for the bees. Sir Rennell Rodd has recorded the loss of an industry to a Greek village which had produced 25,000 lb. of honey in a year, when forest fires had destroyed the vegetation of the mountains round about.[5] Cane and beet sugar have made us almost forget the significance of the bee in ancient life, and how well it had merited the fourth *Georgic*.

We need not recapitulate the many uses served by wood in

1 Van Hise, *Conservation*, p. 104.
2 Irving Manatt, *Aegean Days*, p. 182. Cf. M. I. Newbigin, *Balkan Problems*, p. 161, etc.
3 Aristotle, *Politics*, vii, 1330 b.   4 Xenophon, *Lac. Rep.* 15, 6.
5 Sir Rennell Rodd, *Customs and Lore of Modern Greece*, p. 59. Cf. Sir Thomas Wyse, *Impressions of Greece*, p. 225, Euboea sending 100,000 cwt. of honey to Constantinople.

the daily round of Greek life, nor dwell on the increasing cost of tool and furniture and roof, as population grew and forest declined. But national life depended in the greater centres on the navy, and Greeks quickly saw that command of timber-growing regions, where transport was possible (a matter emphasized later on by Vitruvius in his book on architecture[1]), was of the utmost importance: Megabazus tells King Darius that it was a mistake to let Histiaeus build a fortress on the Thracian coast, where "ship-building timber is boundless".[2] When Amphipolis was lost in 424, there was intense alarm in Athens; loss of revenue was serious, but it was more serious to lose control of the source of the timber which Athens needed for ship-building. A city whose food depended on her rule of the sea must have a navy. The wide range over which Britain in the Napoleonic wars sought her ship-building timber—the Baltic, Nova Scotia, Albania and even Burma (where merchantmen were built for her of teak) —will suffice as a modern illustration. The Athenian oligarch emphasizes the importance of rule of the sea, if Athens is to buy such timber from those whose forests grow it, and urges that Athenians should allow none to go to their rivals.[3] Annexations and alliances turned not infrequently on timber supply. Macedonia was important, because the best timber for the builder—smooth, straight and resinous—was to be had there; the next best was from Pontus.[4] Similarly kings of Egypt, early Pharaohs and later Ptolemies, aimed at control of Lebanon and Cyprus because of their cedar forests.[5]

Here pause: ἄλλην δρῦν βαλάνιζε. We have looked at the use and abuse of the forest, at climate and economics. It is time that Wordsworth, and Euripides with him, should murmur to us of

One impulse from a vernal wood.

---

1 Vitruvius, ii, 9; significance as on the St Lawrence and the Ottawa of river transport; for which compare Strabo, C. 222.
2 Herodotus, v, 23, 2.   3 [Xenophon], *Ath. Rep.* 2, 11; 2, 12.
4 Theophrastus, *Plants*, v, 2, 1; i, 9, 2.
5 Cf. Theophrastus, *Plants*, v, 8, 1; Strabo, C. 684; Pliny, *N.H.* xvi, 203; and Breasted, *History of Egypt*, pp. 515, 387; A. Holm, *History of Greece* (tr.), iv, 125.

THE GREEK FARMER[1]

I

THE farmer, when all is said, has had his full share of literature; perhaps to no other trade, unless the soldier's be excepted, have poets and men of letters given more of their attention. It always seems to remain a question whether it is the real farmer whom they portray, and whether the real farmer ever reads what they write. He of all men is apt to be most practical, and least susceptible to the charm that other men have felt in the *Georgics*. But in the very beginning of Greek literature for once farmer and poet came nearest together. For a poet Hesiod is; and yet his last editor hesitates—the *Works and Days* is "almost a fine poem, but not a complete handbook".[2] Charles Lamb once wrote that to read that poem was like eating good wholesome brown bread.[3] Whatever Greek farmers did with the poem, other Greeks read it and re-read it; and Pausanias says he saw at Helicon the poem inscribed on a lead tablet.[4]

A poet—but a farmer; the union of the two is familiar to every Briton; but Burns wrote no poem to teach farming. Hesiod was no Burns, however. A "clear but clumsy intellect", "a close-fisted poverty-stricken peasant", who preaches "the gospel of getting on"[5]—no one would speak so of Robert Burns; and no one could compare Hesiod's contribution to nation-building with that of the Scottish poet. The spirit of the men is different; two lines of *The Twa Dogs* represent their outlooks. "But surely poor folk maun be wretches" says the dog Caesar, quite in Hesiod's vein—

---

1 Some matters have necessarily to be touched on in this essay, which also come into the survey in two later essays; but perhaps the same reader will not read all three.
2 T. A. Sinclair, *Hesiod, Works and Days*, p. xi.
3 Letter to Sir C. A. Elton, Aug. 1822 (?); E.V. Lucas, *Lamb's Letters*, ii, no. 393.
4 Pausanias, ix, 31, 4.
5 Gomperz, *Greek Thinkers*, i, 38; R. W. Livingstone, *Greek Ideals*, p. 71; T. A. Sinclair, *Works and Days*, p. xxvi.

"Full is the earth of evils, and full the sea"; and Luath
rejoins, with Burns, "They're no sae wretched 's ane wad
think." But, however they judge of country folk and country
life, they both know it from experience.

The first thing for the farmer, says Hesiod, is to "get a
house, and then a woman, and a ploughing ox—a slave-
woman not a wife, who might also follow the cattle; and to
get all gear within the house, lest thou beg of another, and he
deny thee, and thou go lacking and the season pass and thy
work come to nothing" (405 ff.).[1] Of course there are other
things he needs; better have *two* bulls of nine years, in their
prime, to draw the plough and not fight (436); and a watch-
dog (605); and then mules. Hesiod, however, does not
mention horse or ass, which had both long since reached
Greece, the ass at any rate from the Orient, and the Homeric
hero's horse (a small animal) from wherever he got it; the
big horse of Cyrene was to come later. The mule is a tougher
animal than the horse, and takes less feeding; the horse in
the British army is allowed 12 lb. of hay and 12 lb. of corn
a day; the mule much less. All sorts of tools the farmer will
need—a plough of holm oak (429), for that is strongest to
plough with; two ploughs, in fact. The wooden plough
continued in use through all ancient history, and to this day
it is better for certain soils, we have seen, than the iron plough.
The farmer will need a mortar three feet wide and a pestle
three cubits long (423), and of course a waggon—and here
comes a curious cry from the poet's heart: "Fool! he knows
not there are a hundred pieces of wood in a waggon" (456).[2]
Hesiod makes it clear that the farmer would most naturally
be making most of these things for himself—like the Trojan
prince in Homer who makes his own chariot. Adam Smith[3]
has an interesting paragraph on the concentration of many
trades in few hands "in the lone houses and very small
villages which are scattered about in so desert a country as
the highlands of Scotland", noting especially how many arts

---

1 The references are to the *Works and Days*.   2 See also p. 38.
3 *Wealth of Nations*, book i, ch. 3.

the village carpenter and the smith must ply, and how every farmer must be butcher, baker and brewer for his own family. Miss Shackleton[1] notes that the wheelbarrow was only introduced into Lesbos a few years ago, and then by an archaeological party from Europe. Sir Samuel Baker tells of a planter in Ceylon who introduced it on his estate, and, returning unexpectedly from an absence, found his labourers reverting to old ways with the unwelcome innovation, and carrying the wheelbarrows on their heads. We need not make a list of all the tools that Hesiod's farmer would use outdoors, nor of those the wife (it is to be hoped, thrifty, for there are awful mischances in that sex) would want within. It is noted that he says little about sheep, but it is obvious that, in days before Egyptian linen and Indian cotton, all clothing must be woollen; and in the Greek winter the farmer needs a long woollen shirt (*chiton*) reaching to his feet, a soft big cloak of wool, boots of ox-hide with the hair inside, a cap and another big cloak of the skins of kids. (It was the riding peoples of the great plains who separately invented the most comfortable and needful of all garments for the modern farmer— Persia with its *anaxyrides*, and *bracata Gallia*.)

Hesiod sets forth the routine of the farmer's year, season by season, and, like Virgil, and for substantially the same reasons, he dates ploughing and harvest and the rest by the stars and the birds. Months varied in Greek states and might yet vary— to say nothing of quite unmetrical names—while Virgil had seen the Roman calendar three full months wrong—ninety days we are told, when Julius Caesar set it right, to stay right for centuries. The crane's voice in the sky gives the signal for ploughing—about the middle of November (448), when the Pleiades are setting (384); "but if you plough the good ground at the solstice (December), you will reap sitting, grasping a thin crop in your hand, binding the sheaves awry, dusty and not glad at all; and you will bring your crop home in a basket, and few will admire you" (479–82). Reaping will be in early May, when the Pleiades are rising (383), "when the

[1] *Europe, a regional survey,* p. 102.

house-carrier (viz. the snail) climbs up the plants from the earth" (371)—"then is the time to sharpen your sickles and rouse your slaves. No shady seats, no sleeping till dawn in the harvest season, when the sun scorches the flesh.... Dawn takes away a third part of your work, dawn sets a man forward on his journey and sets him forward in his work—dawn which puts many a man on the road, and on many oxen the yokes" (571–81). Thrashing and winnowing will be when stout Orion shows himself (598).

Work is the thing—not dawdling, not putting off, not chattering at the smithy (493); work, well ahead of time, "hope is a poor companion for a man in need" (500). "The man who is rich in fancy thinks his waggon as good as built" (455). No! no! a man must be ready beforehand, must have his tools made before he needs to use them. "Work is no reproach; it is not working that is reproach" (311). And thrift, as Virgil saw too, is the foundation of everything, the first virtue of civilization. "Neither manner of life (*mos*) had they (the old Italians) nor good ways (*cultus*); they knew not to yoke the bulls; they knew not to lay by nor to save what they had gained." So Virgil in the *Aeneid* (viii, 317). The pioneer in North America said the same thing of the Indian. Thrift is the prime duty, Hesiod sees; it leads to wealth and "on wealth virtue and good repute follow" (313);—"virtue" is, of course, always a word that needs definition. Evil anybody can have: "smooth is the way, and near at hand is its dwelling. But in front of virtue the deathless gods have set sweat; long is the path and steep, aye, and rough at the first; but when a man has reached the top, the going is easy" (286–92).

Right conduct helps, too; for where men are straight in their ways, famine consorts not with them, nor war; peace is the nurse of their children; they go about their work with light hearts; earth gives them victual in plenty, the oak on the mountains has acorns on top and bees in the middle; their sheep are heavy with fleeces; their wives bear children like their fathers; they flourish with good things continually;

nor do they go upon ships (225–37). Righteousness indeed pays;—the poet would never have understood Plato's indignation at such a sentiment, nor the irony in the adjective hurled at "the noble Hesiod" (*Rep.* 363A).

But in June the farmer may rest a little—when the artichoke flowers, and the grasshopper on the trees pours his shrill song from under his wings, when goats are fattest and wine sweetest; then is the time for the shady rock, the wine of Biblis, a clot of curds, and milk of the goats, the flesh of an heifer "that has fed in the woods and never calved" and of firstling kids—yes, *then* to sit in the shade, with a good bellyful within, and the fresh West wind in one's face, and from a never-failing spring to mingle three parts of water with one of wine (582–96).

So much for the farmer; but he must think of his neighbours; for in the moment of trouble a neighbour will hasten to you ungirt, but a kinsman will stay to gird himself (345). Always be fair with your neighbours; kind deeds beget kind deeds; add a little when you repay a kindness. "Give is a good girl, but Snatch is a bad girl and brings death" (356). Never taunt a man with his poverty (717–18). Round about are men with trades—free men in rivalry one with another: there is a bad rivalry, and a good, and the good rivalry "stirs even the helpless to labour", and he hastens to plough and to plant and set his house in order—"this strife is *good* for men". So potter is hot with potter, and carpenter with carpenter; yes, and bard with bard (11–26). But there are also "bribe-eating princes"—Homer's old word *Basilées*, which some say might better be rendered barons. They judge suits between men and their neighbours, not always justly. Thrifty and idle craftsman, farmer and sea-faring man—there they are in an iron age; and never a hero among them. It is more like old-time village life in New England, neighbours all, and individualists, a man farming his own land and sometimes able to buy another man's farm (341), some sluggards and some talkers; but work, thrift and wealth the watchwords of the community.

II

Right ways! cries Hesiod, and sacrifice (up to your means) to the immortal gods, "that they may have for you a gracious heart and mind, so that you may buy another's holding and not another yours" (340). Another's holding or lot—the word is the *klêros* familiar in Homer; but, so far as we can see, the conditions on which a *klêros*, a holding, is held, are entirely different. Hesiod thinks of purchase and ownership, apparently in the sense given to these words by the Greeks of the historic period, by the Romans and by ourselves; property in land acquired by purchase. But he would be a bold man who would be definite about such matters in Homer's Greece; the most that could definitely be said is that our way, and Hesiod's way, was not that of the Homeric world. But that world may very well have had several ways. We read at least of what we translate as "common field", of the holding (*klêros*), of the prince's *temenos*, of the enclosed vineyard, the garden obviously enclosed, and of the farm which Laertes "acquired" (κτεάτισσεν), however he did it.

To begin with the common field. "As two men contend about their borderlines, with measuring rods in their hands, ἐπιξύνῳ ἐν ἀρούρῃ, when in narrow space they strive for equal shares" (*Il.* xii, 421). It is the natural thing, at least for the English reader, to translate it "common field"; it is difficult to think of any other possible rendering; but, while there must probably be strong likeness between one "common field" system and another, differences as strongly marked are quite likely. Common field and equal shares—but for how long are these equal shares assigned, and by whom? Would the share be the κλῆρος? Who then holds the *klêros*, some individual or a family in common? What rights has the community, tribe or canton, or have the families that con-stitute it, to the common land? Permanent rights, or rights limited to so many beasts or so many months? In all probability, in newly settled places (one of which is described to us), there will be unreclaimed land, which is also unclaimed, and which is used as pasture for cattle, or sheep, or swine, or all of them, though cattle and sheep at any rate do not like feeding together. When Nausithoos transplanted the Phaeacians to Scherie "aloof from trading folk", he set a wall about the town, built houses, made temples for the gods, and "divided lands" (ἐδάσσατ' ἀρούρας, *Od.* vi, 9, 10). This passage tells the lawyer little; but Homer was not making the *Odyssey* for lawyers; they came later in the world's history, when the heroic age was over. More famous is the passage, where Achilles in Hades tells Odysseus that he would rather be a hired labourer on earth, with a man who had no *klêros* nor much living, than be king of the dead below (ἀνδρὶ παρ' ἀκλήρῳ, *Od.* xi, 490). A man may have many *klêroi* (πολύκληρος, *Od.* xiv, 211). A prince has a *temenos*—why have we been honoured in Lycia with seat and flesh and cup, asks Sarpedon, yes, treated like gods? Why do we hold a *temenos*, a great one, by the banks of Xanthus, a fair one of orchard and wheat-bearing land (φυταλιῆς καὶ ἀρούρης πυροφόροιο, *Il.* xii, 310 ff.)? The elders of the Aetolians besought Meleager to come forth, and they would give him a *temenos*, exceeding good; he should choose it himself, fifty acres (πεντηκοντόγυον), half ploughland (*Il.* ix, 574 ff.).

Analogies there may be many, illustrative but not decisive. So there stands the question of land-tenure in Homer's poems. But when we come to garden and orchard and vineyard, conditions are obviously different. We are told that an olive tree takes eighteen years to reach its prime. It is difficult, then, to think of an olive-yard apart from the idea of some kind of private property; and garden and vineyard are on much the same footing—individual tenure, because individual culture is needed; and there will be some kind of wall or fence or dyke; and so there is—a ἕρκος, built of loose stones (*Od.* xviii, 360). Hedges are English, and chiefly of eighteenth-century production, when land was enclosed to grow turnips—analogy again. Irving Manatt, who knew Greece, speaks of "the sweetest note of country life in all Homer"[1]—"come", says

1 *Aegean Days,* p. 363.

Odysseus to Laertes on the farm which he κτεάτισσεν, "come and I will tell thee the trees through all the terraced garden, which thou gavest me once for mine own, and I was asking thee this and that, being but a little child, and following thee through the garden" (*Od.* xii, 336 ff.).

But Hesiod's is another world; nothing is said of common field, in any sense of the words, nothing of king's holding, nothing of kings at all but that they take bribes by the mouthful. As for the *kléros*, we have seen already that, if you are good and pious, you by grace of the gods may buy another man's lot, and not he yours. We are among peasant farmers who appear to own the land they till; at any rate they buy it. It is the modern world, with a vengeance—modern virtues of the Victorian type, thrift and self-help and hard work; Hesiod would have little but contempt for the labour party of to-day, with its dreams—"rich in fancy"—and its talk and the places where it talks, worse, he would say, than the smithy (*W. and D.* 493). No! no! "best, altogether best, is the man who considers things for himself and makes up his own mind" (*W. and D.* 293); no "standing pat" for Hesiod! He is the true old farmer type, the "hayseed" of old Ontario —except, of course, that the "hayseed" wrote no verse, or none that survives.

When we pass from Hesiod's Boeotia to early Attica, it is another land again, and another story—this time a story of landlords and tenants, of land becoming massed in fewer hands, of debts and mortgages and the sale of debtors. The chief doubt among ancient historians was about the meaning of the term that described the tenants; did the ἑκτημόροι, the "sixth-part-men", pay that sixth part of their produce as rent or keep it to live on and pay as rent five-sixths?[1] To-day a fair rent is one-tenth of the produce of arable land, but land has of late been cheap in England; a good farm all in all could be bought at £20 an acre, I am told, a rate at which you could not replace the buildings. The *Song of*

---

1 Plutarch, *Solon*, 13, says the rent was one-sixth; Photius says it was five-sixths.

Solomon (viii, 11), on the other hand, speaks of a vineyard, for which "Solomon" was to have 1000 pieces of silver and "those that keep the fruit thereof two hundred". Whatever the tenant farmer in Attica had to pay his landlord, changing times developed a series of difficulties—land, we are told, was monopolized by a few persons of noble family, and rents began to be paid in coin instead of produce. So much we learn from the books; but probably at the same time population was increasing,[1] trade perhaps becoming more widely ramified, and prices, now measured by currency, fluctuating in a way that no man could foretell. Good crop or bad crop, somehow some one, neither tenant, nor landlord, seemed to make the profit on the good crop and not to do so badly on the bad crop; we are not the first generation to find the ways of money unintelligible. Add to all the uncertainties debt, which was no uncertainty, and the monstrous law that the insolvent debtor with his wife and his children might all be sold into slavery; and discontent on a wide scale needs no further explaining. Primitive law and modern economics made a bad pair for national prosperity or domestic happiness. The small farmer—the yeoman of old English history—is after all one of the most valuable persons in a community. He has the "stake in the country" of which men speak, and he knows it; he is shrewder than many who despise him; and, though this was less true in antiquity than to-day, he has the advantage over many fellow-citizens that he is doing a whole job and not like them a fractional one. His work means close study of Nature, season, grain, land and beast—beast from birth to butcher; and finally, as an acute observer suggests, it "does not leave him much time to be anything else but honest". There is yet another point; the family of the small farmer—*o fortunatos nimium sua si bona norint*—trained as they are in intimate relation with Nature—*patiens operum parvoque assueta juventus*—are about the best stock put into the body of citizens. This type of man was in danger of disappearing.

At this point (590 B.C.) comes Solon—a great sage, antiquity

1 On this, and on the general situation, see pp. 86 ff.

maintained, a great economist, they say to-day. Fifty years
ago the emphasis was laid on his constitutional schemes;
to-day it falls on his interest in farming and industry, on the
measures he took to save the farmers of Attica and to bring
trades and crafts to Athens, on his strangely comprehensive
view of life and work as a whole, and his sympathy with the
motives of common men. Here we have not to consider his
position as law-giver nor his scheme of votes and councils;
we have only to look at his work for the farmer. The first
thing needful, he saw, was to give men hope; no man will
farm effectively without hope. Men were arguing about
conjectural remedies for the state and the farmer, such as the
cancelling of all debts; perhaps—but it is doubtful at this
date—about a re-division of the land. Solon adopted neither
plan; but he did two things at once that lifted the burden
from the farmer's mind. He enacted that a man's wife and
children should never be sold into slavery to pay his debts,
nor himself either; that saved the family—an unspeakable
relief, as Solon very well understood. Along with this
enactment, he cancelled debts on land, as British Royal
Commissions have done in Ireland. In one of his simple
autobiographical poems he calls on the black Earth, mother
as she is of the Olympian gods, to give her testimony how he
had pulled up the mortgage pillars that men had stuck about
her, and how once she was in slavery, but Solon had made
her free. *Seisachtheia* he called this part of his work—the
shaking off of burdens.

He did other things to help the farmer. He offered a bounty
for wolf killing. From one market he debarred his Attic
farmers; they should not sell their wheat outside Attica—
which meant to Megara; but, to balance this, he encouraged
settlement of men with trades in Athens, which meant a
growing home market. But he had larger views. Attica was
not a wheat country; South Russia (as we call it) was; but
the Greek colonies of South Russia must import all their olive
oil, a main staple of Greek life, a great food primarily, but
also the equivalent then of soap and electric light. If the

Attic farmer would shift from wheat to olive growing, when once the trees were mature, there would be work and profit on the land in abundance, for Attica was eminently a land of the olive. Ancient legend spoke of the olive as Athene's special gift; and a century after Solon the olive of Athens was the theme of lyric song and of national jest;—once call Athens λιπαραί, and she was in a good temper on the spot and would cede anything.[1]

As for the redistribution of the land—a great theme, it is alleged, among democrats—a repudiation of it was said to be included in the Heliastic oath, the oath of the juryman in historic Athens; and as all such ordinances came down from Solon, the inference was obvious. But inference is not evidence; and the Heliastic oath, as it stands in the manuscripts of Demosthenes' speech against Timocrates, is now described as a forgery. Isocrates says this redistribution would be an irremediable disaster;[2] and Aristotle implies that demagogues were apt to toy with the idea, and Plato says the same of would-be tyrants.[3] Mr W. E. Heitland[4] shrewdly asks whether the proposed result would be that citizens would find themselves working with their own hands on their new lots, or whether the dream included some distribution of slaves among them to complete the earthly Paradise. Perhaps as important a question—and one not much easier to answer —would be, Was it ever actually attempted? It was no proposal of Solon's.

The nearest that Athens came to it was in the time of Pisistratus, who, by common dating, became tyrant of Athens thirty years after Solon. He was a man above the run of men in "virtue and understanding", Thucydides says (vi, 54), who gives to "virtue" (aretê) his own meaning, which is not Hesiod's nor the later Stoic's—a more robust and comprehensive meaning, if less suggestive of piety. Pisistratus is credited with the final abolition of the system of ἐκτημόροι, the confiscation of the estates of his opponents, and their

1 Aristophanes. Acharnians, 639.   2 Isocrates, Panathen. 259.
3 Plato, Rep. viii, 566A.   4 Heitland, Agricola, p. 67.

distribution among small farmers. A modern scholar suggests that he aimed more at promoting agriculture than trade. Certainly in modern times we have seen how the French peasant was for keeping Napoleon as Emperor rather than having the Bourbons back; for what would become of his farm and its freehold? In this century the Rumanian government set a system of peasant farmers between them and the Soviet; they took over the great estates and compensated the landlords with paper money, which rapidly fell in value, though not so fast or so far as the Russian rouble. Antiquity was spared the horrors of paper money; there was no paper and no press. Pisistratus, however, would have preferred his opponents to live abroad.

To help his new peasant proprietors Pisistratus devised a system of loans to carry them along till they could stand on their own feet. He also realized, what Varro writes in his *de Re Rustica* (i, 15), that transport is an element in the cost of production; and he did something toward better roads, marking out the distances with *herms*—rough half-finished images of Hermes. This was an anticipation of the milestones of the successors of Alexander, from whom the Romans caught what might be called a real passion for milestones. He also instituted judges of small cases in country districts.[1]

Pisistratus levied a tax upon his farmers of one-twentieth of the produce[2]—or some said a tenth[3]—but he knew when to let it go. He had the habit of moving about the country himself; he could settle disputes in person, and stop (or save) people from making expeditions to the city; they were better at home and at work. So once, they say, he saw an old man busy, digging rocks, and he sent his attendant to ask what he got out of the ground. "All the bothers and pains there are", said the old man, "and of those bothers and pains Pisistratus must take the tenth." He had not recognized Pisistratus, we are duly told; but Pisistratus was delighted with his freedom of speech, and, we are assured, with his

---

1 [Aristotle], *Ath. Rep.* 16, 5.   2 Thucydides, vi, 54.
3 [Aristotle], *Ath. Rep.* 16.

love of work. "I don't want the tenth of his bothers and pains", he said, and remitted the tax; so that ever after the farm was called "the farm without a tax".

It would appear that in the days of Pisistratus Attica took to the wine industry. At any rate the archaeologists assure us that by the end of the sixth century the broken Attic wine jar is more frequent than the Corinthian, implying that Athens has captured the trade; and this again implies the development of vineyards. The vine, we are told, needs more water than the olive, and succeeds better in terraces where the soil is deeper.[1] This shift from grain to trees confirms what the historians tell us of the change in tenure of the land; the owner will sink more capital in the land, if it is only labour and the plants, than the tenant. The gain to the countryside (and to the nation) in stability and contentment is incalculable. It may be noted that the festival of the City Dionysia began in this period, about 534 B.C.—a festival of the wine-god, to be in later days of signal importance in the development of drama and literature.

III

Solon and Pisistratus obviously did immense service to Attic agriculture in giving the small farmers hope, security and new ideas; and, so far as we are informed, the countryside throve till the Peloponnesian war. "Count the city an island", was then one of the watchwords of Pericles. Under the conditions of Greek warfare he could say nothing else; the strength of Athens was on the sea, her land forces could not face the Spartans, and the Spartans were incompetent in siege war. With the Sicilian expedition in full swing, a new type of invasion and devastation was launched upon Attica by the Spartans. Of course the trees perished; they were the first object of attack[2] and would take years to restore; but a historian recently recovered tells us that the very tiles from the roofs were sold to Theban dealers. But, quite apart from

1 M. R. Shackleton, *Europe*, p. 101.   2 Aristophanes, *Acharnians*, 183.

war and such vindictive destruction, Greek agriculture did not generally improve.

In another essay deforestation and its effects are dealt with; here other factors ask for attention. As we have seen, and as we should expect, population increased; the rate of its increase at various periods we have not the data to compute; it must have been rapid in the early days when Greek colonies began to line the coasts of Mediterranean and Euxine. So long as it increased, the demand for food from the land was bound to increase too, and the value of land with it. If we have to realize that this demand was met in the case of Athens by wheat from the Black Sea for decades together, and in the Peloponnese and elsewhere in various measure by wheat from Sicily and Egypt, we have to remember the olive and its share in paying for the wheat. If imported wheat tended to keep down the value of land, the olive and the need of vegetables and fruits would help to keep it up. But in Athens manufactures, the revenues of a great *emporion*, and a large share of the carrying trade and general maritime business of the Mediterranean, would go far to pay for the wheat. In any case our knowledge of the prices of land to buy and land to rent is negligible apart from these general considerations, which do not take us far.

It seems agreed that Greek agriculture did not improve, that it declined, rather. For one thing, it would appear that the farmer's tools were not improved, though the wooden plough is not by itself decisive evidence. We are told that there is some evidence for the draining of swamps and for terracing on the hillsides; but Plato tells us how progressively sterile those hillsides were becoming. Lucretius in the last century B.C. generalizes what he observes; the land grows effete; the world becomes exhausted (ii, 150); and we need not take this as a mere cry of poetic pessimism, a mode familiar in literature.

Probably in a great many places the land was over-used. With fallows the ancients were familiar; but the rotation of crops was not a dominant principle; they did little with

clovers, peas or beans, and the earth had to do without the
nitrogen which leguminous plants gather from the air. Nor
is there evidence that they managed their animals well;
perhaps they could not in their climate. Water and grass—or
failing grass, leaves—required the driving of stock and sheep
to the hills for the summer. There was no folding of them by
night on the arable, to put (as a modern farmer phrases it)
the fertility collected on the hills in the day back into the
cultivated land, in the shape of urine and dung. It is sometimes urged that there was too little manuring altogether.
Evidence is found for this, for instance, in the legend of
Herakles cleaning the byres of Augeas of thirty years'
accumulation of manure by turning a river into the byres
and washing it all away.[1] He was always counted rather a
fool of a hero. Homer, however, describes the dog Argus
lying on the manure heap full in front of Odysseus' palace.[2]
At a much later day, in the times of Alexander the Great,
Theophrastus has a good deal to say in his book on Plants
about manure and its varieties. Thus the pomegranate thrives
if treated with "pig-dung and a great deal of river-water"
(ii, 2, 11); "wheat welcomes abundant rain more than
barley, and bears better on land which is not manured"
(viii, 6, 2); and an authority whom he quotes by name
(though the name seems odd and corrupt) grades the value
of dungs—human is best, next the pig's, third the goat's, and
then in turn that of sheep, oxen and beasts of burden
(ii, 7, 4). Like the modern farmer, he recognizes the value
of litter manure (συρματῖτις, ii, 7, 4); it is for that that byres
to this day are strown with straw.

When we ask about labour on the farm, it seems agreed
that, apart from the farmer and his family, the rest of the
work-people were apt to be slaves. The "divine swineherd"
of the *Odyssey* was a slave, παρ' ὕεσσιν ἀπότροπος—a kidnapped
child, bought from Phoenicians; but one has only to read the
scene in which Telemachus, returning from his voyage, finds

1 Apollodorus, *Bibl.* ii, 5, 5; slightly differently in Pausanias, v, 1, 9–10.
2 *Odyssey,* xvii, 297–9.

Eumaeus entertaining Odysseus, to realize that slavery was not a uniform condition of reluctance and ill-will. "Up started the swineherd in wonder, and from his hands fell the cups, wherein he had been busily mixing the bright wine. And he ran to the prince and kissed him and both his fair eyes and both his hands."[1] Odysseus, in his character of tramp, is offered work for wages of a sort on a farm, where he may sweep stalls and feed kids, or again gather stones for fences and plant trees.[2] Hesiod's farmer, as we saw, began with house, ox, and slave-woman; but, as the poem moves on, there is constant allusion to slaves (δμῶες) working with the master on the land, threshing, building barns; and the farmer is bidden to attend to their food, to "let them rest their knees" when the oxen are unyoked (*W. and D.* 608), and to keep them up to their work.

On a Greek farm, one is not surprised to learn, there was scarcely so much demand for slave labour as in the town factories. But slaves on farms are mentioned from time to time by Aristophanes. Dicaeopolis has his Xanthias; Strepsiades laments that in war-time you cannot lay your hands on your own slaves. Even in the ideal socialist state that the women bring in, when Praxagora is asked who is to till the soil, "the slaves", says she in two words.[3] And Plato comes round to her view, when he remodels his ideal state in the *Laws*; "the more", says Mr Heitland, "he adapts his speculation to the facts of existing civilization, the more positively he accepts slave labour as a necessary basis", though not unaware of the dangers of servile labour on a large scale.[4] Even in the *Republic*, the bad soldier is to be reduced to farm labour.[5] Aristotle also recognizes slavery; the slave is an animated tool; and on a farm the husbandmen should be slaves, but not all of one race.[6] The intention there is obvious. In the household of Ischomachus, the ideal landed proprietor, the genial and humane master and his little wife

1 *Odyssey*, xvi, 12 ff.   2 *Odyssey*, xvii, 223; xviii, 359.
3 Aristophanes, *Ecclesiazusae*, 651.   4 Heitland, *Agricola*, pp. 77, 78.
5 Plato, *Rep.* v, 468 A.   6 Aristotle, *Politics*, vii, 10; p. 1330 a.

recognize the slaves as human, as beings to be cared for, trained (as the dogs and horses, of course, are), punished or rewarded; and there is no reference to hired labour.

IV

When we turn to the produce of the Greek farm, it is needless to repeat what has been said elsewhere in the book about the vegetables grown. It is clear from the references of Aristophanes that they were grown in some considerable variety and marketed. For reasons by now beyond our reach, he decides and reiterates that the mother of Euripides cultivated and sold vegetables, that the poet was bred up among them and was "the child of the field-goddess". Where the sting was in this—in a democracy—it is hard for a foreigner to decide, when the farmer is constantly something of a hero on the comic stage.

Turning then to grain, trees and beasts, we have to note some facts which explain to us a good deal of what we read. In the first place, it is remarked that, quite apart from the disastrous effects of deforestation and Turkish government through the centuries, Greece is in any case so mountainous that only about one-fifth of the total area lends itself to cultivation.[1] Wheat, barley, spelt and millet were grown. Dodwell, travelling in Greece in 1812, tells us that corn— being English, he probably means wheat and not the Indian corn (maize or sweet corn) now grown in some parts of Europe—ripens in Attica twenty-five days earlier than in the Peloponnese or Crete, and that all the grain is harvested and trodden by 15 August.[2] He adds a curious point. The effect of the *lolium*, or tare, that sometimes grows among the wheat, if it be not carefully removed before the wheat is ground and the bread made, is to induce giddiness, headache, and something like intoxication—an observation that adds significance, if the weed meant be the same, to a parable in the Gospel.

The geographers tell us that among fruit trees the olive and the pomegranate appear to be "the only two indubitably

1 M. R. Shackleton, *Europe*, p. 101. 2 Dodwell, *Tour*, ii, 9-11.

native fruits" of the Mediterranean area.[1] The peach was the "Persian apple", the apricot the "Armenian apple", and the orange eventually the "Median"—though we are told that it perhaps came originally from "the summer rain-lands of Southern China". Happily man has found means, by irrigation and by "smudges", to make it feel at home in very many lands. The lemon is still more sensitive to cold than the orange. Athenaeus hails the fig tree as the guide or pioneer of civilization (ἡγεμὼν τοῦ καθαρείου βίου 74d). The old Acharnian, in Aristophanes, promises his love, that, if she will take him—γερόντιον as she may think him, "a bit of an old man"—he will show her his triple husbandry:

First a row of vinelets will I plant prolonged and orderly,
Next the little fig-tree shoots beside them, growing lustily,
Thirdly the domestic vine; although I am so elderly.
Round them all shall olives grow, to form a pleasant
    boundary.[2]

Here one may recall the story told by Aristotle about Thales—a story of universal application, he says.[3] He was reproached for his poverty, which was supposed to show that philosophy was of no use. He knew, however, from his study of the stars, while it was yet winter, that there would be a great harvest of olives; so, having a little capital, he paid deposits for the whole of the olive-presses in Miletus and Chios, which he hired at a low price, as nobody bid against him. When the harvest time came and there was a sudden demand for a great many presses at once, he let them out at any rate which he pleased and made a great deal of money, and proved to the world that it is easy for philosophers to be rich, if they wish. It should be remembered that olives must be pressed at once, just as gooseberries and oranges must be promptly turned into jam and marmalade; and further that Miletus, with its many colonies on the Black Sea, had an important market to think of for its olive oil.

A few words on the animals must conclude this part of our

1 M. R. Shackleton, *Europe*, p. 32.   2 Aristophanes, *Acharnians*, 994.
3 Aristotle, *Politics*, i, 11; p. 1259a.

study. Once more the geographer comes to our aid. In the Mediterranean zone there is little grass, so that the raising of cattle is not very generally important. The aromatic herbage will support sheep and goats, though they do not fatten on it, and their flesh gets a peculiar taste. The beasts, as we saw, are driven up into the mountains for the summer, and live largely on leaves. As they look after themselves, the young trees have little chance to escape them, and re-forestation is almost impossible—no new story, as we have learnt from Plato.[1] The Northern reader of the Classics remarks that milk is chiefly the product of sheep and goats, that butter is a Northern manufacture,[2] but that cheese is familiar to every Greek from Homer's day. When we think of food preservation, one reason for this is obvious. The ancients believed that lucerne—*Medica* they called it—was introduced to Europe by the army of Xerxes. So at least say Pliny, and Servius commenting on Virgil, and the latter adds a pleasant touch—"of this Venetia (Virgil's country) is full."[3] Finally, very little care seems to have been given to breeding. The ox indeed is familiar in our story—for quiet ploughing and hauling; but the ancients did not realize (or if they did, paid little attention to it) that castration is the foundation of the improvement of stock.

V

Oeconomicus—a very dull name (whoever invented it, author or transcriber) for a delightful book. Ruskin had a translation of it made, to be the first volume of his *Bibliotheca Pastorum*, hoping to make it one of "the chief domestic treasures of British peasants". It contains, he said, "the ideal of domestic life"; an ideal which "cannot be changed", he added, and which is "presented with extreme simplicity and modesty of heart...the language of an educated soldier and country

---

1 More fully dealt with in the essay on The Forest.
2 Cf. Pliny, *N.H.* xxviii, 133; *e lacte fit et butyrum, barbararum gen ium lautissimus cibus et qui divites a plebe discernat, plurimum e bubulo,* etc.
3 Virgil, *Georgics*, i, 215, with the commentary of Servius *ad locum*; Pliny, *N.H.* xviii, 16, 144.

gentleman, relating without effort what he has seen, and without pride what he has learned". "This piece of noble Greek thought" is his last word upon it. Mr J. L. Myres, who perhaps came at it from a different angle, speaks of "that most gracious and humorous essay on How to be happy though married".[1] It is the work of Xenophon, "that illustrious commander, the most English of the Athenians", as Andrew Lang called him. Mr J. A. K. Thomson says that his natural tastes were very much those of Sir Walter Scott. In Xenophon, writes Sir Richard Livingstone, "we see humanism at its best". Modern historians have too often a pedantic shake of the head for him; but to humanists he must ever appeal.

It would be pleasant to give again the story of the dear little wife and her training; Xenophon—or Ischomachus, who tells the story—does not look on women with quite the eye of Hesiod, and it is no peasant's household that he is describing. But he too is a firm believer in work and in tidiness. He wants his house kept "shipshape", and he describes the amazing, the enchanting order, in which he found everything on a big Phoenician ship he once visited (8, 11–16). "How beautiful," he says, using the highest word of praise that Greeks knew, "how beautiful it is to see—the shoes laid in a proper row...No serious man would smile when I claim that there is beauty, something eurhythmic, in the order even of pots and pans set out in neat array, even if a wit laugh at the idea." That is the man, grave, courteous, in earnest, bearing, in words that anticipate a line of Tennyson, "the majestic (σεμνόν) name of gentleman", of "the beautiful and good", as the Athenian put it (6, 14).

His theme (and ours) is farming. His father had had a passion for farming (φιλογεωργός) and he would never let Ischomachus buy a well-farmed piece of land; "it costs too much, and it can't be improved", he would say; and, where you could not be improving the estate, there was no real pleasure in it. Ischomachus tells Socrates that they have

1 J. L. Myres, *Political Ideas*, p. 197.

before now increased the value of a property many times over. His father did not learn this business of farming from anybody else, nor from worrying about it; he got it all from loving the job and liking to put his back into it (διὰ τὴν φιλογεωργίαν καὶ φιλοπονίαν, 20, 25).

Farming, he says, is such a friendly and gentle art (οὕτω φιλάνθρωπός ἐστι καὶ πραεῖα τέχνη, 19, 17), that it tells those who have eyes and ears all about itself. The earth is so honest and definite (σαφηνίζει τε καὶ ἀληθεύει, 20, 13); she plays no tricks, but lets you know what she can and what she can't do; treat her well, and she treats you well—everybody knows that (γῆν δὲ πάντες ἴσασιν ὅτι εὖ πάσχουσα εὖ ποιεῖ, 20, 14). You must study the nature of the soil, by watching what it will do and what it won't—look at the next farm; and when you know, it is no use to fight against God (θεομαχεῖν, 16, 3). Even waste land shows its nature in the wild stuff that grows on it. Seasons, too, have to be considered, late or early, for God doesn't take orders in arranging the year (17, 4). Get your mind on winter and the weeds and the wind; reap with your back to the wind, and winnow against it. You will learn by watching men at work; a really good farmer likes you to see him planting and sowing; ask him about what he is doing and he will tell you (15, 10, 11).

We need not follow him into detail, of which he gives a good deal—there are slaves to think of, and there is manure—but we may end our story with the gist of the whole matter. It is not knowledge or want of knowledge that makes a farmer thrive or fail; the real thing is care. People talk of farmers who have found out some clever device and prospered accordingly; but with farmers, as with generals, it is not cleverness that counts but carefulness. Are your men working, for instance, or slacking? (20, 5). There is as much difference between good work and slacking as between industry and doing nothing at all. Suppose the vines are being hoed to clear the ground of weeds; if the hoeing is so badly done that the weeds grow more rank than before, how can you call that anything but idleness? (20, 20).

EMPORIA

A GOOD many years ago I was returning on the Grand Trunk
Railroad to Kingston, Ontario. The long slow journey was
over, and the weary passengers transferred themselves to the
shuttle train that plied to and fro between the Junction on
the main line and the city. For some reason or other the
shuttle train did not start, and I found myself listening
absent-mindedly to the talk of two commercial travellers,
who sat near me and were chatting idly to fill in the time.
Suddenly I began to be interested. "You can always sell
at Quebec", said one of them. "Why?" said the other, "it's
not a big place." (The population was, if I remember, about
60,000 in those days.) "No, it's not," said the first; "but
the English-speaking travellers don't go further than Quebec,
and the people from all those French towns and villages
down the river have to come to Quebec to buy." These
small French places extended on one side of the St Lawrence
and the other for some hundreds of miles. Then the train
started, and I remember no more of my fellow-passengers or
their talk; but they had given me an idea, they had started
for me a new line of observation and reflexion; and to their
weary talk while the train dawdled, I trace back this paper.
Quebec was what the Greeks called an *Emporion*, a centre
where merchants gather—a "centre of distribution" we might
call it to-day.

I am more and more clear that, in all sorts of cases, the
data of ancient historians and of those who excerpt them, who
deal in moral instances, who give us constitutional points and
so forth from a dim past, have to be checked not merely by
the statements of other ancient writers, but by what happens,
by what we can see happening, by what we know to have
happened, in similar cases elsewhere. There is the evidence
of the physical world to be weighed, the evidence of the sea

and the winds, the evidence of the mountains, of climate too, and of deforestation. There are obvious changes in the Mediterranean world resulting from the disappearance of forest; and science men tell us to keep an open mind for changes on a larger scale for which man is not responsible— changes of wet and dry from 1000 B.C., into which I cannot go. But a great deal does not change. Nelson's experience of the shifting and uncertain winds of the Mediterranean and his imperative need of a naval base in Corsica will explain something of Roman history. But I fear we are landsmen all, who deal with the records of the ancient world, and we are amenable to what Colonel Campbell wrote of Napoleon, on Elba: "Napoleon has no idea of the difficulties occasioned by winds and tides, but judges of changes of position in the case of ships as he would with regard to troops on land." The wind drops, and your sailing ship is out of control—and the old currents and the ancient shoals are still there. "A new boat and old rocks", is the pungent Highland proverb.

But now to return to our commercial travellers and Quebec. They remind us how the habits of trade change and do not change. The French, from a hundred little towns and villages, go to Quebec to buy necessary goods from middle-men, who have bought them from the travellers of the manufacturers in Toronto and Buffalo; the goods are at Quebec, but the travellers did not bring them. That is a modern innovation, and there are obviously many. Trains, penny postage, telegrams and cheque books—a whole system of quick communications and of credit and banking differen-tiates modern business from ancient, so far as method goes. Professor Bury urges that commerce had much less influence in ancient politics than we sometimes suppose; and Professor Hasebroek has written a raging tearing book to the same effect. But it comes to this. If we do not find tariff wars in the ancient world (and the Megarians might dispute this), nor Ottawa agreements, nor "protected" industries, nor trades unions (except in a very rudimentary form—in the absence of paper, telegrams and journalism), the sea was

always there, and there were sailing ships, freights and
dealers. The sea did what it does now; sailing ships were
sailing ships; human nature was human nature; and trade
was trade. Even then dealers kept a sharp look-out on prices.
"Praise a little ship, but put your goods on a big ship", said
Hesiod, and so said the modern experts, at any rate before
the late war. Or look at the playful talk of Socrates at the
end of the *Oeconomicus* on the love the merchants (ἔμποροι)
feel for wheat, a love which drives them to sail the seas to
wherever there is most of it; and then they will take it
wherever it is most honoured and people prize it most highly;
he plays on the two meanings of τιμή, honour and price.

Economics is a branch of study, which, I gather, has only
produced one first-rate classic; and that was in the eighteenth
century. Men of letters in ancient days, as nowadays, were
not greatly interested in economics. Thucydides gives no more
than a chapter or two to the finances of the Peloponnesian
war; he makes the Spartan king allude to money, but he
omits the doubling of the League's tribute carried by Cleon;
he tells us that 20,000 slaves escaped from Athens when the
enemy occupied Attica, who are reasonably supposed to have
been in the main skilled artisans. For the rest, he hardly
supposes we should be interested in the monetary aspects of
the war, for he seems not to have been so himself. There is
so much colour for Bury's assertion. But once leave the
texts and the records, and study the sea and the ways of men,
and their tastes in foods, clothes and climates—and we may
not be as sure as Bury was, or as indifferent as Thucydides.

There was, in fact, a great deal of overseas trade. Everybody knows that Athens lived on imported wheat, but not
everybody asks how it was paid for; nor does everybody ask
how the ancients managed their trade. They had not our
modern devices, nor had the medieval people; and they
tended to do things somewhat in the same way. In the
medieval world merchants carried their goods about in bulk
from town to town, and so they did in the ancient world.
There they were in the πωλητήριον; you could buy the lot

and take them away for a cash payment, or another freight.
Then again, just as there are to this day special centres for
special trades; so there were in the middle ages; so there were
in antiquity. Down to the war, perhaps to-day, Liverpool,
one of the world's great ports, had to buy its tea in London.
The world's crops of tea went regularly to London; London
was the great centre of distribution for the tea trade of
Britain. In the middle ages Venice and Genoa were great
centres in the same way; they controlled the Eastern trade
of Europe, and fought often enough for it; the goods of the
Orient, silks, spices, pepper and so forth, went in bulk to
Venice or Genoa as might be; and the people who wanted
such things got them from Venice or Genoa, at the prices
demanded there. No wonder that Wordsworth can write

> Once did she hold the gorgeous East in fee.

II

If a place is to become a real centre of distribution, an
emporion, it must have certain natural advantages; you must
be able to reach it easily and get away easily. If it is on the
sea, it must have, first of all, a good harbour, and not only
a harbour with plenty of room and deep water, but one that
is easy to get into and easy to get out of, with no hostile
current sweeping past it or difficult wind to hold up ships,
and preferably no river bringing down silt. We forget among
the great noises of history, among soldiers, constitution-
builders and politicians, what a factor speed is in commerce.
How long does it take you to get your ship into the harbour,
how long to get out? And (very important, too, as we shall
see) how long will the harbour people, officials, stevedores,
dockers and the rest, keep you hanging about, unable to tie
up, to discharge cargo, to load, and to get your papers?

So much for the harbour; but the harbour is not all. There
are harbours enough among the Greek islands and along the
Eastern shore of the Adriatic. What an *emporion* needs beside
a harbour is a hinterland of some sort, with efficient means

of access to it, real roads that can be travelled or familiar
sea routes. Venice was nothing, and Genoa hardly more, in
the Roman Empire; it took a civilized Germany, France and
Northern Europe generally to make them. Winnipeg and
Vancouver were predestined centres of distribution, but it
needed population and the Canadian Pacific Railway to
bring them into being. Greece had no good trunk-roads; how
could she, when she was cut up by mountains and controlled
in detail by city states? and what city state would dream of
building its section of a trunk-road across its little territory,
to benefit the trade of a neighbour, near or far? The Persians
had their trunk-roads across a continent under a single control
from Susa to the Aegaean; and Rome early signalized her
dominance in Italy by building across the country roads to
last for eternity. Such roads fix the future course of trade,
just as the railways do to-day; a sea port served by a railway
will be a difficult competitor for an aspiring town with poor
railway connexions.

Greece, then, had no trunk-roads of any consequence, and
thus the sea remained the chief means of transit; the sea took
the place of roads, as it did in early New England; and this
is important to remember. For Greece trade depends on the
sea, and the Mediterranean is tideless. As a result a harbour
is always a harbour; deep water and a good access once there,
they stay. Even if there had been roads, we have to remember
what Adam Smith points out, that freight by water is
infinitely cheaper than by land, by one ship than by many
waggons; and Greek land-transport was done by mule. Once
a ship is loaded, says Sir Douglas Owen, an extra hundred
miles, or a thousand, makes very little difference. Sea routes
or land ways, the main thing is for our *emporion* to be in the
centre of a large enough group of accessible subsidiary
markets; and this Athens was.

Much of what I have been saying, with my mind on Venice
and Montreal and similar places in the medieval or the
modern world, and starting from my fellow-travellers and
Quebec, was said long ago in Athens. A tract on Revenues

is generally printed among the works of Xenophon. Of course its authorship is doubted; the function of scholars is always to hesitate—except perhaps in cases where there is no evidence. Scholars generally, noting a reference to an event of 361 B.C., date the pamphlet about 355 B.C., but the general conditions described had prevailed long before that. Athens, with her trade and her empire, was laid low, as we all know, at the end of the Peloponnesian war in 404; and her recovery was one to amaze people who thought about it. The tract, even if it is a generation later, explains this. The reason lay in the Peiraieus, the ideal *emporion*, and the conservative habits of business men; before the war they had always taken their goods to Athens—where else should they take them now? The author of the *Revenues* (*Poroi*) reads the situation exactly.

"One might reasonably suppose that the city lies at the centre of Greece, nay, of the whole inhabited world...every traveller, who would go from one end of Greece to the other end, passes Athens as if the centre of a circle, whether he goes by sea or land. She is not wholly sea-girt; but, as if she were an island, every wind that blows lets her fetch what she needs or export what she will. For she is on two seas, and by land she receives much from the merchants (*emporoi*)"; and, he adds, she is untroubled by barbarian neighbours, which was not true of some notable *emporia*, as we may see. One part of his policy is a more generous welcome to foreign merchants who want to reside in Athens (*metics*); they are a great source of revenue, and self-supporting, and ask nothing for their services but leave to stay. All that is needed is to remove certain burdens that do not really benefit the state, and seem to put some disability (ἀτιμίας τι) upon them. Why for instance should they be made to serve in the infantry? Do Lydians, Phrygians, Syrians and other barbarians really strengthen Athenian troops? Such service interrupts their commerce. Could they not also be allowed to hold land and houses of their own? If so, probably more would come, and men of a better class. For Athens is the pleasantest and most profitable city to which merchants can resort (ἐμπορεύεσθαι).

He surveys her advantages—"the finest and safest accommodation for shipping", no risks in bad weather, and no delays. "At most other ports merchants are compelled to take return freights, for the local currency has no circulation outside; but at Athens there is abundance of goods, so that they can carry away what freight they will; and, if they find no convenient return freight, it is very good business to take Athenian currency abroad. Wherever they sell it, they are apt to make a good profit." The great thing is speed, as little demurrage as possible. Athens ought to encourage the harbour authorities to make the speediest settlements of any disagreements. That would encourage business and be all to the good of Athens. Everything should be done to get *emporoi* to use the *emporion*—good seats in the theatre, hospitality, better hotels (καταγώγια), shops and exchanges (πωλητήρια). Imports, exports, sales, rents, and customs would all be benefited. After discussing a further suggestion about silver-mining, he returns to this desirability of bringing visitors from outside—"ship-owners (ναύκληροι) and merchants to begin", people with wine, oil, cattle, people who "can make profits by use of judgment and of money", artisans (χειροτέχναι), poets and philosophers. "Yes, all those who want to effect a rapid sale or purchase of a thousand commodities, where could they find what they want better than at Athens?"

It is a strange new note that rings in our ears here—"what we want is not an empire, but better hotels". Yet the central fact of the *emporion*, the centre of distribution, was not new. Pericles hints at it, even in the great Funeral Oration: "Because of the greatness of our city the fruits of the whole earth flow in upon us; so that we enjoy the goods of other countries as freely as of our own" (Thuc. ii, 38). The Athenian Oligarch, about 424, touches on the same point, and links it with command of the sea—the products of Sicily, Italy, Cyprus, Egypt, Pontus, etc. are all gathered in Athens. Timber for ship-building is a matter lightly noticed in our histories, but it was immensely significant in a world reckless in deforestation, and it gave new importance to Macedon, Lebanon, Cyprus and Pontus. The Oligarch does not over-look it; of course, timber will come to the mistress of the seas; and brass, linen, wax—all needed for shipping and ship-building; no other city has all these together, and Athens can prohibit their export. So much for her rivals!

Strabo is interpreting Greek history aright, and eminently Athenian history, when he says that "in a certain sense we are amphibious, and belong no more to the land than to the sea" (C. 8). It is a poor theory that will not explain more facts than it was initially intended to cover. Strabo gives us here a real clue to all human experience; we are made by Nature to need both sea and land.

III

I propose now to take two or three typical instances of the *emporion* in Greek waters, and from them to return to Athens, as everybody inevitably does who thinks about anything Greek.

Marseilles shall be our starting-point. Its foundation was dated traditionally about 600 B.C. The known story of colonization should incline us to accept without much scepticism the date of a colonial foundation; for it is generally the thought-out act of a civilized people, and colonists have good reason as a rule to remember years. Massilia, then, curiously recalls early settlements in the New World. Those who read Parkman will recall the divine visions and revela-tions that led to the foundation of Montreal by Maisonneuve in 1642; and Strabo tells a somewhat similar tale of Ephesian Artemis bidding first the Phocaeans to get a guide from Ephesus, and then bidding Aristarche, "one of the women held in high honour" there, to go with them, and to take with her apparently a reproduction of certain sacred things. So, when the colony was duly founded, a temple of Ephesian Artemis was built, and Aristarche was made its priestess.[1]

1 Strabo, C. 179.

Montreal had nuns, with a garrison to protect them from the Indians, and a saint of a painfully ascetic type. Marseilles had a Pocahontas too. For Nanus (Jullian[1] calls him Nann) was marrying his daughter Petta when the Phocaeans came, and he invited them to the function. It was the usage that, after the banquet, the maiden to be married should come in with a cup of water and give it to him among the suitors whom she should choose, and he should be the bridegroom. So, when Petta came in and looked round, she gave the cup to one of the Greeks; and her father, counting it something of a divine coincidence, agreed with her choice, and they were married. Petta received a new Greek name, and perhaps her husband did, too; for they lived together as Aristoxene and Euxenus, and from them came the well-known family of the Protiadai. Either their son was Protis, or else that was the husband's original name.

Outside the region of romance, the story of Marseilles closely recalls that of Montreal or New York. It did not actually stand on the river, as those cities do. The nature of the country and of the river was against this (Strabo, C. 183). The city stood rather to the east of the Rhone mouth, on a harbour only equalled (says Jullian) in the Western Mediterranean by that of Carthage, a harbour screened by islands from the storms of the Gulf of Lyons and by a mountain ridge from the landward wind, the Mistral (Μελαμβόρειος, Strabo, iv, C. 182 calls it). Strabo (C. 188) would have us remark the harmoniousness, the concord (ὁμολογίαν) of the countryside with the rivers and the two seas, Mediterranean and Atlantic—

large part of the excellence of the place is the ease with which the necessaries of life are interchanged by everybody with everybody else, and the profits that all share....One might (he adds) cite it as evidence for the work of Providence, that the regions are laid out, not in a fortuitous way, but as though on a thought-out plan. For the Rhone is navigable, for a long way and by big ships; it reaches many parts of the country,

1 Camille Jullian, *Histoire de la Gaule*, i, ch. 5, p. 204.

for the rivers that fall into it are navigable and in turn receive
traffic to a very great extent.... (From these) the commerce
goes overland to the Seine and then down to the Ocean...
whence it is less than a day's run (δρόμος) to Britain.

Some indeed of the traffic, owing to the force of the Rhone,
goes up by land, as the New York Central runs up the
Hudson and the Mohawk. How like the New World it all is—
the great ships to Montreal, 800 miles from Belle Isle—the
bateaux and canals above the rapids, the lakes, the Ottawa
river trade with the portage across to the rivers that flow into
Lake Huron. The likeness to the New World is helped further
by the savage fighting between two races to control this inter-
Ocean trade, in which at last the Greeks beat the Cartha-
ginians, and by the immense influence of Greek ways in Gaul
as of French ways among the Indians. Probably Petta was
no more than Pocahontas the last native girl to prefer a
husband from overseas. The Gauls, Strabo says, loved Greek
ways so much that they wrote their contracts in Greek. If the
alternative was a Semitic script, their practice is quite
intelligible and laudable. A hundred and fifty years after
Strabo there were Christian martyrs at Lyons whose story
was written in Greek; and the chief heretic of the Celtic
stock in the fifth century A.D. changed his name into Greek,
from Morgan to Pelagius.

Strabo is very clear on the advantages of Gaul; there were
gold mines with slabs (πλάκες) of gold the size of your hand,
gold dust and nuggets—all placer mining; iron mines—and
very pretty ones (ἀστεῖα); good water supplies; hot springs;
and (we may note) *emporia* dotted about the country. The tin
trade from the Isle of Wight, following the Seine and Rhone
route, with its ingots carried on pony-back, is familiar to
everybody. Less familiar is the fancy of the Britons (recorded
by Strabo) for ivory necklaces, which must have come from
Africa or India, from Carthage or from Alexandria. For
centuries, once the Punic menace was averted, Marseilles
dominated the Gallic tribes—*not* conquering them, be it
noted. The city was a model of high order and aristocratic

government, like Renaissance Venice; and again like Venice "she must espouse the everlasting sea"—or, in Strabo's simpler words (C. 179), they "trusted the sea more than the land".

The ivory necklaces reminded us of Alexandria. Its story is endless and most various, with every kind of literary, scientific, and religious interest. But to confine ourselves to our special theme, one section of Strabo must suffice, and that much abridged (C. 798). "Chief among the happy advantages of the city is this, that it is the only place in all Egypt blest by nature in both ways—seaward, by having good harbours, landward because the river easily conveys and concentrates everything on the place, which is the greatest *emporion* of the world." He quotes Cicero to the effect that under Ptolemy Auletes the annual revenues of Egypt were 12,500 talents.

If then the worst and idlest administrator of the kingdom made such a revenue, what must one think of the present management (under the Romans), when such care is shown, and trade with India and the Troglodytes has been so much increased? In earlier days not twenty vessels would dare to pass down the Arabian Gulf (the modern Red Sea) just to peep outside the Straits (Bab el Mandeb); but now great fleets go as far as India and the headlands of Ethiopia, from which the most valuable freights are brought to Egypt, and from Egypt exported to other regions, so that double duties are collected on entrance and on export....In fact, it is a case of monopolies; for Alexandria is not only the receptacle of goods of this kind, but is the source of supply to the outside world.

An *emporion* emphatically, a Venice with Eastern trade and Western and Northern customers—Strabo says elsewhere that 120 ships in a year would sail to India. I forbear to discuss the monsoon, the "Hippalus", and the explanation of the rising of the Nile, and only hint at the trade in living elephants and tigers, spices and pearls.

IV

From various sources we get pictures of the actual life in an
emporion—from Aristophanes eminently. Take the questions
addressed by Dionysus to Herakles about conditions in the
world of the dead—

> Tell me what friends received
> And entertained you when you went below;
> And tell me too the havens, fountains, shops,
> Roads, restingplaces, stews, refreshment rooms,
> Towns, lodgings, hostesses, with fewest bugs.
>
> (*Frogs*, 112)

Clearly the writer of the *Revenues* tract might suggest better
hotels in Hades. Retail dealers must be prominent features
in any *emporion*. A quick short visit—run in, discharge cargo,
sell it, get fresh cargo, and out again, and the minimum of
delay and demurrage; and anything you buy will be in the
smallest possible quantities, unless you are provisioning your
ship. No wonder Aristophanes talks of dynasties of dealers,
culminating in the sausage-seller vulgarian-in-chief to the
state, of the abusive language of the women who sell loaves
(*Frogs*, 858), and the men who sell charcoal by the basket
(*Ach.* 325). Athenaeus quotes a comic poet who enumerates
ten sorts of peddlers (-πώλας), hawking anchovies, charcoal,
dried figs, hides, barley, spoons, books, sieves, sweet-cakes,
and seed (iv, 126e). No wonder that thoughtful people
reflected on the κάπηλος, the retail-dealer—his origin, habits,
and acquired character; how could the growers and producers
hawk their own wares or sell them retail? A poor class the
κάπηλοι! How could they be anything else—people who trade
in penn'orths? Distinguish, says the philosopher (*Rep.* ii,
371 D); the *emporoi* travel, the *kapêloi* sit, while the αὐτοπώλης
(*Pol.* 260c) sells the goods he makes himself and is not a
kapêlos. Did not the Lydians originate κάπηλοι and coinage?
asks the historian. Incidentally we are brought face to face
with the fact that the *emporion* means not only sound currency
—"owls" to take all over the Mediterranean—but small

currency, the little bits of coins that you carry in your mouth and that look like fish-scales. Nothing that bears on profit is counted disgraceful at Carthage, says Polybius (vi, 56). But look at the type! The Reckless Man in Theophrastus "is apt to become an inn-keeper or a tax-farmer; he will decline no disgraceful trade, but he will be a crier, a cook, a gambler, he will neglect to maintain his mother, will be arrested for theft, and spend more time in gaol than at home".[1]

I must not linger to tell of money-changers and bankers—inevitable, with all the many currencies of the myriad independent cities. They were at least spared paper-money. Visitors to Athens by sea to-day see their successors, with the glass-covered *tables* and an amazing variety of coinages, lining the street where you land in the Peiraieus. Picture Phormion, cringing meanly along—betraying his miserable mind in his pitiful gait, cries his wastrel stepson who need not be quite believed. Nor must I do more than remind you of the foreigners who brought gods and demons and cults with them, and set up their shrines on Attic soil. Here indeed were people from the sea bringing in new ideas—and amazingly infectious ideas, fertile of evil and of good, of superstition and philosophy.

The rude young gentleman among the Phaeacians tells Ulysses that he classes him

> with the ship-frequenting kind
> Of traders, overseers of merchandise,
> Whose talk is all of cargoes, and their mind
> Dreams of unjust gains, and doth bargains prize.[2]

Plutarch is careful to apologize for Solon having lived the life of an *emporos*, a merchant; but that life used "to make men at home in the affairs of foreigners, win them the friendship of kings, and give them a broad experience—some merchants have actually been founders of great cities, as Protis was of Marseilles" (*Solon*, 2).[3] A taunt and an apology; and the ideal city should not, Aristotle thought, have traders

1 Theophrastus, *Characters*, 16—with a good bit more.
2 Homer, *Odyssey*, viii, 161.   3 See also p. 80.

and dealers among its citizens. They might under conditions be there as an unenfranchised class.

Plato, as we all know, mistrusted the sea and those who haunt it; they picked up new notions and they had a bad influence; the ideal city should stand at a reasonable distance from the sea, safeguarded against foreign traders and their ideas, generally so bad, so alien to a philosophic state, so untrue to real conceptions of godhead. Yet even he admits that a city on a spot or in a region where no imports are required is well-nigh impossible (*Rep.* ii, 370). Utopia, it is abundantly clear, ought to be on an island, but even then it is difficult to keep it from contact with the sea. Americans and Phaeacians have alike found it impossible to have the best clippers afloat and yet keep out of the world. Neither Plato nor Thomas Jefferson, under the most ideal conditions, could maintain an embargo.

Yet I feel that it was generally in the *emporion* that enlightenment came to Greece; that it was, in large measure, this dubious class, the *emporoi*, carrying their cargoes about the seas, who opened up the world to the Greeks, and, if you will forgive the antithesis, opened up the Greek mind to the world. Athenian orators would trace law, order and civilization to Solon, the ideal law-giver; and he was himself an ἔμπορος, and at the centre of his law-giving was the conception of the *emporion*.[1] Alexander the Great had the same idea for Alexandria, with the larger conceptions which come so naturally from it. The one made the very nidus for Greek poetry, Greek art, Greek philosophy; and the other gave Greece the second great centre of living thought, the *emporion*, where science and learning and religion found a new home, and throve to the everlasting profit of us all. It takes a whole world to make a real philosopher; wonder, says Aristotle, is the mother of philosophy; and a despised class, as so often in human history, revealed the world—

The beauty and the wonder and the power.

1 Cf. pp. 59-61.

FEEDING THE ATHENIANS

I

THERE is a story in Strabo's *Geography* (C. 486), which has often come back to me during the Hitler War. Each fresh enactment of Lord Woolton gave it weight. It was to the effect that on the island of Ceos (Zia nowadays) there was a law—or so Greeks said—which enacted that, when man or woman reached the age of sixty, hemlock should be administered to them. It was to economize on the island's food. The botanist Theophrastus tells us that hemlock meant a "swift and easy release".[1] We all remember the last scene in the *Phaedo*: "when the cold reaches the heart, τότε οἰχήσεται, our friend will be gone"; and so it proved; but till then the discussion went on nobly. I give Strabo's story as he gives it, not forgetting that in Greek island and city states there was a certain readiness to accept and spread stories about rival communities, without excessive pedantry in historical inquiry. Failing authentication, it seemed useless to propose the scheme to Lord Woolton; the Cabinet might have been against it.

True or false, the story illustrates what we understand to have been the constant difficulty of most Greek states, especially city states. The standard crops of Greece were grain, wine and oil, but the scantiness of arable land is repeatedly emphasized. "Of course, there must be food; it is a first necessity", is Aristotle's dictum. Few would dispute it; but the question was where and how to get the food. Colonization was one of the remedies; and Plato[2] recognizes over-population as one of the grounds for planting colonies; not hemlock but emigration should solve the food problem.

---

1 Theophrastus, *Plants*, ix, 168, a combination devised by Thrasyas of Mantinea, of hemlock, poppy and some other things, for which there was no cure. In Ceos, he adds, they did not compound it, they bruised it, added water, and death was swift and easy.

2 Plato, *Laws*, iv, 708.

An immense number of colonies were planted; Miletus, according to ancient reckoning, planted eighty or ninety, largely on the Black Sea. The inference is drawn that the birth-rate must have been high, and not balanced, as so long in England and elsewhere, by a high infant mortality—a fair indication, one would think, of wholesomeness of diet, whatever the difficulties about quantity. Sir John Mahaffy[1] suggested that in later days Greeks became less prolific; certainly population in old Greece declined, but emigration and the deliberate destruction of the newly born are outstanding causes. Greek comedies and novels are very apt to use the recognition of a daughter exposed at birth as a reasonably probable part of the plot. The call for mercenary soldiers all over the nearer East took men away from the days of the younger Cyrus; and the foundation of new Greek cities all over his empire by Alexander had the same effect. In the earlier generations the settlers in those new cities fetched wives from Greece. But all this was later than the great period of Athenian history, which begins with a crisis, or a combination of crises, of some magnitude.

Attica was overcrowded, and there was agricultural distress, debt and discontent. Poverty, as Aristotle repeats,[2] is again and again the cause of revolution; and in a Greek community poverty meant hunger without state aid for the hungry, a dangerously narrow margin between life of a sort and sheer starvation—a condition only too apt to produce riot with murder on a savage scale. Politics could be furious among Greeks; they can still; but politics reinforced by hunger—we have had for decades no such experience in Britain. Ancients and moderns alike, from Thucydides[3] to Mrs R. C. Bosanquet,[4] suggest that Attica had not been richly blessed by Nature, from an agricultural point of view; but the country had been from early times an asylum, and so the population had grown. By 590 B.C. difficulties were

---

1 Mahaffy, *Rambles and Studies*, p. 194.
2 Aristotle, *Politics*, ii, 6, 13; p. 1265b; iii, 8, 7; p. 1279b.
3 Thucydides, i, 2. 4 *Days in Attica*, p. 66.

very great. How Solon solved the agricultural problems is dealt with in another essay.[1] There remains Athens, to be considered—and to be fed. Let us look ahead.

It is difficult to estimate a population without an exact census. Cambridge in the census of 1931 had some 60,000 people—or a few thousands more; ten years later, with "evacuees", troops and the students of shifted colleges, people conjectured there would be 120,000. A very few facts, on which we can really rely, are available for any ancient town. Thucydides says that one consequence of the Spartans fortifying Deceleia in 413 B.C. was that more than 20,000 slaves deserted.[2] Exactitude, τὸ ἀκριβές, was one of his passions; so we can accept the figure; and it is generally thought, in view of other facts incidentally gained as to life at Athens, that a large proportion of these slaves would be artisans employed in industries in Athens and the Peiraieus. We are told that the theatre of Athens would seat 30,000 people; they would not all be residents. All things considered, the population of Athens may be guessed to have been 200,000—a guess, but not an extravagant one;[3] and every mouth had to be filled every day, and the land was not equal to it. But there was the sea.

It would undoubtedly be better (wrote Aristotle),[4] both with a view to safety and to the provision of necessaries, that the city and territory [he is framing an ideal state] should be connected with the sea; the defenders of a country, if they are to maintain themselves against an enemy, should be easily relieved.... Moreover, it is necessary that they should import from abroad what is not found in their own country, and that they should export what they have in excess; for a city ought to be a market, not indeed for others, but for herself.

1 See p. 60.
2 Thucydides, vii, 27.
3 Glotz, *Ancient Greece at Work*, p. 257, suggests 350,000. Neither estimate can be relied on for Solon's date, when the population, though seeming large to those who looked back, cannot have been as great as in the time of Pericles and the Peloponnesian war.
4 Aristotle, *Politics*, vii, 6, 2; p. 1327a.

Obvious enough to us all. But a great idealist who had planned an imaginary state before Aristotle wanted it to be at some distance from the sea. Sailors, sea-faring men, merchants and people who came from overseas had a bad effect on a community; they suggested changes, even if they did not advocate them; they had other customs and induced criticisms of home ways, which might lead to the upset of the ideal founder's plans. The history of New England and its neighbours is commentary enough. But we are not dealing with an imaginary state, or a Quaker colony, or a Jesuit paradise in Paraguay. Athens was on the sea; at least the Peiraieus was on the sea and was linked by long walls to Athens—one city with it. So, of course, what was not found in Attica would have to come in from overseas, and in considerable quantity. That was admitted then; Pericles boasts of it [1]—"we enjoy the goods of other countries as freely as our own"; and historians have had no doubt about it.

The American historian and politician, Henry Cabot Lodge—the enemy of Woodrow Wilson, who wrecked the President's League of Nations plans—in one of his better moments gave us a great principle; one fact, a single fact, he suggested, was mere gossip; two facts related to each other were History. Here, then, is a second fact. Athens had to get her food by sea; but in the winter months, roughly from the end of October to April, there was no navigation. This appears alike in authors so severed in date and in interests as Hesiod, Thucydides and St Luke.[2] Hesiod says the ship must be beached; Thucydides says there was no communication, or only with difficulty, with Sicily during the four winter months; and St Paul's voyage is familiar to us all. Mountain lands, towering islands, narrow seas—and North winds from across the Steppes of Russia, and South winds from the flat Sahara—all the conditions to make sailing uneasy; and we read without surprise that Aegaean navigation was full of perilous uncertainty in early spring, the islands "scourged"

1 Thucydides, ii, 38.
2 Hesiod, *Works and Days*, 619 ff.; Thucydides, vi, 21, 2; Acts xxvii. 9.

by the North wind, the two great counter currents of wind
the formative causes of the Balkan climate.[1] Seneca, in his
Natural Questions (v, 18), with some little rhetoric, applies to
the winds the remark made first about Julius Caesar—that it
was doubtful whether his birth was a blessing or a curse to the
state; but he will not saddle the Creator, God or Nature,
with the sins and follies and greed of man; death is always
with us; why seek it?

Another fact is to be remembered, though often forgotten
by landsmen, which most historians are; the ships of the
Greeks were all sailing ships. As we noted before (p. 73)
Colonel Campbell on Elba remarked with surprise that
Napoleon, for all his experience, seemed not to understand
that ships cannot be pushed about and stationed here and there
as if they are regiments. Landsmen never quite understand
what can be done and what cannot be done with ships; and
men who only know the sea as passengers on steamers are
poor judges of navigation, when it has to be conducted in
sailing ships, and those small. Grote[2] did not see why
Thucydides called the boast of Cleon—that he would fetch
the Spartans prisoners from Pylos in three weeks—"madman's talk".[3] He forgot that, fifteen years or so after Cleon,
the Spartans retook Sphacteria because the winds would
not let an Athenian relieving fleet get round Cape Malea
(Matapan);[4] he forgot that in 1453 a sailing fleet failed to
save Constantinople because it was held up outside the
Dardanelles.

Take it, then, that the food of Athens had to come in by
sea, and that in winter next to nothing could come in. What
follows? Obviously that all the food for those four or five
winter months had to be in Athens before November began
or very little later. This, because it was not practicable to
rely on road-borne food. One of the things with which Adam
Smith begins is the immensely greater cost of sending by land

---

1 D. G. Hogarth, *The Nearer East*, p. 100.   2 Grote, *History*, vi, 127.
3 Thucydides, iv, 28, κουφολογία; 39, μανιώδης.
4 Diodorus, xiii, 64; **and** rather dimly, Xenophon, *Hell.* i, 2, 18.

from Aberdeen to London on so many waggons with so many horses and so many men what would go on one ship with no horses and far fewer men. But Greece had not even such roads as Britain could boast (little room for boasting) in the eighteenth century. A poverty-stricken series of city states—how should they make trunk roads through one another's territory?[1] A glance at the map reveals that rivers would not serve; Greece south of Salonica has no navigable rivers. That made the fascination of Nile and Euphrates for the Greek traveller. Then, neither by sea, nor by land, will food reach Athens in winter—food, that is, in anything like the quantities needed.

Yet another fact confronts us, which (I think) has not had from historians the full attention it requires. If food in large quantities has to be in Athens by November to last till April, it is clear, to those who will think about food, that its preservation must have been a major problem; and with that goes the other question (if it is not really the same question)—What food, suitable for 200,000 people, can be kept for four or five months? There are preferences, wherever food is concerned; but the blockade of Britain in two wars brought us to the position noticed by the Lydian as permanent in Greece—they eat not what they would like but what they have got. Greeks had their theories about the relation between food and health, though they knew nothing of calories and vitamins. Hippocrates—whatever his date in whole or in part—offers suggestions as to diet for the seasons; winter is the relevant season for this inquiry of ours; in winter then "a man should have one meal a day only, unless he have a very dry belly; in that case let him take a light luncheon (μικρὸν ἀριστῆν)"—and the foods should be wheaten bread rather than barley, roasted meat rather than boiled; drink dark and slightly diluted wine, and not much of it; vegetables, as little as possible, "except such as are warming and dry";

---

1 On roads, even in modern Greece, see Dodwell, *Tour* (1819), i, 115; Mahaffy, *Rambles*, pp. 158-9; Mrs R. C. Bosanquet, *Days in Attica*, p. 259; R. C. Jebb, *Modern Greece*, p. 109.

and a minimum of barley water; plenty of exercise, a hard bed, and, "if a bath is desired", cold after exercise; and an emetic twice or thrice a month, according to your constitution, dry or moist—especially after drunkenness, surfeit, or change of food or change of residence; caution near the Solstice; and a different regime when Spring comes.[1] There is little sickness in India, says Strabo (C. 706), because of the simplicity (λιτότητα) of their diet.

II

Food, then, has to be imported, and has to be preserved, to cover a period of four or five months. The main items to be imported are three; three more items may be home-grown, perhaps reinforced from abroad. We shall consider them in turn. The first three, the most important in their way, are wheat, fish and cheese; the second three are olive oil, honey and wine. A consideration of Athenian water supply should follow; and finally there are other things, almost luxuries, such as small fresh fish and small birds, fruits dried or fresh, and vegetables. A few words may be added on the small significance of milk and the absence of butter. Finally, some brief reference might be made to Greek methods of cookery in a land rather scant of fuel.

The historians from Herodotus to Polybius notice the significance of the Black Sea, and especially of Byzantium on the Bosphorus, in the trade of Athens, and indeed in her existence. When Herodotus speaks of the Scythians in South Russia, he tells us they are "tillers of the land, who sow grain not for eating but for selling" (ἐπὶ πρήσι). When Xerxes reached Abydos on his great expedition, he saw the wheat ships passing down the Dardanelles "on their way to Aegina and the Peloponnese"; his staff were for capturing the ships at once, but the king's view was that he was going to the same destination, and that the ships were taking food there for him and his forces.[2] It is noted that among the earliest

1 Hippocrates, *Regimen*, iii, 68 (Loeb, iv, 368).
2 Herodotus, iv, 17; vii, 147.

things the Greeks attempted after breaking the power of Xerxes at Salamis and Plataea was to free the Hellespont and the Bosphorus from Persian control; and they were successful. While the Confederacy of Delos lasted, the wheat supply was secure. When at Aegospotami in 404 Athens lost her last fleet, her fall was inevitable, a mere matter for her enemies of prolonging her starvation. Again in 387–386 Antalkidas stopped the ships from the Black Sea from sailing to Athens and sent them to the allies of the Spartans. Then, when Philip aims at control of Greece, and fails in Euboea, he looks out for some other position from which he can attack Athens (ἕτερον κατὰ τῆς πόλεως ἐπιτειχισμόν). "He saw", continues Demosthenes,[1] "that we use more imported wheat than any other men, and with the aim of controlling the wheat trade he advanced to Thrace, and his first endeavour was to ask the Byzantines, his allies, to join him in war against *you*", and when they refused, he besieged Byzantium; and Demosthenes reminds his hearers how "you—I mean the city" prevented the Hellespont from falling into Philip's hands at that time, and how he himself had had no small part in stirring them up to this great success, which, in addition to the great glory it brought, kept Athens supplied with the necessaries of life. Two centuries later Polybius speaks of the Black Sea region being rich in what all the world requires for the support of life, and of the Byzantines being absolute masters of all such things. He specifies cattle and slaves, in larger numbers and better quality than from other regions; honey, wax, and salt fish; and on occasion they also send grain to Mediterranean Greece, "while they take our superfluous stock of olive oil and every kind of wine".[2] Theophrastus tells us that of the various wheats imported into Greece this from the Black Sea was the lightest, the Sicilian heavier than

---

1 Demosthenes, *On the Crown*, 87–9. In *Lept.* 31 he uses the same phrase, σίτῳ πάντων ἀνθρώπων πλείστῳ χρώμεθ᾽ ἐπεισάκτῳ, adding that wheat from the Black Sea is roughly equal to what comes from all other ἐμπόρια. M. R. Shackleton, *Europe*, pp. 112, 113, says that the list of Greek imports is still usually headed by grain, though reclamation of basins in Macedonia, Thrace and Thessaly is increasing the home supply.

2 Polybius, iv, 38.

most imported kinds, but not as heavy as the Boeotian; these characters depend on soil and climate.[1] With care there was no great difficulty in keeping wheat, as long as it was unground; and it was stored in pits. India had not yet made her most significant contribution to the West; the rat was still unknown in Europe. Glotz tells us that merchant ships were built up to a tonnage of 360 tons (or, in Greek reckoning, 10,000 talents), carrying 7000 bushels of wheat.[2] He conjectures a consumption of something about 8 bushels *per annum per* person[3]—the figure allowed some years ago in France per person being 8 bushels as against the average American consumption of 6 bushels.

It is important to remember a few elementary facts about Greek navigation. The captain of the ship had, it would seem, no charts—none at all events to match the Admiralty charts carried by every British ship—and certainly no compass. The compass is a medieval invention or discovery, and is associated with Amalfi.[4] The seas were not lighted, nor were buoys put out and marked. The steersman had to carry all in his head, steering by headlands and the shape of the land, by the sun, and by the stars if he sailed at night. He had no anchor till the seventh century B.C. He had, moreover, to reckon on the chance of meeting pirates. The island harbours of the Aegaean, like the winding creeks and bays of the Adriatic, offered ideal opportunities for piracy, which have been used again and again when there has been no strong naval power to protect shipping. The pirates had agents in the ports, and, as the regular shipping routes followed the shores, there was little difficulty in guessing where the victims might be. There must have been many who sympathized with the comic poet quoted by Athenaeus (154 f.):

$$\text{ὁ μὴ πεπλευκὼς οὐδὲν ἑόρακεν κακόν.}$$

Hesiod had been of the same opinion—the sea was "full of

---

1 Theophrastus, *Plants*, viii, 4, 5.
2 Glotz, *Ancient Greece at Work*, p. 293.   3 Glotz, *ib.* p. 257.
4 See R. Beazley, *Dawn of Modern Geography*, ii, 398; *prima dedit nautis usum magnetis Amalphis.*

evils": he said the same, to be sure, of the land; his own voyage had been across from Boeotia to Euboea, a distance to be measured in yards, and afterwards bridged by the Boeotians to block Athenian use of the Euripus on the Black Sea voyage.

The Black Sea provided also the second great staple of Athenian diet—fish. "Ten thousand and beyond ken are the tribes that move and swim in the depths of the sea", writes Oppian in his poem on fisheries (i, 80), "and none could name them certainly; for no man hath reached the limit of the sea; but unto three hundred fathom, less or more, men know it and have explored Amphitrite." He understates the number of varieties by now classified, unless his "ten thousand" is to be taken as infinite. Modern men of science speak of 19,000 known species, but they know other seas beyond the common reach of Mediterranean peoples; they confirm Oppian, however, as to depth. No fishing ground of any consequence is known deeper than 270 fathoms; profitable fisheries are where the depth is about 110 fathoms, and sunlight makes plant life possible, and cold and warm waters meet.[1] The Banks of Newfoundland, rich perhaps beyond all other fisheries, lie on the shelf of the continent and receive the silt that comes down the St Lawrence from the regions drained by the Ottawa river; the depth is 100 fathoms, though just outside the Atlantic bottom is 1000 to 4000 fathoms down. The area of the Banks is about the size of Ireland.[2] The ancients recognized the bearing of depth, temperature and salinity.[3] The Mediterranean is salter than the English Channel, as 39 to 35; the water on the Banks of Newfoundland is on the same ratio 32·8; in Cabot Straits it is down to 26·2.[4] The Black Sea received masses of fresh water and its current was uniformly outward through the Bosphorus;[5] and there are no tides.

The Mediterranean is not regarded as very rich in fish,

1 Herubel, *Sea Fisheries*, pp. 55, 188.
2 These figures are from Herubel, *Sea Fisheries*, pp. 166, 61.
3 Athenaeus, 319 f.   4 Herubel, *Sea Fisheries*, p. 71.
5 Polybius, iv, 43.

and it has not many rivers to attract them. Where streams and lakes have outlets into the sea, says Athenaeus (358a), or where there are large lagoons or bogs, fish are more liquid and rich; they are pleasanter to eat, but not so good for digestion or nourishment. Strabo (C. 145) speaks of tunnies frequenting the shores of Spain, to feed on acorns that fall into the sea; and Aristotle says that inshore is better feeding. It was recognized that the tunnies made for the Black Sea to breed, keeping to the right shore as they entered.[1] The young fish are hatched in the Sea of Azov,[2] and when they are a little grown (they grow rapidly, adds Pliny), they rush from that sea into the Black Sea in shoals—"like city communities or armies", says Oppian (i, 438)—and move along the Asiatic coast as far as Trapezus, where men begin to fish them, though the catch is so far small; when they reach Sinope, they are worth taking and salting. Next comes the Bosphorus, their only way out; and there, we are told, a white rock projecting from the Asiatic shore near Chalcedon seems to alarm them, and they swing off and are at once caught by the current and swept over to Byzantium—into "the Horn" and its stag-like branches, to be trapped in the narrow waters with no exit, and masses of their kin pressing on them from behind. Little skill was required to catch and kill them. They were like the salmon in old days on the Fraser river, caught in baskets by the Indians. Indeed Aeschylus, describing the battle of Salamis, says that, when disaster overtook the Persians, it was like killing tunnies with broken oars and fragments of wreckage; the men helpless in the water, and any weapon that would deal a blow would finish them.[3] Chalcedon, Strabo adds, has no share in the great revenue that the tunnies bring to Byzantium. The tunny, it should be added, may grow to be ten feet long and weigh half a ton; oxen had to be used now and then to drag them

---

1 Aristotle, *Hist. Anim.* 598a, 6.
2 The sentences that follow are from Strabo, C. 320. See also Procopius, *Wars*, viii, 6, a long chapter on the rivers and currents of the Black Sea. Cf. also Pliny, *N.H.* ix, 20, 50, much on Strabo's lines; the Golden Horn owes its adjective to the tunny.   3 Aeschylus, *Persae*, 424.

out of the water; "tunny fishing was not regarded in the least as an art or a sport", says Mr Wethered.[1]

Once caught the tunnies have to be cured, and Nature has been kind enough to the Black Sea region to give it natural deposits of salt and, at any rate, one lagoon where it can readily be made.[2] We may realize the significance of this from the record of great loss to Newfoundland in one season, when the salt ships were wrecked. Athenaeus (116 c) quotes at second hand (or third hand?) an alleged passage of Hesiod, which he really thinks, he says, more like the work of a cook than of "most musical Hesiod", about pickled and salted fish from the Bosphorus, sturgeon and pike; "and again, of tunnies pickled in the right season, Byzantium is mother"—dubious maternity! And he adds that "over the Ionian wave men from Italy will bring as freight from Cadiz or holy Tarentum huge tunny hearts, which are packed tightly in jars and await the beginning of dinner". Probably it is not Hesiod; but Strabo (C. 144) confirms the statement about the Spanish pickled tunny, "not worse than the Black Sea sort". Another authority quoted by Athenaeus (116 c), viz. Diocles of Carystos, writing on hygiene, says that the young tunny is the best among all lean varieties of salt fish, but of all fat fish the grown tunny is the best. Some shook their heads as to whether it was supremely digestible, but Archestratus, the epic poet of cookery, bids his friend, if ever he goes to Byzantium, to be sure to have a slice of *hôraion*, a variety whose very name would confirm his assurance that it is "good and tender".

Little wonder that at Athens the wind that brought the fish was a good one, and the winds from North or South that held up the ships were bad ones, bad as Phayllos whose greed will sweep the whole catch off the market. His preference may have been for the small fresh fish to which we shall return. But the Athenians, we read, had such enthusiasm

---

1 H. N. Wethered, *The Mind of the Ancient World*, p. 103; an interesting book, based on Philemon Holland's translation of Pliny.
2 Herodotus, iv, 53; and Strabo, C. 312.

(σπουδὴν) for salt fish that they gave their citizenship to the sons of Chaerephilus, an outstanding dealer in it—not the only one of the trade whose name survives.[1]

We must not linger over the sturgeon, which, says Herodotus,[2] has no backbone (it has to be content with cartilage, say modern naturalists), nor "the ass whose heart is in its belly"[3]—in plainer English, the codfish, nor the mackerel. Chief of all is the tunny; and the salted fish of the Black Sea is, like the Newfoundland cod of to-day, the staple of diet. There were fishmongers enough in Athens, but no great fishing industry such as Byzantium and Tarentum knew.[4]

Less need be said about cheese and its part in Athenian life. It was made in ancient days, as in more modern Greece, from goat's milk. The meal that Dodwell had on Aegina consisted of goat's milk cheese, olives and figs, and brown bread soaked in water. Greece imported cheese, along with hides and lard[5] from Sicily. When Bdelycleon arranges a law-court at home for his foolish old father, the dog Labes is prosecuted,

> For that, embezzling a Sicilian cheese,
> Alone he ate it.[6]

"I used to think", says Philemon in the play entitled *The Sicilian*, "that Sicily produced just this one speciality, its fine cheese."[7]

III

We may now pass to those articles of diet which could be produced nearer home, and first among them we may set the olive, the special gift of Athene to her city—

> Looking out on the hills olive-laden
>> Enchanted, where first from the earth
> The grey-gleaming fruit of the Maiden
>> Athene had birth;
> A soft grey crown for a city
> Belovèd, a City of Light.[8]

1 Athenaeus, 338d; 119f.   2 Herodotus, iv, 53.   3 Athenaeus, 315e.
4 Aristotle, *Politics*, iv, 4, 21; p. 1291b.   5 Plutarch, *Nicias*, 1.
6 Aristophanes, *Wasps*, 896.   7 Athenaeus, 658a.
8 Euripides, *Troades*, 801, Gilbert Murray's translation.

After that, it would be flippant to linger over the joke of Aristophanes about the adjective λιπαραί, which as applied to Athens has a magic effect in softening the Athenian heart, though really a word more applicable to sardines.[1] The nature of Attic land was peculiarly fitted for the cultivation of the olive, and the fruit and the oil made from it had a high value, particularly, we are told, in the nourishment of children.[2] The story of Thales and the oil-presses is told elsewhere, though it is not irrelevant here.[3] Mr Tozer tells us that the olive crop is good in alternate years—perhaps not alone among fruit crops.

Honey had a large role in ancient life, which has gradually in the West been usurped by sugar, another and happier contribution to European life from India. Athenaeus, who has many references to honey and its uses, quotes the comic poet Antiphanes, one of whose characters boasts of products of Attica that beat the whole world, and the first he names is honey and shortly after it thyme,[4] and concludes his list with admirable water—you would know it in a minute (43 b). Mahaffy was not very enthusiastic about the honey of Hymettus, his daily food in Athens, though one judges that he did not, like Democritus, confine himself to honey—"honey inside and oil outside", was that philosopher's rule.[5] Mahaffy did not like either its flavour or its colour; it was too dark, and not so good as what he got at Thebes and Corinth, not to mention (he adds) the heather hills of Scotland.[6] But he tells us that Hymettus is so bare that he wonders where the bees can find honey at all. Mrs Bosanquet explains that the ceaseless consumption of brushwood in field ovens is to blame. The mountain even in Dodwell's time had hardly any soil, but about its base. Yet Aristotle reckoned bee-keeping as one division of the true or proper

---

1 Aristophanes, *Acharnians*, 639.
2 See Varro, *de Re Rustica*, i, 55; and Sir A. Zimmern, *Greek Commonwealth*, pp. 53, 54.
3 See p. 68.
4 On the thyme, see Theophrastus, *Plants*, vi, 2, 3, the source of honey.
5 Athenaeus, 46f.   6 Mahaffy, *Rambles and Studies*, p. 131.

art of money-making.¹ Virgil's fourth *Georgic* is a little remote
from Attica and the food of Athens, and it might tempt us
into a digression on Theology.²

When one comes to wines, one can only echo Professor
Michell's word, when he says that the list given by Athenaeus
is prodigious, though only a few of them were famous.
Hippocrates discusses the effect on the human system of one
and another wine—soft dark, sweet dark, dark and harsh,
harsh white, thin, and acid.³ As every traveller tells us, the
modern Greek adds resin to his wine, and Pliny discusses the
vinum resinatum of the ancients.⁴ Athenaeus (33 b), perhaps
more surprisingly, adds that they sometimes, on Cos and at
Halicarnassus, added sea water to wine, and did it "sufficiently" (ἱκανῶς), and that wine so treated will stand dilution
with "hard" water if the water is filtered. In the absence of
coffee and tea, not to be known in the West for some two
thousand years, wine diluted in some way was the only drink
apart from water; only foreigners such as Egyptians and
Germans knew anything of a Dionysus of barley;⁵ and Plato,
discussing wine as a beverage, makes the points that it is
"cheap and an innocent way of training character".⁶

Water appears to have been an age-long difficulty in
Attica. Greece is not a land of rivers, though travellers speak
of springs, often with sycamores flourishing over them, in
every glen, even on the mountain tops, as for instance on
Acrocorinthus and above Mycene. Manatt tells us that the
limestone drinks up the rain and leaves the land thirsty; and
streams that disappear in the limestone, to reappear later in
volume, known as *katavothra*, are a feature of the country.
Some springs have quite disappeared, as a result, it is believed,
of earthquakes. Thebes, says Dodwell, has the best water
supply in Greece, while no part of the land is so ill supplied

---

1 Aristotle, *Politics*, i, 11, 2; p. 1258 b.
2 Varro, *de Re Rustica*, iii, 16, has a long chapter on bees.
3 Hippocrates, *Regimen*, ii, 52 (Loeb, iv, 324).
4 Pliny, *N.H.* xxiii, 1, 24, 45. He thinks the addition of sea-water useless.
5 Cf. Herodotus, ii, 77; Polybius, xxxiv, 9, 15 οἴνου κριθίνου and the
   Emperor Julian's epigram.
6 Plato, *Laws*, i, 650.

with water as Attica.[1] This poverty in water was one of the problems that Solon had to face.

Since the country was not supplied sufficiently with water either by ever-flowing rivers, or by lakes, or copious springs, and most of the inhabitants used artificial wells, he made a law that where there was a public well within a distance of four furlongs (ἐντὸς ἱππικοῦ) people should use that, but where the distance was greater, they must look for water of their own; but if, after digging down ten fathoms on their own land, they do not find it, then they may take it from a neighbour's well, filling a five gallon jar twice a day.[2]

It is not generally known, but perhaps not irrelevant to mention here, that to the left of the great gate of Trinity College, Cambridge, is a tap, connected with a spring or springs on the Madingley hills two miles away, from which tap citizens of Cambridge are entitled to help themselves to water—an old endowment; but I have never heard of anybody actually doing it. Mr Ernest Gardner, in his book *Ancient Athens*, discusses the whole question of water at Athens, the deficient streams, and the work of Pisistratus and his family in constructing the fountain Enneacrounos ("nine spouts")[3] and the rock-cuttings made to collect water. It is of interest to recall other tyrants whose names are associated with the provision of water—Polycrates with his big water tunnel through the hill at Samos of which Herodotus speaks, and which has been discovered and cleared, more or less, in modern times; and Theagenes with his water basin at Megara, which Pausanias mentions in one of a number of passages that deal with hot and cold springs, people who bathe in tubs ancient fashion, and waters of strange colours.[4] Vitruvius, in his work on Architecture (book viii), deals with the water question and the tests by which good water may be recognized. Athenaeus, like Robert Burton, discusses

---

1 Cf. H. F. Tozer, *Geography of Greece*, p. 100; Manatt, *Aegean Days*, p. 182; Dodwell, *Tour*, i, 267, 468, and ii, 7, on the extreme dryness of the air in Attica.

2 Plutarch, *Solon*, 23.   3 Thucydides, ii, 15.

4 Pausanias, i, 40, 1; stranger waters, in iv, 35, 8-12.

waters of different weights; Attic water, by the way, if scarce, is pure and light, Mrs Bosanquet says. The Turks, during their supremacy, did as they have done elsewhere, and built fountains about Athens. The Greeks, once free, destroyed the Turkish fountains along with the minarets and the cypresses, to abolish every reminder of that hated tyranny. To-day, since the great transfers of population from Asia Minor made in 1922, the water problem of Athens has again become serious.

IV

So much then for the great staples of life in Athens, to the significance of which we must return. But first a rapid review may be made of things that the Athenians liked to eat, and did eat when occasion served, things that could not always be counted upon, but varied and freshened the standard diet. They were devoted, we are told, to the salted fish from the Black Sea, but we can understand that they found fresh fish attractive. Railways in Britain, and the use of ice, have made fresh fish, and very fine fish, available all over the country. We read in Cowper's letters of salmon and so forth sent to him at Olney by his friends in London, but perhaps that was as far as it could go. In Greece fresh fish, if it was to be fresh, must be caught locally; and we read a great deal in Athenaeus and elsewhere—more, as a rule, than we want to read—of the small fish, of the ἀφύη kind, sprats, sardines and other small things—"the sort which we eat, bones and all" (says Athenaeus, 357 e). This the fishmongers retailed, with great insolence to customers and sundry tricks to make it look fresher than it was—e.g. a well-staged free fight among themselves, which would end in buckets of water being tipped over the fish, a perfectly well understood performance. Then there is the hare, coming over and over again as a dish in Aristophanes, and the subject of a long chapter in Xenophon's tract on hunting; his hares were very much alive, and their capture was both "art and sport", a pursuit he thoroughly enjoyed. He even makes

Socrates discuss hare-catching with a young woman at Athens, which seems to take the philosopher further afield than the *Phaedrus* would lead us to believe he ever penetrated into the country. And there is that "engaging passion for snaring small birds" which, though not really a gentleman's amusement, appealed too much, Plato says,[1] to small boys, just as in Canada in old days you would see them go out shooting red squirrels. There were fruits, too, preserved and fresh—raisins and dates (not nearly as good as the dates Xenophon tasted by the Euphrates) and figs—but also fresh figs and myrtle berries, sometimes to be had even in winter with a sprinkling of snow over the basket—apples—and on a lowlier level turnips and garlic. Little was done with milk, but to make cheese of it. Butter was strange on the whole to the Mediterranean peoples. There was not much pasture; and, though the animals like leaf-feeding, it does not much help dairying. Even by the Renaissance butter in Britain was a food of the lower class.[2] In 1672 Madame de Sévigné wrote to her daughter: "I cannot pity you for having no butter in Provence, because you have admirable oil and excellent fish." So she might have written to the Athenians.

A glance at the eatables mentioned in Aristophanes' *Acharnians*, when once Dicaeopolis has made his private "thirty-years peace" with Sparta, may sum up the bill of fare: garlic, of course, from Megara; and the noble eel from Boeotia, "eldest of Copais' fifty daughters", meet to be compared (wickedly enough) with Alcestis herself; little fish; ducks and other wild fowl; sprats from Phalerum; thrushes, tripe and cuttle fish; cakes and "slices" (probably tunny). Dicaeopolis believed in "doing himself well", but none of this seems very extravagant. Athenian meals were a byword; Greeks (so the Persians said)[3] always left off eating while still hungry. Amphion, most musical of men, was told to emigrate to Athens, where the sons of the Cecropidae luxuriously

1 Plato, *Laws*, vii, 823 E; cf. Manatt, *Aegean Days*, p. 175.
2 See Drummond and Wilbraham, *The Englishman's Food*, p. 127.
3 Herodotus, i, 133.

—starve, gulping down the breezes and feeding on hopes.[1]
If you dined with Plato, you could count on having no
indigestion next day. The Athenians were not Boeotians, who
were the best of men at eating all day long.[2] It was no good
to envy them; but the comic poets picture what things were
like in the Golden Age (the date doubtful), when barley
cakes jostled with wheaten to get into the mouths of men,
when fish would bake themselves and come spontaneously to
table ready cooked, when a river of broth flowed by the
couches, and thrushes positively flew into your gullet, and
so forth—everything so automatic and so delightful, but not
wild luxury.[3]

When viands take to cooking themselves, no reader will
want to spend time on handmills and field-ovens, on brazier,
charcoal and fan; so, with a reference to the use of these last
three in the *Acharnians*, we may leave cookery behind us.
There may be those who will remember that Charles Kingsley
in his fairy tale picked up this ready-to-eat idea, and spoke of
little pigs, already roasted, running about and crying "Come
and eat me", while the happy people just waited till the
pigs ran against their mouths, and then took a bite and were
content. But Kingsley was a field naturalist, and adds a
caution—roast pigs could not be expected to have little ones.
So we return to the real world; and where Greeks were, the
world was very apt to be real—in lots of ways.

V

We have surveyed the feeding of Athens, and have seen how
year by year the ships brought into her harbours by November
the food that was to last till April, and to keep her great
population in health and fit for work. An immense number
of men must have been employed in the various branches of
this trade—merchants who went themselves to South Russia,
to the wheat fields and the fishing grounds; sea-faring men
of every grade; dealers and retailers in Peiraieus and Athens;

1 Eubulus, the comic poet, cited by Athenaeus, 47b.
2 Athenaeus, 417c.   3 Athenaeus, 267b.

every one of these occupations calling for practical sense, for business capacity and the quick eye. Aristotle stresses the value to a community of a middle class, "the natural elements of a state"—"great is the good fortune of a state in which the citizens have a moderate and sufficient property".[1] He quotes Phocylides; "many things are best for them of middle rank; I would be of middle rank in my city".[2] Aristotle indeed shakes his head at times when he thinks of the art of money-making ($\chi\rho\eta\mu\alpha\tau\iota\sigma\tau\iota\kappa\dot{\eta}$); true, money is needed to pay for imports, he admits that; and Athens did pay for her imports, and her currency was good, her "owls" as good as British sovereigns, familiar in our youth, the world over. She paid in goods, and ships, and service. Yet the philosopher can tell us that men who work with their hands making those goods, artisans and mechanics, cannot "practice virtue".[3] That is his phrase; and much may turn on what he means by "virtue". To pursue that philosophical inquiry is not our present task. Doubtless men engaged in the industries and retail trades of Athens suffered, as people noticed, in body and mind; they paid in measure as we all do somehow for our profession; all specialization seems to mean limitation of some sort. The dyer's hand is subdued to that it works in; clerk or fishmonger or cleric, we all live fractional lives, and so far miss what Greeks at large counted the "virtue" of a man, the full circle of insight and capacity.

Writers apologized for merchants and persons in trade, when they did not abuse them; and, broadly speaking, apology and abuse imply the same thing—it is only the accent that differs. Plutarch writes a chapter[4] on the subject of Solon being a trader—his father had reduced the family estate (by his philanthropies); the young Solon was too proud to depend on relatives; and indeed there are some who say

1 Aristotle, *Politics*, iv, 11, 8-11; p. 1295 b.
2 Cf. Goethe to Eckermann (24 February 1825): "A certain middle rank is much more favourable to talent, on which account we find all great artists and poets in the middle classes."
3 Aristotle, *Politics*, iii, 5, 5; p. 1278 a.
4 Plutarch, *Solon*, 2. Big and little dealers are discussed also by Cicero, *de Officiis*, i, 42, 151.

he travelled to gain experience and to learn, rather than to make money; and, of course, he was till old age ready to learn; he "grows old, learning many things". Yet, elsewhere among his poems, we read:

> Wealth I desire; but wrongfully to get it
> I do not wish. Justice, if slow, is sure.

A good statesman would be reasonable, surely, neither ambitious of superfluous wealth nor careless as to what is necessary. Besides, in those old days, as Hesiod says, "work was no disgrace", nor did a trade involve social inferiority, while the calling of a merchant (ἐμπορία) was really respected; it gave a man a chance of familiarity with the barbarian world, of friendship with kings, and of large experience in affairs. Plutarch speaks of Protis of Marseilles, of Thales and Hippocrates the mathematician, and of Plato selling oil in Egypt. Still one does notice, he adds, traces of the mercantile life in Solon's attitude to pleasures, which suggests the market (φορτικώτατον) rather than the academy. It is an apology, and perhaps one or two more apologies may clear our minds as to its value. "No generous youth (εὐφνής, i.e. of good blood and breeding) would wish, as a result of seeing the Zeus of Olympia, to be Pheidias; nor to be Anacreon, or Philetas, or Archilochus, because he enjoyed their poems. Delight in a graceful piece of work does not necessarily mean that you should respect the maker of it."[1] Even Athenaeus (543 c) criticizes Parrhasius for luxury "above his station as a painter", in spite of his claim to "virtue".

There seems to be some dislocation of ideas in all this, some confusion of mind, some surrender to convention, to "the gentleman code". Apology? apology for the men who made Athens, the strong capable men who mastered crafts and understood the significance of trade and the sea, and built up the reserves that made civilization, developed the skill and invention that led the world to hail things Athenian; and in the apology are included the supreme artists of Greece.

[1] Plutarch, *Pericles*, 2.

To pay for foreign wheat, or—for Solon deliberately appealed to the domestic emotions of common people—to pay for the people's food, Solon headed Athens to industry and opened her doors wide to the skilled man. The Revocation of the Edict of Nantes gave thousands of new citizens to Britain and to Prussia—not paupers and failures with assisted passages, the remittance-men that our Dominions knew—but men of character and faith, prepared to make sacrifices for ideals, men of enterprise and skill, who brought not only their trades and crafts but a great tradition, and those habits of mind that make men and train their children, and help to mould a national character. It was not Huguenots who came to Athens at Solon's call, but yet the "men with trades", who brought their families, knew what they wanted; they wanted a peaceful life, to be rid of *stasis*, faction, revolution and street murders; they wanted opportunity. And they found what they sought at Athens; but it is more than arguable that they gave Athens as much as she gave them, or more. They made the *nidus*, so to say, the *milieu* (what a pity to have to use foreign words!) in which, through the clashes and the sympathies of active intelligences in shop and market—and in hours of rest and idleness—through the habitual handling of new ideas and experiments—

> (There's pleasure in it,
> When some idea, a new one, strikes a man,
> To make it known to all.[1])

—the Athenian habit of mind was evolved, that attitude to life, which meant for the world, and still means for us as much as ever, art, drama, letters, architecture and philosophy. It is a great story, and it goes back to one man—a merchant, who knew the Eastern Mediterranean and the Black Sea, and understood what he learnt—a strange blend of a man, shrewd trader and simple-hearted poet, quick to see what was happening around him, and not less quick, as a poet who appealed to the simplest emotions, to understand ordinary

1 Anaxandrides, quoted by Athenaeus, 222 b.

people. Solon saw what should be done, and how to do it, and he was able to get it started. The Greeks as ever, with their minds running on politics and political definitions, thought of his political work—how he blended features of every kind of constitution, giving *dêmos*, not just the strength enough that he alleged, but a great lever for altering all he did.[1] Of course, his political work counted. Athens would hardly have attributed every good law and every sound institution to him otherwise. But modern thinkers see more in his work as the greatest economist of the Greek world.

"Let us remember", says Aristotle,[1] "that we should not disregard the experience of ages." Experience is the test— as Longinus saw, in literature—as Athens saw, in politics. The great economist threw tradition to the winds—Athens could be, and should be, independent of home-grown food; she could do better with her rocky soil, her harbours, and the brains of her people. Solon, above all men, evidently counted the Athenian his city's chief asset—untied his hands, set him free from old restrictions, flung everything open to the energy and brains of the individual. Ships should feed Athens, and trades should pay for ships and food—and eventually for Parthenons, Olympian temples and great festivals. And they did.

It has been suggested, shrewdly, too—though I forget the name of the thinker—that it is a poor solution which does no more than solve the problem that actually called it forth. Solon had above all a food problem to solve—of course, with many more involved in it; and his solution did far more than "roll the load" from the hearts of poor farmers (much as that was) and find food for a town population. He saved the small farmer of Attica; he built up a great city with a great population, a people of surprising intelligence; his plans brought them wealth, gave them the insight that enabled them to face the Persian menace and save Greek liberty, and then to found a confederacy, an empire. So much for the people of Athens; and for all of us, his work meant eventually,

1 Aristotle, *Politics*, ii, 12, 2; p. 1273 b.

and still means, the highest ideals of democracy on the one hand, and of art and letters on the other, that mankind has yet seen.

Notes on Athenian Foods

Percentage of Nutrients in various fish as given in Dr. Robert Hutchison's *Food and the Principles of Dietetics* (Edward Arnold, 3rd edition).

1. Those eaten by Ancient Greeks:

Tunny	36·51	Sardines	52·92
Herrings	34·54	Eels	33·96
Salt herrings	53·97	Mackerel	24·03

Popular fish eaten to-day:

Salmon	32·02	Plaice	20·14
Haddock	17·64	Sole	16·06
Halibut	23·78		

2. Percentages of solids in dry fish.

	Fat	Proteid
Tunny	30·68	66·08
Herrings	25·25	67·07
Salt herrings	21·90	38·88
Sardines	33·49	55·44
Eels	44·68	42·88
Mackerel	25·73	62·32

Non-Greek:

Salmon	29·43	56·65
Haddock	1·29	79·57
Halibut	15·81	79·67
Plaice	9·84	75·16
Sole	1·71	86·71

3. Vitamins (as given by Professor R. H. A. Plimmer, *Food, Health and Vitamins*, Longmans, 5th edition, 1932).

		Found in
A	which prevents colds and eye diseases and fosters healthy growth in children	cheese and green vegetables

		Found in
B_1	which helps the nerves and appetite	wholemeal wheat, dried peas and lentils
B_2	which prevents skin diseases	fish, cheese and lean meat
C	which prevents scurvy and helps the blood	raw and lightly cooked vegetables, citrons and other fruits
D	which helps the bones and prevents rickets	cheese and animal fat
E	which helps babies before birth	oil of the wheat germ

I am indebted to my friend Mr Charles Ray for these notes.

THE FAIRY TALE

I

ONCE upon a time there were three brothers, who lived in Russia, when hardly anybody else lived there. Their father was the son of Zeus and of a daughter of the river Dnieper; and he named the three brothers Lipoxais and Arpoxais and the youngest Colaxais. We do not know who their mother was, but it can be easily seen that they came of good fairy blood. One day there fell from heaven certain things wrought of gold—to wit, a golden plough, a golden yoke, a golden axe and a golden cup. The eldest brother thought to take them; but, when he drew near, the gold blazed with fire; so he went away. Then the second brother approached, and again the fire blazed. But when the third brother, the youngest, came, the flame was quenched; and he was able to take the things to his house; and his elder brothers declared that he should be king. From these three brothers are descended the Scythian races of Russia; from the youngest the Royal tribe. The golden gear is still there, guarded by the kings and honoured every year with a sacrifice. For the land is large; and Colaxais had, like his father, three sons and made them all kings; and to the North of their country are regions where none can see and where none can travel, for earth and air are full of feathers that fall from the sky. Colaxais became king a thousand years before Darius attacked the Scythians.

That is the Scythian story about themselves, but the Greeks have a different one. Herakles, as all know, captured the cattle of Geryones who lived near Cadiz in Spain, and came on his return through the land of Russia which was then desert. A storm came up, icy cold; and he wrapped himself in his lion's skin and went to sleep. When he woke, the mares, which he had unharnessed from his chariot, were gone. He went over the whole land and could not find them. At last he came to a certain cave, where was a strange creature, the

upper half of her a woman, the lower half a snake.[1] He
marvelled to see her, and asked her about his mares. She
said she had them herself and would give them back, if he
would lie with her. So the bargain was struck, and, when the
time came to part, she asked what she should do with the
three sons that would be born to her; should she settle them
in Scythia, or send them to Herakles? He gave her a bow
and a girdle which had at the end of its clasp a golden cup;
and he said that the son that should be able to stretch the
bow and be girded with the girdle, should settle the land;
and the others should go away. So, when her three sons were
born and grown, the youngest of the three, whose name was
Scythes, performed the task; Agathyrsos and Gelonos had to
go; and from each is descended and named a tribe of men.
And to this day the Scythians carry cups attached to their
girdles.[2]

Now whatever else may be gathered from these stories—
and people who think of Scythian gold ornaments, 20,000 of
which were at one time gathered in the Hermitage at
Petrograd, will hail the evidence for gold in Russia in
1500 B.C.—they are fairy stories of a type that all the world
likes and all the world tells. Of course there is magic gold;
and of course it is the third son who achieves the task; and
the world was full—or had been full—of fairies who wanted
human husbands. But sometimes it was a masculine fairy
who wanted a human wife. Everybody knew of such things;
they came into history and were confirmed by the gods. Why,
in the great hour of need in the Persian invasion, an oracle,
men said, bade the Athenians call on their brother by
marriage to be their helper. And the Athenians remembered
their ancient history, how Oreithyia the daughter of King
Erechtheus became the wife of Boreas, the North wind. So
while their ships lay at Chalcis in Euboea, they sacrificed to
Boreas and his wife, and called on them to destroy the fleet

---

1 Pausanias, viii, 41, 6, is told about an image, perhaps of a daughter of
  Ocean (that was disputed), half woman, half fish; but he did not see it.
2 These stories come from Herodotus, iv, 5-10.

of the Barbarians. Whether it was for this reason that Boreas
fell on the Barbarians as they lay at anchor, Herodotus is not
able to say; but he did fall on them with great effect, and
when the Athenians returned home they set up a temple for
Boreas by the river Ilissus.[1]

Now turn to Plato.[2] Socrates is out in the country with
Phaedrus; let us go to the Ilissus, he says; and they do, and
being barefoot they cool their feet in the water. Wasn't it
somewhere hereabouts, says Phaedrus, that Boreas caught
and carried off Oreithyia? So people say. But might not this
be the exact spot? the little stream is delightfully clear and
bright; and Phaedrus could imagine the girls playing there.
No, not exactly here, says Socrates; but about a quarter of a
mile down; there is some sort of altar to Boreas there. But
does Socrates really believe the story? Well, some clever
people are doubtful; so Socrates would not be singular if he
also doubted; perhaps, he suggests, the girls were playing
together, and Boreas swept Oreithyia over the rocks; that
might account for the tale. An allegory, you see, and quite
pretty; but if you once begin to allegorize, there is no stopping;
think of centaurs and chimaeras, and Gorgons and winged
horses, and all sorts of strange things. It would be a crude
philosophy, bumpkin work, to elaborate them all into some
kind of probability. The Delphic oracle bade "Know thyself";
and, till Socrates does know himself, the common opinion
will serve about all those things (πειθόμενος τῷ νομιζομένῳ).
A later generation allegorized the old tales, fearfully and
wonderfully,[3] hardly realizing that it was all guess-work and
aside from the thought of the ancients who told the tales.
Some try to rationalize the legends; that very ancient king
of Athens who had a serpent's tail, could not he be reduced
to history by cutting off the tail? But surgical operations of
that sort are rarely successful.

Much has been written on Animism, and the supposed
frames of mind that preceded it, including the -ism of the

1 Herodotus, vii, 189.   2 Plato, *Phaedrus*, 229.
3 See p. 203, the cave of the nymphs.

ugly name, Animatism; but I do not propose to add to the
volume of fact or conjecture about these matters. For our
present purpose it will suffice to recall that Boreas was not the
only wind-god, that trees and springs were homes of gods or
spirits of some sort, or even were not their homes but were
somehow identical with themselves. The river might in legend
take the form of bull or man, and have a double capacity.
Nereids still haunt Greece, and Dryads protect their trees.
There were sea nymphs, too; Virgil gives us the names of
a good few, and we shall meet Thetis by and by. What is
more, "the legate of Gaul wrote to the Emperor Augustus
that several (*complures*) Nereids had been found lying dead on
the sea-shore";[1] one must feel that it can only have been the
Atlantic coast of France; such mortality could hardly have
been possible in the Mediterranean, though tree-nymphs
died with their trees, as we read in the passage in the
Homeric *Hymn to Aphrodite*.[2]

"Once I did see a nymph," writes John Cuthbert Lawson,[3]
"or what my guide took for one—moving about in an olive-
grove near Sparta"; and, he continues, "there certainly was
the semblance of a female figure draped in white and tall
beyond human stature, flitting in the dusk between the
gnarled and twisted boles of an old olive-yard. What the
apparition was, I had no leisure to investigate; for my guide
with many signs of the cross and muttered invocations of the
Virgin urged my mule to perilous haste along the rough
mountain-path." He concludes that, if he had had the
guide's early faith in Nereids and a gift for mendacity, he
might have corroborated the highly coloured tale the man
told in the next village, where the ready credence given to it
made it clear that personal encounter with Nereids was quite
in the way of everyday life. Guardian spirits or *genii* of one
sort or another are still believed in; and persons born on a
Saturday are reputed able to see them.[4] It is better, Greeks

1 Pliny, *N.H.* ix, 5, 9.   2 Quoted on p. 36.
3 Passages in his *Modern Greek Folklore*, pp. 48, 131; the same episode, I think.
4 J. C. Lawson, *ib.* p. 288.

say, not to risk contacts with nymphs; it is safer not to rest
under a suspected tree, or the nymph may punish you with
madness; such trees have to be felled with great care, and
the woodcutter does well to prostrate himself and put a stone
on the trunk to prevent the spirit from getting out.[1] That is
what they say to-day; and the same sort of story is told by
Apollonius Rhodius; the Hamadryad wept and prayed to
have her tree spared, the tree coeval with herself, and, when
it was not spared, she made her death a curse to the man and
his children.[2]

Gods and daemons are indistinguishable in Homer, and
Plutarch reckoned it a forward step in religion when the
difference between them was made clear. The full natural
history of daemons will be found in the tract by Apuleius
"On the god of Socrates".[3] Something is added to this by
the fathers of the church, who are clear that the daemons
are after all the angels that fell. *Non enim uno modo sacrificatur*
transgressoribus angelis, says Augustine.[4] But we are drifting
to Theology, which is not our subject here. Enough has been
said to show the background of our stories; the appeal of the
stories is another thing.

> Θεόσυτος ἢ βρότειος ἢ κεκραμένη,
> Be it from god or man, or both conjoined,

there is a charm, a fascination in them. "We must not",
writes Sir James Frazer, "look for a myth or a rite behind
every tale, like a bull behind every hedge.... Men have told
stories for the sheer joy of telling them."[5] It is the old idea
of Apuleius in his Golden Ass: *Lector intende*; *laetaberis*. "Give
me", wrote J. R. Lowell, "the writers who take me for a
while out of myself and (with pardon be it spoken) away from
my neighbours."[6] It is not necessary, however, for the story

---

1 Theodore Bent, *Cyclades*, pp. 85, 27, 456. Cf. Rennell Rodd, *Customs and*
Lore of Modern Greece, p. 171.
2 Apollonius Rhodius, ii, 477. Pausanias, x, 32, 9, on tree nymphs, especially
of oak trees.
3 Perhaps I may refer the reader to an essay on Daemons in *Greek Byways*.
4 Augustine, *Conf.* i, 17, 27.
5 Preface to Apollodorus (Loeb Library, i, pp. xxix, xxx).
6 Essay on *Don Quixote*.

to be charming; you may be more thrilled, if it is not. Prudentius, said a French critic, had like a Spaniard *le goût de l'horrible*; and we remember Catharine Morland in *Northanger Abbey* asking her friend about the books recommended. "Are you sure they are all horrid?"

Of course there are objections. Plato, as we know, was hostile to stories that misrepresented the divine nature; and god, nymph or, as we say, fairy were in his day very much in one order of being. There were fathers of the church who deprecated such tales—lying tales of daemons. How can the Classical teacher claim to be loyal to his pledge to renounce the devil and his angels, if he makes his living by pounding them into boys? Clement of Alexandria was less tragic about these matters; he loved Greek literature; the gods were, of course, none of his, and the great books were too good to let go. But in modern times, "educationists" (as they are called in present-day jargon) have tried to exclude the fairies from the children's bookshelf. Some will remember the fun which Charles Kingsley made of these theorists in *Water Babies*, but as late as 1929 the Teachers' College of Columbia University has been at it again, solemnly excommunicating fairies and nursery rhymes in the interest of Natural Science for the nursery. Poor children! But such institutions are clean against what the Greeks called φύσις, Nature. There is a vigorous letter of Charles Lamb's to Coleridge on the subject (23 October 1802):

Science has succeeded to poetry no less in the little walks of children than with men. Is there no possibility of averting this sore evil? Think what you would have been now, if, instead of being fed with tales of old wives' fables in childhood, you had been crammed with geography and natural history! Hang them!—I mean the cursed Barbauld crew, those blights and blasts of all that is human in man and child.

"Oh! give us", cries Wordsworth,[1]

> Oh! give us once again the wishing cap
> Of Fortunatus, and the invisible coat

1 *Prelude*, v, 341–6 (=364–9).

Of Jack the Giant-Killer, Robin Hood,
And Sabra in the forest with St George!
The child whose love is here, at least, doth reap
One precious gain that he forgets himself.

And his language a little further on is almost as fierce as
Charles Lamb's.

It is to be understood that it is of the essence of the fairy
tale that it is serious and not comic, a tale of good faith, told
with the unsmiling gravity of which they tell us Cervantes
was supreme master. But—well, so much is improbable!
Yes, but as Aristotle says about the Greek play, the im-
probability is "outside the tragedy"; you accept it for the
moment, and the rest follows. It is what Coleridge calls "the
willing suspension of disbelief which constitutes poetic faith".
Perhaps Lamb had the *Ancient Mariner* in mind, when he
wrote that letter. At all events the fairy tale has an age-long
appeal which the "Chemistry for Schools" has rarely
possessed; and I remark that outstanding men of science are
found who "do not believe in school science" or themselves
only began their scientific work when they came up to the
university with scholarships awarded for Classics.

II

Now let us turn back to our stories—and "all the dear
familiar marvels old child-hearted singers knew".

It is an escape from a humdrum world that is too much
with us, that we want—from routine into a happier region of
gayer possibilities—from limitation into freedom.

Was it Puss-in-Boots who wore seven-league boots? No
matter; a nobler figure had foot-gear less clumsy but as
miraculous. Here is Hermes, and Zeus bids him go to
Calypso:

He spake; nor did the fleetfoot shining One
Fail of obedience, but at once laced on
Beneath his feet the imperishable fair
Sandals of gold, that when he would be gone

> Over the wet sea or the boundless land
> Bore him like blowing wind; and took in hand
> The rod wherewith he charms men's eyes to sleep
> Or makes the sleeper to awake and stand.[1]

We need hardly follow him as he goes, like a sea-eagle.

Or here, in Walter Leaf's prose, is Athene arming herself:

She put on her the tunic of Zeus the cloud-gatherer, and arrayed her in her armour for dolorous battle. About her shoulders cast she the tasselled aegis terrible, whereon is Panic as a crown all round about, and Strife is therein and Valour and horrible Onslaught withal, and therein is the dreadful monster's Gorgon head, dreadful and grim, portent of aegis-bearing Zeus. Upon her head set she the two-crested golden helm with fourfold plate, bedecked with men-at-arms of a hundred cities.[2]

A little lower down it is another helmet—the "helmet of Hades, that terrible Ares might not behold her".[3] A helmet we meet again in the *Acharnians*—

O why keep putting off with that shilly-shally air?
Hieronymus may lend you, for anything I care,
The shaggy "Cap of Darkness" from his tangle-matted hair.

Other poets speak of the helmet that makes you invisible; but my own affection centres on Mambrino's helmet. I forget, of course, who Mambrino was; but I know who wore the helmet and love him, as one loves few figures in literature. Was it a mere barber's basin, worth I forget how many maravedi? Nonsense! Look at the Knight of the Rueful Countenance wearing it, and believing in it—the finest helmet in human history; for the helmet of Hades was a god's.

But it was not always a helmet that hid you from your enemy's eyes. There is the story of Gyges, who became king of Lydia. Herodotus tells us that his predecessor on the throne grew so infatuated with the queen's beauty, that he made

1 *Odyssey*, v, 43 ff.; translation of J. W. Mackail.
2 *Iliad*, v, 736 f.   3 *Iliad*, v, 845.
4 Aristophanes, *Acharnians*, 390.

Gyges hide in the bedroom to see her as she stripped and got into bed; but the queen saw Gyges, and next day told him that he or the king must die for it; so Gyges killed his foolish master, married the queen and reigned for years.[1] That is a story with a good deal of character about it, but not a hint of fairydom. Plato in the *Republic* has a more thrilling version.[2] Gyges was a shepherd in the king's service, and one day storm and earthquake made an opening in the earth near where he was feeding his flock. Gyges went down into the cavity; and, among other curious things, he found a hollow horse of brass, with a hole or two (like so many Japanese things, always called incense-burners) through which he could look. Inside he saw a dead man's body, bigger than mortal, it seemed to him, and naked but for a gold ring. The ring he took from the dead and climbed out. When he rejoined the gathering of the shepherds with the ring on his finger, he chanced to turn it round so that the collet (σφενδόνη), that would normally hold the gem, was inside his hand. He noticed that the other shepherds began to talk of him as if he were not there; and, sure enough, he found he had become invisible. When he turned the ring round again, they saw him. He tried it several times, and the magic always worked. So he got himself sent on some errand to the king; and at the court, with the aid of the ring and his being invisible, he seduced the queen, and with her help killed the king; and so he reigned. Now, says Glaucon, is there anybody who, with a ring like that, would be so adamantine as to stick to justice and upright conduct, when he could have all the advantages of dishonesty without the less fortunate consequences? A very searching question, but we need not try to answer it, nor dispute with scholars whether the Gyges of the ring was the Gyges of the bedroom or some ancestor. Cicero had no such doubts.[3]

Apollodorus, in his so-called *Library*, tells us that when Achilles was born, his mother Thetis used to hide the baby in

1 Herodotus, i, 8-12.   2 Plato, *Rep.* ii, 359-60.
3 Cicero, *de Officiis*, iii, 9, 38; 19, 78.

the fire at night in order to destroy the mortal element in him, which came from his father Peleus, and by day she anointed him with ambrosia. But one night Peleus watched and saw the child writhing on the fire, and cried out. Thereupon Thetis, vexed at being frustrated, forsook them, father and son, and went off among the Nereids, of whom she came. Apollonius Rhodius had told the story before him in the dreary fourth book of his epic. But the oldest form of it is told of Demeter in the Homeric hymn addressed to her or written of her.[1] When her daughter was caught away to Hades, she forsook the company of the gods and high Olympus, and wandered on earth in disguise. At Eleusis the king and queen, Celeos and Metaneira, took her in, at their daughter's suggestion, and she was given the charge of the youngest child, the son much prayed for, a baby in arms. No witchcraft shall hurt him, she said, from any heedlessness of his nurse, nor yet the Undercutter; for she knew charms to protect him from both. The Undercutter (Woodcutter in the next line) is supposed to be the worm that makes teething uncomfortable for the child and toothache for the grown-up. And the child did well, for she anointed him with ambrosia by day, and at night she hid him like a brand in the heart of the fire, till—till his mother saw it and cried out. And the goddess was angry and declared herself; a light shone from her, and a fragrance came from her, and the house was filled with the brightness; and the goddess was gone.

Among happy marvels we must reckon the ships of the Phaeacians, swift and safe beyond the common man's dream. Odysseus shall go aboard, and wake in his own country, even if it were further away than Euboea, farthest of lands that Phaeacians have seen—

> Yet one day then sufficed to go and come
> Unlabouring, and fulfil their journey home;
> And you shall know too how no ships nor lads
> With swifter oars than mine throw up the foam.

[1] *Hymn to Demeter*, 90–300.

But alas! it was the last of such voyages; for, as the ship, after they had put Odysseus ashore in Ithaca, came running home, the angry Poseidon turned her into stone, a ship-like rock full in sight of the harbour.[1] One more marvel, and we pass to grave problems; but whether this marvel is the gift of fairies or of Nature, or a legend, the reader must decide. Pausanias, who began by doubting on occasion the stories told him by Greeks but came to think there might be something in them,[2] says there is among the Achaeans a river called Selemnus; and he has heard that the water of it is a cure for love in man or woman, for they wash in the river and forget their love. If there is any truth in this story, he concludes, great riches are less precious to mankind than the water of Selemnus.[3] He feels bound to record Greek traditions, and he does it with a fullness for which every intelligent reader must be grateful; but he adds that he does not feel bound to believe all he records.[4]

III

A little Geography now, but without isotherms. Strabo (C. 150) thinks that Homer had heard of Spain, and, learning about the wealth and other virtues of the land, placed there in fancy ($\pi\lambda\acute{a}\sigma\alpha\varsigma$) the abode of the blest and the Elysian plain, where Proteus tells Menelaus he is destined to go to dwell—

> But you the everlasting Gods shall send
> To the Elysian plain at the world's end,
> Where fair-haired Rhadamanthys dwells, and where
> Life is for men most pleasant: there descend
>
> No violent tempests, neither rain nor snow;
> But shrill from ocean Western breezes blow
> Even to cool men's drought; since you for wife
> Have Helen, and are kin to Godhead so.[5]

1 *Odyssey*, vii, 317–28; xiii, 160ff.   2 Pausanias, viii, 8, 3.
3 Pausanias, vii, 23, 3. They say that Pausanias has no humour; but perhaps he came near it on this occasion.
4 Pausanias, vi, 3, 8.   5 *Odyssey*, iv, 563.

The description applies perhaps even better to California, a land that owes its name to romance, though how the name came to be transferred from the tale of chivalry, no one knows. The region, whether Elysian or Californian, was long supposed to be an island.

Islands abound in fairyland. The kind Phaeacians dwelt on an island, Scherie; the Cyclops and the terrible Laestrygonians on other islands; Circe and Calypso again had island homes. When Swift wrote the travels of Lemuel Gulliver, it appeared that he was shipwrecked on one island after another. Robinson Crusoe again made one island famous. Sir John Mandeville transforms every country of Further Asia, even Cathay and Tibet, into an island, which, with some other facts, has led moderns to suppose his travels were less in other men's lands than in their books. Sindbad, too, prince of Arab voyagers, saw many islands; but some of his islands were real, such as Ceylon. Rather to the North of Britain is a large island, one geographer tells us, an island called Ierne, where the people are said to be cannibals, though he is not quite certain of this.[1]

Odysseus, as we all know, touched at two islands inhabited by giants. The tale of his putting out the eye of the Cyclops delighted ancient readers,[2] and it was borrowed by Sindbad the Sailor, who met a somewhat similar giant on his third voyage and treated him in the same way. The Laestrygonians, again, were giants, horrible to behold. Giants have always appealed to story-tellers and their readers; we remember how Don Quixote was haunted by the thought of them and the glory of cutting them in two through the middle, which was a Knight Errant's privilege and duty. And then Pausanias tells us that the giants are not an invention; their bones have been found of superhuman size—in one case almost identified.[3] We can readily believe that bones of superhuman size were found; but were they human? The local poet of Lyme Regis records a similar story with another explanation,

1 Strabo, C. 201. 2 See p. 198.
3 Pausanias, iii, 22, 9; viii, 32, 5.

and a moral so sound, that it is almost impossible not to quote him:

> Miss Anning, when a child, ne'er passed
>   A pin upon the ground
> But picked it up; and so at last
>   An ichthyosaurus found.
>
> All ye who have a fossil mind,
>   Or care for ancient bones,
> Lyme Regis is the place to find
>   Those creatures turned to stones.

But Pausanias was more careful than might be supposed. There was a silly story, he said, that giants have serpents instead of feet; and so indeed we see them pictured in ancient art—a mode of progression that looks singularly inconvenient. But he says that, when the river Orontes near Antioch in Syria was diverted to a canal, a coffin eleven ells long was found; a man's remains were in it and filled it, a giant indeed with human feet. An oracle revealed that he had been an Indian, from a country which to this day produces beasts of extraordinary size and strange appearance; so why not men?[1] Once again, as with the stranded Nereids in France, we find the fairy tale confirmed by science.

There were stranger things than giants—the Minotaur in Crete, the phoenix in Egypt, the ant-gold in India, the *martichoras* in India (or at least Ctesias says so, and he describes it—three rows of teeth, and prickles on its tail, which it shoots like the porcupine of fable),[2] wild men in Libya,[3] dog-headed men,

> and men whose heads
> Do grow beneath their shoulders.[4]

But do these belong to fairy tales? They are at least akin to the creatures that Hercules had to deal with in his endless adventures from Spain to Scythia, and that Odysseus

---

1 Pausanias, viii, 29, 3.   2 Pausanias, ix, 21, 4.
3 Pausanias, ii, 21, 6.   4 Herodotus, iv, 191.

encountered in one island after another. Those oxen of the Sun which his foolish sailors killed and cooked, and which bellowed from the spit, sound like a fairy tale, but we read elsewhere how three bad Irishmen of the Ui Meith Mendait Tire stole and ate one of two goats that used to carry water for St Patrick, and came to swear a lie; but the goat bleated from the bellies of the three. "My God's doom!" said Patrick, "the goat himself hides not the stead wherein he is."[1]

The more or less human people, that heroes meet, were strange enough—transforming other people and themselves into all kinds of queer things. "That a man should be turned into a bird is to me incredible", says Pausanias,[2] but he inclines to believe in lycanthropy—the man turned into a wolf. "For my own part I believe the tale; it has been handed down among the Arcadians from antiquity, and probability is in its favour." For in those ancient days men were guests of the gods, who honoured good men and punished bad. Some human beings even became gods—like the Cretan damsel, Britomart, Hercules and the Dioscuri. So Lycaon may well have been turned into a wolf, and Niobe into stone. But in our day wickedness grows so vast, so universal, that it is only in flattery and rhetoric that men become gods; and the punishment of the wicked is reserved for hereafter. He adds a story, a doubtful one—for people will pile a superstructure of falsehood upon a foundation of truth—a story of men transformed to wolves but permitted, if they abstain from human flesh for eight years, to recover their human form; but not otherwise.[3] Proteus, the old man of the sea, resists Menelaus by transforming himself, and

first became
A deep-maned lion, then a serpent, then
A panther, and a boar of mighty frame,

1 Whitley Stokes, *Tripartite Life of St Patrick*, ii, 467.
2 Pausanias, i, 30, 3. Ovid's *Metamorphoses* are the work of a very clever man, too conscious of his cleverness to let the book be quite sincere, but it has had a long and deep influence in literature.
3 Pausanias, viii, 2, 4–6.

And water wet and a high-foliaged tree;
Yet fast we held him down immovably,
Until the ancient wizard, wearied out,
Broke into speech, and thus he questioned me.[1]

It was Proteus' own daughter, a good fairy indeed—or a sea-nymph if we must be sternly classical—who gave "the old man" away, and hid Menelaus in ambush among the seals, with a fresh seal's pelt upon him, and ambrosia at his nose.[2] Another sea-nymph, Thetis herself, tried the tricks of Proteus[3] to avoid the caresses of her mortal husand, Peleus, whom, as we saw, she eventually left. The same story is told of Nereus.[4] But Circe's habit of turning unsuspecting guests into animals, with the added cruelty of their minds remaining human, was far more dreadful, as we can believe.

No wonder that protection against fairy, nymph and daemon was an urgent matter, and that it was indeed a godsend to Odysseus, when Hermes met him and warned him against Circe, and gave him the magical *moly*, which protected him so well. It is always so, where these semi-supernatural people are concerned. You must have a rowan, with its red berries, near your farmhouse, if you live in the North of Scotland; fairies are such uncomfortable neighbours, and have such uncertain tempers and unpredictable habits.[5] If it is in the Southern States you live, a rabbit's foot is the thing to carry; the negro there always feels safer when he has a "hand"—a queer little bundle of protective oddments—to keep off a "ha'nt".[6] We read in Athenaeus (548) of

---

1 *Odyssey*, iv, 456.
2 *Odyssey*, iv, 365 ff. Theodore Bent, *Cyclades*, p. 422, confirms from experience near Antiparos the desirability of ambrosia, when you are among seals.
3 Apollodorus, iii, 13, 5.   4 Apollodorus, ii, 5, 11.
5 See the charming book of J. M. McPherson, *Primitive Beliefs in the North East of Scotland*, pp. 219, 221 the rowan; and p. 99 the delightful story of the fairy who came drest in bright green with a long wand in her hand to protest against the shepherd's wife emptying dirty water "my gate", and "makin' a jaw-hole o' ma best chaumers". I sympathize with her indignation.
6 On these Southern safeguards see N. N. Puckett, *Folk Beliefs of the Southern Negro*, a treasure house of fascinating information.

"Ephesian letters" being useful in the same way, but the rabbit's foot and the red rowan berries are more easily obtainable, and there is no evidence that "ha'nts" and Scottish fairies read Greek.

Protection was indeed needed. For the nymph or even the goddess would fall in love with a man; they still do in the Greek world; and the Scottish and English ballads hint the same danger. Theodore Bent tells of Nereids on the island of Ceos having children by human fathers, very uncomfortable youngsters, too like their mothers, malicious and ill-disposed. It is a taunt to naughty children that their mother must have been a Nereid.[1] There is a story from the Hebrides of a fisherman catching a sea-nymph, who was half-seal;—he caught her by hiding her seal-pelt when she was swimming, a girl with others, half-seal half-girl friends; and he had children by her; and then on a sad day she found her pelt, had it on in a moment and was into the sea, a long "Good-bye" (or none) to husband and children. We must be just to the children, however; the most famous of all "goddess-born" were Achilles and Aeneas, the most splendid hero and the most well-balanced in all legend. Achilles has indeed the temper of the nymph; but it would be hard to imagine a child more unlike its parents than the "pious Aeneas"—nothing of the eager impulsive Anchises about him, and still less (apart from physical beauty—*quam forti pectore et armis*) of his bewitching mother. Heredity failed; he was "the noblest Roman of them all". But, quite apart from offspring, to mate with a Nereid or a goddess might undo a man. Odysseus made Circe do a good deal of swearing before he consented to her desires, and she kept her promises. Anchises was greatly alarmed when he found his bedfellow had been Aphrodite, and she warns him it will be disastrous if he reveals who was the mother of Aeneas, for she tells him on the spot she has conceived a son. He did tell; and we read in the *Aeneid* that he paid for it.[2] Tithonus suffered from the

---

1 J. T. Bent, *Cyclades*, p. 456.
2 *Odyssey*, x, 339; *Hymn to Aphrodite*, 189; *Aeneid*, ii, 647.

absent-mindedness of the Dawn-goddess in asking immortality for him and forgetting to add eternal youth.

Whether it would be right to group the visits paid by Odysseus and Aeneas to the world of the dead with the kidnapping of True Thomas and others into fairyland, might be a question; but there are points of contact. Persephone ought not to have tasted the pomegranate, and True Thomas had to be warned against certain fruit; but both of them drifted back to the mysterious sphere to which they had been taken. But the sixth *Aeneid* belongs to philosophy rather than to fairy lore; but the best things always go that way; was not literature, according to Matthew Arnold, the interpretation of life?

One last phase of the fairy tale—the last for the present— remains to be noticed—a point with which indeed we began —the triumph of the youngest brother, of the unexpected. There is always the return of the lost child to be thought of; Oedipus fulfils the oracles; Romulus is rescued from the Tiber and founds a city and a race; Cyrus, who is more historical by a great deal than either of them, has his legend which tells how he came back, fulfilled oracles, and founded an empire. Cinderella's slipper finds her the prince, as, long before, in Egypt, the slipper that the eagle caught away and dropped in the king's lap found a royal husband for Rhodopis. Jack always seems equal to dealing with the giant; and Brer Rabbit ("bred en bawn in a brier-patch, Brer Fox!") triumphs in one negro story after another. It seems a permanent human trait to wish success to the little one, to the third brother—and a lovable trait.

IV

A few words only remain to be said on the fairy tale in literature. We have seen already what Lamb and Wordsworth felt about its value as background. The tale is always simple, always intelligible, always sincere. It touches mystery, as life does; it uses the common motives, that we all understand from the cradle. Of course Lipoxais and his brothers wanted those golden things from heaven; we are all of us acquisitive, as the pedants call it to-day. We all of us love adventure; if we do not actually wish to be pirates ourselves, nor indeed to sail with John Silver, we draw to him when he is in a book. "I would sooner have *written* the *Iliad*," Charles James Fox is reputed to have said, "but I would sooner *read* the *Odyssey*." So would we all; and perhaps a majority would pick the books in which Odysseus tells the Phaeacians of his wanderings. The story never dies; the good story never does, and men want to hear it again—perhaps in new words, but as likely as not in the old. It is like Goethe's nightingale—

> Die Nachtigall sie war entfernt,
>   Der Frühling lockt sie wieder;
> Was Neues hat sie nicht gelernt,
>   Singt alte liebe Lieder.[1]

"Alte liebe Lieder"—that is true; it is they that appeal.

Apuleius, so far as we know, was the first to tell the story of Cupid and Psyche; but do we know? At all events his is the oldest extant rendering, in a Latin that nobody else wrote.[2] *Erant in quadam civitate rex et regina*—of course, there were; and you are launched into the story as swiftly as Bunyan gets you started with the man who has a book in his hand and a burden on his back. The king and queen naturally had three daughters, and the youngest is the heroine. It is a wonderful piece of Latin and of story-telling—something too peregrinate, some might say, and you need to be at leisure; but it is a story, and a good story deserves leisure. In nineteenth-century England two men told it over again, each in his mannered way—Pater in the fifth chapter of his *Marius*, William Morris in *The Earthly Paradise*. Or take something much simpler, to which reference has been made— the Homeric *Hymn to Aphrodite* that tells the story of Anchises and the goddess. The author is not Homer, he and the goddess keep explaining things so much; it is not the *non secus ac notas*

---

1 The first quatrain of Goethe's *Ländlich*.   2 Apuleius, *Met.* books iv–vi.

of Homer; other stories come in, and the goddess is a shade discursive. Anchises is not discursive; he is quite direct. But take it as it stands, telling of what it does; it is a poem that one is glad to read again; it has a freshness, a life and an appeal. The most beautiful line in the *Pervigilium Veneris* might be taken to characterize it—would it be too fanciful? It is all youth and happiness and beauty.

Ver novum, ver jam canorum, ver renatus orbis est.
New spring, singing spring, spring the world reborn.

At all events the fairy tale has entered literature. The *Midsummer Night's Dream* is not its first appearance in the literature of Britain. Chaucer shows us the Wife of Bath telling a fairy story long before; and gradually the ballads have found fit audience. In the last century, the brothers Grimm gave Europe the fairy tales of our Northern ancestors; and Hans Christian Andersen invented some new ones which Europe took to its heart—not all his tales, of course. Oxford, too, gave us one—or is it two?—the finest contribution Oxford has made to literature—in *Alice*. Once again, the tale has to be simple and sincere; and everybody that Alice meets in her two great adventures is intensely real, and instantly intelligible and permanently lovable. Perhaps you would not use the last adjective of the Red Queen or Humpty-Dumpty? But put it in another way—could you wish to be without them? They belong to us as John Silver does, or even more.

What motives the fairy tale reveals—gravity, imagination, simplicity, essential human nature, romance, adventure, beauty. Sentimentalism, too, comes in—a very human trait —at any rate in Andersen. The appeal is to our sense of the old, to the essential child that survives in every real person, to our longing to escape, to widen our range. Charles Lamb, once more, shall tell us what we want to say. In 1803 he learnt with dismay that his friend Thomas Manning was thinking of going to the Far East. It is delightful to read again and again the letter that Lamb wrote to him (19 February 1803); it would be relevant to quote it all here;

but a sentence or two will say what we want said. "I am afraid 'tis the reading of Chaucer has misled you; his foolish stories about Cambuscan, and the ring, and the horse of brass. Believe me, there's no such thing, 'tis all the poet's *invention*; but if there were such *darling* things as old Chaucer sings, I would *up* behind you on the Horse of Brass, and frisk off for Prester John's Country." Of course!

THE GASTRONOMERS

I

As literature it is valueless; a bedside book, a book to dip
into, merely, otherwise tedious; a vast hodge-podge; one
more example of a bad habit in a world of scholars grown
lazy, writers content to amass and not create;—so men speak
to-day of the book of Athenaeus.[1] It would surely have
astonished him; for he wrote along the lines of a great
tradition. Plato had perfected the pattern of dialogue; and
Athenaeus begins with a clear imitation of the *Phaedo*; friends
meet, and one undertakes to tell the other of a notable
conversation. True, the subjects are different; but so they
should be; and here Athenaeus had another precedent in the
Table Talk of Plutarch—"the world is so full of a number of
things". If the pedigree of his book was so unassailable,
posterity bore witness to its value. We may set aside Aelian,
who borrowed passages from it for his congeries (it is little
else) on Natural History. Macrobius, in his *Saturnalia*, that
story of a most memorable feast, illuminated by a great
commentary on Rome's greatest poet, and duly diversified,
is said to have had the work of Athenaeus in mind as a model;
at any rate there are great resemblances between them.
Finally, a man more charming and more quaint than either
of them avows that in his *Anatomy of Melancholy* he is imitating
Macrobius, and in fact borrows his dictum, *omne meum, nihil
meum*, and sails away into the infinite with his immense
freight, a mixed cargo indeed. Those who love arithmetic
may count whether Burton or Athenaeus has read more books
and conned more authors for relevant or genially irrelevant
quotation. So, looking before and after, Athenaeus might

[1] I would like to express some gratitude for the help I have had from
Professor Gulick's text and translation in the Loeb Classical Library.
The title which I have used was the invention of the great scholar, Basil
Gildersleeve of Johns Hopkins University; the book is more commonly
called by a transliteration of its Greek title, *The Deipnosophists*.

well be pleased with his achievement, based on a great model and itself the model for books that mankind has loved; and he might wonder again at those English critics of these last hundred years who will only dip into learning.

How else was learning to be put before the world? If philosophy needed the charm of talk, of the quick reaction of mind upon mind, and lived because it had thus been brought into the business and bosom of mankind; if Clement of Alexandria (whom he does not quote, and would not quote, but might have quoted) uses the omnium gatherum method to propagate his new religion in what he calls his *Stromateis*—counterpanes stitched together of bits and ends of borrowings; why should not learning and literature be allowed a similar opportunity? Gellius had done the thing in Latin, had emptied capacious notebooks into a long series of books and chapters, none very relevant or cognate to the next; he had gracefully called the whole *Attic Nights*; and the Latin generations kept his book as the Greeks kept Plutarch's narratives of his family and friends at table. Why, then, should not Athenaeus with a more clearly defined purpose, and perhaps a less wandering eye, gather his interests into a book of his own, full of references to his library, to letters and to drama, to natural history, natural science and philosophy, with gleams of borrowed humour and a little of his own, all linked with what through the ages has been man's central preoccupation—dinner?

Macrobius admits that his Table Talk had not been talked and had not been at table; but table talk had been and was yet to be the base of real books. Presumably Plato's books had rested on talk; it was well known how Socrates had talked for years with all sorts of persons. At a later date St Augustine had notes taken, perhaps in shorthand, of his discussions at Cassisiacum. Doubtless both authors revised their material, and, as Spurgeon said of the shorthand reports of his sermons, "altered them to keep them the same". So we have two types—the faithful reproduction used by St Augustine and the work of art created with a free hand by Plato, "combing, curling, and grooming every way his dialogues, at eighty years of age".[1] But in both cases it is real discussion, and discussion of great themes.

Here the critic will challenge Athenaeus, and will allege two grave failures of judgment. Sheer erudition, the conveyance of information on a large scale—wholesale, if the phrase may be pardoned—blends ill with dinner. Even philosophy was abandoning the fiction of dialogue. Seneca wrote letters, embodying his doctrine. Arrian transcribed the lectures of Epictetus as lectures; he did not play with a dinner-party and an objector. Stoics, it might be supposed, had simpler menus than fill the imagination of Athenaeus or would permit his immense length. Athenaeus is fusing two types of literature, if literature they both deserve to be called —the dialogue and the dictionary, which will not be fused. He is endeavouring to create a literary hippogriff, or chimaera rather; he of all men cannot object if we quote Homer—

πρόσθε λέων, ὄπιθεν δὲ δράκων, μέσση δὲ χίμαιρα[2]

—a thing lion in front, snake behind, and goat in the middle. Such things may do in art; they flourish in legend; but in literature they need no Bellerophon to kill them, for they never live. The plan is a misconception from the first, and there is trouble in its execution. The discussion lasted—how long? One day, three days, "new every day"? At one stage he seems to forget, unless it is an epitomator forgetting it for him, that there was a time-scheme at all. But that need not greatly trouble us. Readers of *Don Quixote* remember with joy the amazing supper on the last night at the inn (in the First Part) when everybody meets everybody else, and all the parted lovers are reunited, and the author clean forgets when supper began and how many hours go to a night. But there is not the same exhilaration at the table of Athenaeus.

The second phase of failure is in the dramatis personae. They are all worked out and listed by careful editors, and it

1 Dionysius of Halicarnassus, *de Comp. Verb.* 25.   2 *Iliad*, vi, 181.

is noted that a number of them were real people, as were the talkers in the *Saturnalia* of Macrobius—at least some were more or less real, though not so well known as the characters of Macrobius. But it is difficult to take any interest in them. There is a cynic who affects the rough rude style of his school; there is a pedant with a taste for the wild etymology of an age before language knew science. But one forgets they are there. The author has so little dramatic gift, and is so much more interested in lexicography than in character. He remembers at times to do his best for them; he prods them into badinage, rather traditional badinage, reminding one of virtuous persons of our day doing their best to be hearty. He even lets the cynic, who is dozing, have his face smeared with perfume (686 c). It has been aptly said that in most literary dialogues one of the speakers tends to drop out, and the thing to become what it really is, a monologue. The whole lot might evaporate from Athenaeus' pages, and few readers, if any, would miss them, or want them back. Historical figures they may have been; their names, some of them, are historical; real they are not. It is as if the volumes of a cyclopaedia engaged in controversy and bantered one another. And then at the very end one of them shows signs of life—by dying; "not many days after that, as if he himself had had a premonition of the silence that was to be his, he [Ulpian] died happily ($\epsilon \vec{v} \tau v \chi \hat{\omega} s$), allowing no time for illness, but causing grief to us his companions" (xv, 686 c). It was urged at one time that this was the well-known Ulpian, murdered in A.D. 228; but surely the adverb is against this identification; Tacitus' phrase *felix opportunitate mortis* is beyond Athenaeus' compass. This sudden inrush of fact and feeling strikes the reader very strangely after fourteen long books in which, so to speak, nobody is anybody. Athenaeus, in spite of the badinage, fails to create character, and has actually led some critics to doubt if he has any sense of humour. He recalls the comment of J. R. Lowell's biographer, who spoke with some surprise of England's appreciation of humour in others, having so little of her own. But, if as a humourist Athenaeus fails, he responds in a grave but rather pleasant way to humour in others as we shall see.

But who *was* Athenaeus? He is almost as elusive as Homer himself, but he vouchsafes us one or two facts about his life. He belonged to Naucratis in Egypt originally, and he is rather later in date than Oppian (13 c). There are problems about the date of Oppian, about the poems on Hunting (really a charming little poem on Natural History) and on Fishing (more certainly authentic, if less charming); and this passage is used to help in fixing Oppian's date. Athenaeus alludes twice to the Emperor Commodus (398 c; 537 f) and the second reference is taken to imply that Commodus is dead; he died in A.D. 192. Athenaeus speaks now and then of Naucratis, discusses the "Naucratite wreath" (675 f), and praises the "excellent *kylikes* (jugs or flagons) made in Naucratis, the native city of our fellow-diner Athenaeus" (480 d)—these are not made on a wheel, but as if fashioned by the finger; they have four handles and a broad base; and there are many potters in Naucratis in the quarter near the gate called after them. It may be permissible to recall that, when Naucratis was excavated early in this century, a clay vessel was found, broken indeed, but bearing most of the letters of the name Herodotus, which prompted the happy guess that it was an offering made by the historian. Athenaeus refers from time to time to "the beautiful city Alexandria" (673 d); he quotes the wicked lines of Timon of Phlius about the many scholars "quarrelling for ever in the bird-cage of the Muses" (22 d)—in the Museum, that is, of Alexandria; and he refers to lowlier institutions known as ἐφθοπώλια, "boiled-meat shops", where feet, heads, tripe, and tongues, etc. were sold, and to a special industry in glassware (784 c; transferred in the Loeb Library to vol. v, p. 54). His language implies knowledge of Rome; borrowing a phrase from the sophist Polemon, he says "one would not shoot wide of the mark if he called the city of Rome an epitome of the world" (20 b). A modern writer has written a book entitled *Round the World in New York*, a survey of the amazing number of nationalities domiciled there.

He is only to be known—once more like Homer, and in some measure like Shakespeare—through the range of his interests. Some men escape biography. The writer of the article about him in Smith's *Dictionary* speaks of his "enormous reading, his extreme love of good eating and his respectable ability". The old engraving of Erasmus bore the legend: "The better likeness his writings will give." The pages that follow endeavour to present in outline a survey of what interested Athenaeus; here a mere list must suffice, there a little more character will slip in. First and last, he gives us a great deal. Like Eusebius (whom he does not otherwise resemble) he helps us most by his habit of quotation; it runs away with him at times, but our knowledge of antiquity would have been much less, if among the 238 Greek MSS. brought to Cardinal Bessarion by Aurispa from Constantinople in 1423[1] there had not been the *Gastronomers* of Athenaeus. No one will call him a great man or a great writer, and many will wish he had thought of other matters than dishes and lexicography when he was quoting. But, as Sir Walter Scott once said, "the character of a nation is not to be learnt from its fine folks"; and the curious picture of the ancient Greek world produced by this amazing massing of commonplace details has, with all the limitations of its author, a singular interest for any one to whom a people's life and mind are of importance. "My subject", wrote the elder Pliny in the preface to his *Natural History* (§ 13), "is a barren one"—he explains that the moving accident is not his trade—"it is the world of nature, *hoc est vita*, in other words *life*; and that subject in its least elevated (*sordidissima*) department." Athenaeus' subject is dinner, a theme lowly enough at first sight. We shall associate with cooks and learn how they look at their own art, but their dishes do not remain in the kitchen, nor shall we; and we shall meet a large variety of interesting people, poets, philosophers and kings, medical men and naturalists, taking them as we find them, in their hours of leisure and enjoyment, content not to be impressive,

1 Sandys, *Harvard Lectures*, p. 182.

occupied with meat and drink, but Greeks still, open-eyed for the world and not altogether missing it, even at table. "We feed on questions", he says (398 b).

II

"We feed on questions" (ζητήσεις, 398 b). The phrase recalls two famous ones. "My story sought (ἐδίζητο) additions (or digressions) from the start", says Herodotus (iv, 30). "Then", says Xenophon, "a question is education too" (*Oecon.* 19, 15). Our gastronomers ask and answer a good many questions as they go. But we had better begin with a rapid survey of what they are doing. Nominally they are dining; actually they are making an encyclopaedia of diet and dishes, of cooks and kitchens, and incidentally of the things brought into kitchens and the sources from which they come. In the reading book of English youth sixty years ago was "The Pudding that took a Thousand people to make"; it was not an appeal to greed but to imagination, and the child ranged over the world that furnished his parents' cook with the materials that made the Christmas pudding—the seven seas and Natural History, plants and animals, ships and sailors. In a certain degree the book of Athenaeus does the same thing for us; we start at the table and survey the world known to the Greeks, and sometimes the company with whom we travel are more amusing than the worthy people we met in the reading book.

A rapid glance, then, at his topics, more or less in his order; but a little irrelevance, as he saw, helps a book now and then. That is why some people have found him a better "bedside book" than any encyclopaedia. His sections on diet may recall Burton's chapters on the foods that conduce to melancholy, but he has not that alarming array of medical opinion to deprecate every item in turn—every item, that is, that any one would want to eat. He does, however, give us as he goes along the judgment of authorities as to the purgative and diuretic effects of various dishes; this or that food will lie on top of the stomach. There have been so many fresh lights on food in these seventy years that one hardly feels it worth while to weigh his comments of this type. The recommendation of Burton may suffice when he assures us that "Cardan's rule is best, to keep that we are accustomed to"; and, if it needs support, there is Cicero's dictum: *Ignoratio futurorum malorum utilior est quam scientia.*[1]

We begin then with Homeric fare. The warriors chiefly ate roast meat; no fish (except in emergency), though the Hellespont, as Homer knew, teemed with fish, nor fruit on the table, nor garlands, nor unguents, and the wine was Pramneian, "which, we know, was heavy and filling". This diet, prepared by themselves and accompanied by violent exercise, was at least wholesome (9, 10, 18). There follows a survey of the various Greek wines of the Classical period (28 onward), with cautious rules as to the proportion of water to be added; as the proverb puts it, "drink either five or three or at least not four", i.e. two parts of wine to five of water, or one of wine to three of water (426 d); and in the old days, Theophrastus tells us, they put the water in first (782 b; Loeb, vol. v, p. 41). Then comes a digression on water, which, he truly says, varies a great deal from place to place. In fact, as we read in Dr Drummond's *Englishman's Food*, water was, before the water companies were amalgamated, a very uncertain and insecure drink in England. The waters of Attica were "hard" ($\sigma\kappa\lambda\eta\rho\acute{a}$, 33 b), coming from springs, and, he adds, rain, which is disconcerting, if "hard" means charged with lime from a limestone region; but "cold waters are hard" (42 d), and mountain water is better than water on plains, because it has less solid matter in it. Nile water (there the man from Egypt quotes Theophrastus) is fertilizing and fresh, and having an element of soda ($\lambda\iota\tau\rho\acute{\omega}\delta\eta$) is useful for the bowels (41 f). There have been people who drank nothing but water, like the orator Demosthenes for a time (44 e) and the Spaniards (44 b). Opinion varied as to this practice; "every faculty in us is nourished by water" (43 c), and it makes those who drink it and nothing else

1 Cicero, *de Divinatione*, ii, 9, 23.

ingenious (43 f); but the comic poet Amphis makes one of his characters say "there is reason after all in wine, it appears, and some people through sticking to water are silly fools" (ἀβέλτεροι, 44 a). Others counted the teetotaller "un-profitable" to the community (ἀλυσιτελής, 163 c), a taunt later on directed against Christians. Yet one authority, perhaps medical, maintained that water is a better aid to digestion (45 d). Athenaeus has more to say on the com-parative weights of various waters, on bitter waters, and water from snow. But let us pass on to fruit.

Alexander the Great, like his father, was "a lover of apples", and it is recorded that he found them particularly good in Babylonia and filled his ships with them—even organizing an "apple-fight" which made a very delightful spectacle (276 f, 277 a). Augustus, we read in Suetonius, was another adherent of apples. The nearer East sent Greece the peach or "Persian apple", a more nourishing fruit than ordinary apples (82 f), though it did not quite please every-body. There was citrus too. But the "pioneer of civilization" was the fig (74 d), which throve admirably in Attica (652 b); and Aristophanes is quoted in praise of Athens to the effect that even in mid-winter baskets of apparently fresh figs and myrtle berries could be seen in Athens covered with snow (372 c).

On fish Athenaeus gives us interminable information, tunny (301 e), sprats (or such small creatures), mackerel and eels, with which I deal elsewhere; but one may pause to note one of his interests before we go on. Ἑψητός is the subject, a term used for tiny fish—boiled, say Liddell and Scott, and we might let it go; but, no, says Athenaeus, and piles up no less than ten references to it in various comedies—just plain references, sheer lexicography. It at least illustrates Athenian taste in diet, and one of his own major passions in literature.

Thrushes and other small birds may come next, finches, blackbirds and sparrows. Thrushes come into the legend of Homer; he was given them when he sang his *Epikichlides* to children, a poem we have lost (65 a). In the absence of meat,

Athenians had a great fancy for these little birds, as we see in Aristophanes; and Plato himself has to deprecate the "engaging passion for catching birds" which Athenian boys felt, "not a very gentlemanly pursuit" (πτηνῶν θήρας αἱμύλος ἔρως, οὐ σφόδρα ἐλευθέριος, *Laws*, vii, 823 Ε). The eating of sparrows has a bad effect on the passions (391 e); this is not even hinted at in the Gospels.

On the large number of varieties of bread (109) and the alphabet of cakes (604–8) we need hardly linger, except of course to note the superiority of Athenian bread (112). Cheese came from Sicily (27); it was Sicily's pride (658 a). A pleasant extract from Hermippus in hexameters gives a whole inventory of imports to Athens—including a cargo of lies from King Perdiccas, and among things more edible, pears, apples, almonds and dates, cheese and pigs from Syracuse, with carpets and cushions from Carthage (27 e). Couches came from Miletus (486), shoes and cloaks from Sparta (483); and we read how King Artaxerxes gave a Greek a silver-footed bed, alleging that the Greeks did not understand bedmaking (ὑποστρωννύειν, 48 e). Cups and platters may follow, but need not delay us with their great variety and numbers, though we should note, when we are told that the ancients used small cups, that Odysseus must have tendered the Cyclops a pretty big one, if the wine was to have any effect on the monster—unless indeed the wine was specially potent, as Homer in fact states, or the Cyclops was unaccustomed to it, as being usually a milk-drinker (461 d). The reader must choose his own theory there. The Cyclops, at all events, did not know, or did not think, of the Greek prescription of cabbage to avert or mend drunkenness (34 c).

Drunkenness, gluttony and luxury fill many pages. Lists of the outstanding gluttons of history (413, 417, 418), supplemented by other lists to be mentioned, incline one to feel that Athenaeus deserved the label that has been attached to him—"the great scandal-monger of antiquity". It would seem that there was literary or historical authority for what he tells us, though we are assured that the book of scandals compiled by Aristoxenus has little pretence to truth, even if they are transcribed by Diogenes Laertius, the historian of philosophy.[1] But these things appear to have interested Athenaeus, and he is not the only man who has found them a corrective to easy optimism about the race. Does not Charles Lamb praise Burnet's *History* because it is "full of scandal, which all true history is"?[2] One feels, however, that some people, and our author among them, carry their enjoyment of scandal too far. Athenaeus devotes a great deal of space to the *hetairai* of Athens; they too had had their chroniclers in verse and prose who registered their names and their associates, and even recorded their jests, which were not always high flights of humour, but more often took the form of puns that require a knowledge of vulgar slang.[3] Very generally these women were slaves, at any rate in their early days, as a play of Aristophanes and a speech of Apollodorus make clear. About A.D. 100 a feeling protest had been made by Dio Chrysostom[4] against union without love and intercourse without affection, exercised for the sake of gain, an Aphrodite who brings no result in child-bearing and is so far against Nature; but nothing of this kind is to be found in our author or indeed in any other of those times that I remember outside the Christian church.

A pleasanter subject is that of joking in general and riddles, to which Athenaeus gives some attention. A riddle, so he quotes from Clearchus, is "a problem put in jest, requiring, by searching the mind, the answer to the problem to be given for a prize or a forfeit" (448 c); it follows, as Clearchus also says, that "the solution of riddles is not alien to philosophy" (457 c). This is dignified language, but one is tempted to turn back to the ribaldry of the comic poet, Epicrates, who describes a team of lads in the grounds of the Academy busy

---

1 Enough will be found about Aristoxenus in D. R. Stuart's book, *Epochs of Greek and Roman Biography*, pp. 129 ff., 158 ff.
2 Letter to Manning, 1 March 1800.
3 E. F. Benson, in his *As We Were*, has an amusing passage on Walter Headlam's pursuit of this theme, till something else diverted his attention.
4 Dio Chrysostom, *Or.* vii, *Euboicus*, 133 ff.

with definitions of Nature, sorting beasts and trees and vegetables into categories, and concentrating on the pumpkin; and what did they make of it? Well, they reflected for a long time in silence and then opined, one that it is a round vegetable, another that it is grass, and a third a tree; which was too much for a Sicilian doctor who was listening (59 e). Let us test ourselves on a riddle and see how near akin we are to philosophers. "A beast without foot, without spine, without bone, with a shell on his back and long eyes that pop in and pop out" (455 e). It resembles the riddles which Theodore Bent, in his charming book *The Cyclades*, tells us the modern Greeks are still asking in those islands, or were in the 'eighties. If any reader's philosophy fails him for the moment, the answer to the riddle is "the snail". The practice of allowing men to joke and pay no scot for a dinner has the most impressive ancestry; it goes back to Rhadamanthus (614 c). But there must be some sympathy for Anacharsis the Scythian. Some Greek professional laughter-makers had failed to make him laugh, but a monkey was brought in and he laughed in spite of himself; and gave it as his opinion that the monkey is funny by nature, but man has to make an effort, to practise in fact, if he wishes to be funny (613 d).

A mere reference must suffice to garlands and perfumes. Sancho Panza, it will be recalled, asked the antiquary, who was busy with the history of mankind, who it was that first scratched his head. One or two such problems are mentioned by Athenaeus, and we learn that it was the Roman god Janus who invented wreaths (692 d). Perfumes, odious by now to civilized man, meant much to the ancient; put on the head they modified the violent effects of wine (692 b), they soothed the brain (687 d), and, applied to the breast, they benefited the soul which, in whole or part, resided in the heart (687 f). As we also learn elsewhere, myrrh was supplied in alabaster vessels (686 c, 691 e). Solon, however, despite the virtues of perfumes, forbade men to sell them (687 a), and the Spartans positively expelled their makers (686 f).

Enough of lists; let us turn to his authorities.

III

In the first place, it is to be noted, as might have been expected, that his authorities are uniformly Greek. The Greeks did not read Latin literature. One quotation from Horace in Plutarch, on some detail of historical fact, does not invalidate this statement. Athenaeus once refers to Varro, ancestor of Larensius the host of the Gastronomers, and adds that "most Roman grammarians, not having been conversant with many Greek poets and historians, are unaware of the source of the proverb which Varro quotes about putting perfume in the soup" (τὸ ἐπὶ τῇ φακῇ μύρον, 160 e). This criticism of the Romans is a trifle naive.

The Greeks quoted by Athenaeus fall roughly into three main classes—historians of repute, such as "the most admirable and honey-voiced Herodotus" (78 e), Polybius, and the universal Posidonius who took the world for his parish; comic poets; and writers on cookery.

"I myself", says one of his speakers, "have read more than eight hundred plays of the so-called Middle Comedy, and have made excerpts from them" (336 d). One would guess it was Athenaeus himself; and the speaker goes on to refer to catalogues of plays made by Callimachus, by Aristophanes of Byzantium and by Pergamene scholars. One might wonder whether eight hundred were not a cheerful round number, like the Latin *sexcenti*, for elsewhere we read of Alexander the Great providing 800 talents for Aristotle's researches into Natural History (398 e); but a modern scholar has counted quotations in Athenaeus from nearly 800 writers and from some 1200 books or plays. So we may perhaps take the eight hundred comedies literally. His quotations, as we have seen, are often short, sometimes no more than three or four words, and he gives us little information as to plot or purpose in the plays quoted, apart from the names the authors gave them. Once only, I think, he pauses to speak of the theme of a play, and devotes five lines to an account of Aristophanes' *Birds* (386 f). Probably we have lost little by this abstention;

résumés and outlines, necessarily brief, of eight hundred plays would be intolerably tedious, as dull as Parthenius' handbook of love-tales. Lexicographers, perhaps, do not really *love* literature; it is words that fascinate them; and neither they nor commentators do very much to illuminate poets or to endear them; so we may be content. Aristarchus made it clear that the real interpreter of Homer is Homer himself, just as to understand Wordsworth the concordance to his poems is far more helpful than any dictionary.

Other poems beside plays Athenaeus quotes freely enough, such as Nicander's *Georgics*, the poem that Cicero praises but which has not reached us, though his *Theriaca* (a sort of epic on remedies for snake bite) more than suffices to console us for our loss. Thus we are given glimpses of the side streets, as it were, of Greek literature. He takes us for short walks in those suburbs of Poetry, where Truth and Resolution dwell, but Genius will not visit, where men invoke the Muses without response and then bravely construct poems full of useful information, decorating them as best they may, regardless of Pindar and Plato and the "madness of the Muses". The Greeks were not alone in this. Readers of Boswell recall the laughter roused at Sir Joshua's by Grainger's *Sugar-Cane*, "Now, Muse, let's sing of rats"—a quotation which suggests that a single line may after all sufficiently reveal a talent. Or there is Coleridge's quotation—

> Inoculation, heavenly Maid, descend!

Some of Athenaeus' quotations are equally enlightening. It was John Bunyan who wrote

> Some things are of that nature as to make
> One's fancy checkle while his heart doth ache.

It may be noticed, in passing, that several times he quotes identical lines from different plays by different authors. Greeks, says Mr Tarn, had no feeling about plagiarism; and Athenaeus himself pillaged Plutarch and Lucian as Macrobius did Gellius.

It is when we come to the cooks that Athenaeus, in Sainte-

Beuve's phrase, makes the heart beat. The literature is so large and lavish. There are glossaries of cookery (387 d), handbooks, poems galore, Philemon, Matron, Heracleides, and above all Archestratus. Matron, for example, has a mock-Homeric poem of some 120 lines, beginning with a parody of the opening of the *Odyssey*—

δεῖπνά μοι ἔννεπε Μοῦσα,

with Homeric echoes in most of the lines, for which Kaibel line by line supplies the reference (137 c). People who enjoy parodies will find it repay attention—*si vacet*, as Quintilian prudently adds to his praise of some author. Athenaeus quotes two poets who gaily expound the scientific aspects of cookery and its subsidiary arts, in passages which we must, alas! abridge. It was Sicon who was the founder of the art; he taught us (the cooks) first to practise astrology and after that architecture; he had by heart all the treatises on Nature, and on top of them the science of strategy. All these were propaedeutic to The Art. Foods vary in flavour with the revolutions of the universal system. Draughts of air carry smoke hither and thither, again affecting dishes; so architecture is vital. And as for strategy, order (ἡ τάξις) is a wise thing everywhere, supreme in our art. Thus the cook in Sosipater's *False Accuser* (377–8). Nicomachus has another cook, who has as high a standard; the subsidiary arts are astrology, geometry, and medicine; we must regard the kitchen as a globe (σφαῖραν), divide it into segments, each appropriate to its phase of the art. As for medicine, it is enough to say that he anticipates the science of the dietician, who saves us from dining on "hostile food" and supplies the antidote. And the military art comes in again—reason and harmony, the knowing where to post each unit (291). We may go further yet. Another cook maintains that his art has contributed, above all other things, to piety, lifting men above the life of beast and savage, leading them from cannibalism to order and civilization; and so forth in a passage fit to place with Charles Lamb's *Roast Pig* (660–1).

Archestratus is the name that recurs—the very Hesiod of cookery, or, if you prefer, the Theognis (310 a). He wrote an epic poem on the subject, and no trifling one. Ennius imitated it in Latin; and on the scientific side, Aristotle, we learn, used it in writing of fishes.

This is a perfunctory treatment of a great subject, which has occupied ancient and modern, Frenchmen and Englishmen and Mrs Beeton. How much we should have lost, if we had not had Athenaeus; for the half has not been told in this constricted page. *Artis poeticae est non . omnia dicere*, wrote Servius.[1]

IV

Let observation with extensive view
Survey mankind from China to Peru;

but a great theme is surely needed, if observation is to do this. It has already been suggested that Athenaeus, in pursuit of his subject, and sometimes just for a change, ranges over the whole ancient world and its races and history. The briefest survey must here suffice; gastronomy was to be our subject, and history is subsidiary. But he makes contributions to our knowledge which are not to be despised. We have noted references to Alexandria and to Rome; Athens is the very centre of all his literary interests, Attic fare and Attic poets; Sparta and Sybaris afford a contrast. Foreigners, too, have their interest as diners; witness the luxurious habits of the Etruscans (517); the rude ways of the Thracians as seen by Xenophon (151); the Arabs and their polite habit of imitating their king, even with a limp (249); and the manners of the Celts, cleanly feeders with lion-like appetites, grasping whole joints with their hands and using their teeth on them, their great hospitality (151, 154), and their bards (βάρδοι) hymning the praises of their chiefs (246 d).

Posidonius is one of the authorities upon the Celts and he supplies a panegyric of old Roman ways. "Their ancestral

1 Servius, *ad Aen.* i.

traits used to be rugged endurance, a frugal way of life, a plain and simple use of material possessions, in general, a religion wonderful in its devotion to the divine; and justice and upright dealing with all men; and withal the pursuit of agriculture." In festival, garb, fare, all was simple and noble (274). No wonder the Romans used the word *antiquitas* as a short epitome of all the virtues. But it may be noted that the larger part of the life of Posidonius fell in the first century B.C., a time when men were very conscious that their ancestors had been virtuous.

In violent contrast with old Roman simplicity of life and worship are the portentous pageants of Hellenistic kings, two of which are described at enormous length. He borrows from Polybius the account of the parade of Antiochus Epiphanes, and other details of the half mad king's (Epimanes) proceedings (193 d–195 f); and from Callixenus of Rhodes the programme of a similarly extravagant triumph of Ptolemy Philadelphus (196–203)—too long, too magnificent, and too stupid to quote. After all this the record of the number of gold and silver cups and so forth in the booty of Alexander seems trifling (781 f, 784 a; Loeb, vol. v). The magnificent ship of Hiero of Syracuse, which contained a library and positively a bathroom with three bronze baths and a marble washstand, and was adorned with paintings, suggests the modern luxury liner (207 e). A less famous figure of this period slides oddly into English literature. Some years ago Mr Charles Seltman bought from a Farringdon Road bookstall a copy of the Bohn translation of Athenaeus once the property of Robert Browning, who had read it and marked it. Théophile Gautier once said that the dictionary was the ideal reading for a poet; and it would seem that Browning leant that way. Among other things marked were the two lines in which a comic poet says that Lachares stripped Athene naked (405 f). This was only too literally true. In 304 B.C. Demetrius Poliorcetes wintered at Athens, and domiciled himself, being, as we shall see, a kind of god, in the Parthenon, whence, as he was in need of money, he "borrowed" the treasures of his "sister" Athene. Four years later Lachares, a mercenary captain, made himself master of the Acropolis and tyrant of Athens, and, as there was little treasure left, he dismantled the chryselephantine statue of Pheidias and coined the forty talents of gold he took from the goddess. Some of his coins are still extant, but one is glad to know he had to flee Athens in disguise. Browning marked this passage and used it in *Aristophanes' Apology*, against all chronology. The explanation was a slip of memory; his mind was running on work of the sculptor Leochares, brought to the British Museum from Halicarnassus about 1859. William Morris, in like manner, tangled Rhodopis and Rhodope.

But to return to Demetrius. We owe to Athenaeus, who took it from the history of Demochares, the most singular hymn of antiquity or of all time, an *ithyphallic* hymn, addressed by the Athenians to Demetrius. The visits of gods coincide, it begins; Demeter and Demetrius arrive together, she for the mysteries of her daughter, he debonair (like a god), beautiful and laughing. Something august he seemeth; all his friends are round about him like stars, himself in the middle like the sun. And they pray him, as son of Poseidon and Aphrodite, to bring peace. "Other gods are either far away, or have not ears, or are not at all, or heed us not; thee we see amongst us, not a wooden god, nor one of stone, but a true god. Bring us peace, O dearest! for thou hast the power!" This very present god should deal with the new Sphinx, to wit the Aetolian freebooter, or at least find an Oedipus to do it. The song, says Professor W. S. Ferguson,[1] "suited the merry mood of Demetrius; it must not be taken too seriously; its puns betray its frivolity". Puns, alas! do not always mean frivolity; does not Charles Lamb speak of pun-divinity? "This was the song of the victors of Marathon", writes Athenaeus, caustic enough, or, if he is quoting, it is with clear sympathy (253). One thinks of Lucan beseeching Nero that, when he takes his seat in Heaven, he will be careful not to tip the universe over.[2]

[1] W. S. Ferguson, *Hellenistic Athens*, p. 143.   [2] Lucan, *Pharsalia*, i, 56.

Politics Athenaeus eschews, ancient and modern. He has a kind word for Hadrian "best every way and most enlightened (μουσικωτάτου) of Emperors", founder of the temple of the Fortune of Rome (361 f). Politics are better left alone in empires of that type and some modern types; and besides they were irrelevant to his theme, though this was surely a minor consideration. It was a period when men were intensely interested in religion, attacking or defending the old faith or the new—Plutarch (whom he read) defending the old; Clement, his contemporary and an Alexandrian, maintaining the new; but Athenaeus has not a word of defence or attack for either; and I think he does not even mention the Jews. The Greeks and their traditions, literary, philosophical and gastronomic, suffice.

v

Let us turn to the philosophers, for whom his sympathy is limited. "Word-diarrhoea!" is the ejaculation of his Cynic guest (159 e). "Polymathy", he quotes from "the divine Heraclitus", "does not teach sense"; or, as a later writer put it, "Much learning,—and nothing emptier than that" (610 b). Another speaker puts a question: "Am I not right in hating all you philosophers, seeing you hate men of letters?" (μισοφιλολόγους, 610 d). An exaggeration, rather than a lie. They are a quarrelsome lot, the philosophers— "with a natural tendency to abusiveness beyond the comic poets" (220 a). There is the illustrious Plato, jealous of Xenophon; in fact, both are envious; each wrote a *Symposium*; Plato does not mention Xenophon as present at the last scene of all; he glorifies Menon the traitor of the Ten Thousand, and has little good to say of the first great Cyrus. And how he abuses Gorgias, and plays the mischief with chronology, bringing people together who could not have met! Did not Gorgias say, when he read the dialogue bearing his name, that he had never said a word of it? Plato attacks everybody; look at the *Ion*! first the poets, then the popular leaders, then

King Archelaos, everybody! (504–7). But he met his match in Aristippus, who had been buying fish for two obols. "I could have bought them for that", said Plato. "You could? You see, then, Plato, that it isn't I who am greedy for fish, but you who love money!" (343 d). As to his doctrine of the immortality of the soul, "even if it is Plato's, I cannot see what help we have had from him. For even though one concede that the souls of the dead change into other natures and mount to the higher and purer region, what is the good of it to us? For we have neither remembrance of what we once were, nor consciousness that we ever existed at all; so what pleasure (χάρις) is there in that sort of immortality?" (507 f). It is the argument familiar in Lucretius (iii, 851)—

Interrupta semel cum sit repetentia nostri.

It is not the usual way in which ancient men of letters speak of Plato. But before we quite leave transmigration of the soul, there are the last words of book viii to recall; he tells friend Timocrates that he will stop at this point "lest some one suppose that we, like Empedocles, were once fish. For that natural philosopher says, 'Before now I was a girl, and a boy, a bush and a bird, and a fish faring from the sea'" (365 e). Aristotle had been the great authority on fish, quoted for ever (πολυθρύλητον) by the sages; but how did he get hold of all his knowledge? Did some Proteus or Nereus, coming up out of the depths, tell him what the fishes do, and how they go to bed, and how they spend the day? (352 d). The Stoics have their turn, holding as they do the dogma that the sage will do everything right, even to the wise seasoning of soup (158 a).

Perhaps it is clear that Athenaeus had little of the philosopher about him, but he has a shrewd touch at the Epicureans. "Some people say that pleasure is Nature's law (κατὰ φύσιν) because all living beings are enslaved to it—as if cowardice and fear and other feelings as well did not exist in all alike!" (511 a). Epicurus was not a man of any real education and

seems to have admitted it (588 a). Epicurus was also quite
frank in avowing that he could not conceive of the Good
apart from pleasures of the body or entertainments of ear
and eye (546 e). A nobler figure surely was Pythagoras, who
offered a hecatomb to celebrate his discovery that in a
right-angled triangle the hypotenuse squared is equal to the
squares on the enclosing sides; and Pythagoras was a moderate
drinker (ὀλιγοπότης, 418–19 a).

To natural science Athenaeus has a good many allusions—
miscellaneous observations; there are cattle so large in the
horn that they have to graze backward (221 e); frogs and
fish sometimes come down in rain from the sky (333 a)—a
matter discussed by Frank Buckland in his *Curiosities of Natural
History*, and touched on by Burton; timber cut by moonlight
is more apt to rot (276 e); mistletoe grows from seeds dropped
by the rock-dove (394 e); the ring-dove lives to forty and is
monogamous (394 b); and so forth; but he returns to the
table—"the fish *batis* (the ray) is about as good eating as a
boiled shirt" (337 d). We have already had suggestions about
medicine and medical men; but one of the guests leaves no
more to be said, by the blunt assertion that, "if there were
not physicians, there would be nothing stupider than professors" (τῶν γραμματικῶν, 666 a).[1] And there we can
leave it.

Philosophers and medical men touched off—what remains?
What we really began with—menus, and cookery books and
etymologies—the last as flighty and as fantastic as Plato or
Macrobius could give us, where Fancy, not where Science
led the way. About eight hundred comedies remain, coming
down from the days when popularity with the masses was a
sign of bad art (τὸ παρὰ τοῖς ὄχλοις εὐδοκιμεῖν σημεῖον ἦν
κακοτεχνίας, 631 f). "What do *you* know of gastronomy?"
asked my friend, the publisher. Little enough, I admitted;
but I modestly claimed (and he allowed my claim) to understand irrelevance; and there lies the fascination of Athenaeus.

---

1 One may compare Petronius, *Trimalch.* 42, *Medicus enim nihil aliud est
quam animi consolatio.*

Life is generally more or less irrelevant. "Yokel Fortune, which knows no culture" (280 e) does so much; or, as another of his poets says—

> Luck rules our mortal lives; and Providence
> Is a blind thing, old sir,—haphazard, too. (693 a.)

So there is much to divert, however thick on the page come etymologies and lexicography. Witness the Spartan at the feast where sea-urchins were served, an unfamiliar viand; without watching his fellow-guests, he put one in his mouth, shell and all (about the prickles I am not sure); it was a tough job to crunch it up, but he was intrepid: "You won't have me beat; but I won't take another" (91 d). Witness the humourist, ordered to execution, but pleading for time for one last jest, to be his swan-song (616 b), like McPherson with the fiddle, of whom Robert Burns sings—

> Sae rantingly, sae wantonly,
> Sae dauntingly gaed he;
> He play'd a spring, and danc'd it round,
> Below the gallows-tree.

Witness the madcap crew of youngsters at Tarentum who got so drunk that they imagined they were on a trireme in a storm at sea, and to lighten the ship heaved the furniture out of the windows, and, when the magistrates looked in to inquire, hailed them as so many saviour gods, Triton and others, to whom they would rear altars when safe ashore (37 b).[1] Witness the jovial painter Parrhasius, ἁβροδίαιτος ἀνήρ as he described himself—"a dainty liver who honoured virtue"—and a first-rate painter, he modestly added; he positively "sang while he painted" (543 e–f). You can add the climate of Aenos, so like the legend of early days in Alberta, "eight months cold and four months winter" (351 c)—only in Alberta the four seasons were June, July, August and Winter; the practice of shaving the beard, introduced in the time of Alexander, a great epoch (564 e);

---

[1] Burton borrows this story (Part 1; Sec. 2; Mem. 4; Subs. 7), but puts it at Agrigentum. "Many such accidents", he adds, "happen upon these unknown occasions."

the revel poems (462–4); the trick verses on the Pythagoreans, resembling the elegiac couplet in four words in the *Comic Latin Grammar* of 1840 (162 a), and the constant parodies, and much else that is irrelevant and engaging.

When you are a guest at a college feast, what is it that you remember? The dishes? More probably (unless luck is against you) the company and the talk; and you may be keeping the menu for the sake of the song on the back of it, sung during dessert. And Athenaeus ends with songs, *skolia*, sung long ago at Athenian parties. Here are two of them—

> Oh! could one but open the breast of a man
>> And look at the thought that within you'd find,
> Then close it again, and be sure thenceforth
>> The man is a friend and honest of mind.   (694 d.)

> Best of all boons for man count health;
>> Next, if fair form be not denied you;
> The third place give to honest wealth;
>> Fourth, to be young with friends beside you.
>>>> (694 d)

Let us, as he says, "since the matters here recorded have reached a sufficient length, let us stop our discourse at this time, friend Timocrates" (185 f, 275 b), and let us end with the not-quite-paean that Aristotle made for his friend Hermeias of Atarneus (696), as another sage wrote verses for Robert Levett—

> Yet still he fills affection's eye.

The version here given is not the work of a supreme poet, nor indeed was the original.

> Virtue, our life's most lovely prize,
>> Thee by long toil we mortals gain.
> Happy the Greek, for thee who dies,
>> Who doth thy virgin grace attain;
> Such is the fruit thou dost bestow
> Like that the blest Immortals know;
> Not gold, not noble ancestry,
> Not gentle sleep, compares with thee!

For thee the son of Zeus, for thee
Toiled Leda's brood; and Peleus' son
Died, and the child of Telamon
Died likewise, both for love of thee.

For thee Atarneus' son to Fate
Yielded his life; and desolate
　　He left the genial day;
Then Muses praise his glorious deed,
Praise friendship's god, let friendship's meed
　　His glorious end repay.

ICED WATER

IT was Smyrna, and July, and very hot; and in those days (1903) I went on foot; indeed most people did in Smyrna. So, when I reached the station (Basmaghané) to take the little train to Bournabat, I was ready for temptation, and it met me. There stood a man selling lemon drinks. There was no medical man with me to warn me about typhoid and water supplies; so I tendered my coin and he filled me a glass. And then came the moment that I never forgot—he reached back his hand to the wallet on his shoulders and threw a handful of snow into my lemon. At the club at Bournabat they explained that in winter the people concerned go out on to the mountains (famous otherwise for brigands and snow-drops) and roll the snow into hollows out of the sun, and there it lasts till summer.

Some years ago I was walking the deck of a C.P.R. liner with a distinguished Canadian doctor, and the question of iced water came up, and the English disapproval of it; What did he think of it? He thought two things, apparently,—one, that the English *have* no ice, and the other that the Americans drink iced water all the time and don't die. And I hasten to add that they are not now so dyspeptic a race as the advertisements used to suggest. One can often get light upon the health and tastes of a community from the dominant advertisements in popular magazines. They are the work of practical and shrewd people, who may be supposed to know their public. The advertisers then have ceased to believe in universal dyspepsia; they devote their genius to other themes, perhaps as profitable to themselves, and as illuminative to the historian. The traditional type of Uncle Sam, lean and hatchet-faced, is a figure of the past, and Americans uniformly look healthy and eupeptic—even plump; and in their diet iced water and ice-cream have a place, which England has never given them. So we have got back to ice again.

But why have the English frowned on it all? I offer two reasons. English people always disapprove of the unfamiliar, the things foreigners do. And their disapproval has a high and impressive medical tradition behind it. Following another trail I came on a chapter in Aulus Gellius' *Attic Nights*,[1] which seems to me very possibly to lie behind this solemn English tradition. I will abridge a little.

It was the hottest season of the year, and Gellius had gone with some student friends to the country place of a rich friend of his at Tivoli. It was very hot, and they drank a good deal of water made of melted snow. There was among them a worthy and well-trained Aristotelian, and he tried to check them—he scolded them severely, in fact. Snow water—he cited Aristotle for it—was beneficial for crops and trees, but very unwholesome if drunk in any quantity by human beings; it produced wasting and disease in the intestines, not at once, but gradually "rotting their guts".

They recognized his prudent care and his goodwill, but it was so hot that they went on drinking snow-water; there was no halt in it. So he got from the temple of Hercules in Tivoli, which had a pretty fair library, a volume of Aristotle, turned up the relevant passage, and besought them to believe the wisest of men, and cease ruining their constitutions. Water from snow, the philosopher had written, was very bad to drink, as also was that water more solidly congealed which the Greeks call κρύσταλλος or clear ice. And Gellius quotes Aristotle's explanation, which you will also find elsewhere.[2] When water melts after being frozen, there is observably less than there was before it froze; some of it has evaporated. What has gone—this is argument, not observation—will have been the thinnest and lightest part of it (τὸ λεπτότατον καὶ κουφότατον ἐξατμίζει); therefore what is left is less wholesome. This does not refer to earth or other impurities, but to the water itself.

So Gellius, like Hannibal against the Romans, declared war and hatred for ever against snow; but his friends were

1 xix, 5.   2 Compare Pliny, *N.H.* xxxi, 33.

less fanatic and were for making some temporizing covenant with it.

Now if you turn to that engaging encyclopaedia of gastronomy that Athenaeus compiled (the subject of a previous essay in this volume), you will find a good many literary antecedents for the use of snow water.[1] I was in the best tradition at Smyrna in spite of Aristotle. One dramatist after another speaks of it—"if I get drunk and drink snow, and am an expert in myrrh", says one; "what you want is wine cooled in the well and mixed with snow", says another; "so and so", says a third, "is the first man to know when snow is to be bought in the market". Elsewhere he has the story of the girl telling Diphilus the poet: "No, it's not snow the wine is cooled with, we put one of your prologues in it." Seneca long after[2] speaks of the same craving for cold— "Nothing is cold enough for some people—hot dishes and snow drinks—and now and then you will see them throw lumps of snow into their cups." I don't blame them. I have done it with ice-cubes from a frigidaire. I note that St Matthew has the adjective "cold" attached to the "cup of water".

Athenaeus speaks of refrigerating pits (ψυχεῖα ὀρυκτά) on the island of Cimolus, into which jars of water are lowered and come out very cold. More interesting it is to read that Alexander, besieging the Indian town of Petra, had thirty of these pits dug which he filled with snow and covered with oak boughs, for in this way the snow will last a longer time. So there we touch the story I was told at Bournabat; and anyone familiar with the Canadian ice cutting on Lake Ontario (most charming of winter scenes), and the solidly packed ice house, will believe it. Seneca says the snow has to be packed hard together.[3]

1 iii, 123, 124. 2 *Nat. Qu.* iv, 13.
3 *Nat. Qu.* iv, 13, 2, *stiparemus*. Pliny, *N.H.* xxxi, 40, tells us that Nero devised the plan of boiling the water and then packing snow round the glass container, "and thus is gained the pleasure of the coldness without the bad effects of the snow". The younger Pliny writes to a friend, who failed to come to dinner, and humorously tells him he will charge the cost of it all to him, including the snow—"yes, especially the snow, which melted in the dish" (*Epp.* i, 15).

When I turn to Hippocrates, it is to find once more the ancient medical opinion against snow-water, a hundred years before Aristotle.[1] "Waters from snow and ice are all bad. For, once frozen, water never recovers its original nature; the clear light sweet part is separated out and disappears, but the muddiest and heaviest part remains"; and he also tells you to notice the diminution in volume. So water from ice and snow is the worst for any purpose.

At this point, I may be forgiven for one or two observations, drawn from more modern sources. So far as I know, the chemical constitution of water is not changed by freezing or by boiling, though both processes will affect what the water may be carrying. Physiologists tell us of the effect on the human frame of drinking for long periods water, which, like snow or new-caught rain, has not been through the earth, and which is therefore the purest H_2O, and has no salts (especially iodides) or lime, elements of high value to man. So far they would agree with the ancients, but for very different reasons.

I learn, further, of a difference between ice and snow which bears on ancient practice. I am told that the aged admiral who plumed himself on having supplied an early Antarctic expedition for three years with water from snow, gathered and melted, might have learned better from whalers and scientific people. Explorers as early as 1500 remarked that water from icebergs was fresh.[2] Sea water in freezing sheds its salt, and when the ice becomes hummocky, the brine runs off. The admiral, if he had used hummock-ice, would not have had to heat to 33° F. the air which is intermixed in the snow and gives it its white appearance; but for a less expenditure of heat (and doubtless of labour) he would have had more water. My informant points out that snow in their wine gave the ancients the cold that they wanted and diluted the wine less than ice would have done.

But there is yet another issue which one could feel looming up behind those comic poets cited by Athenaeus and the

---

1 περὶ ἀέρων κτλ, viii, 50 (Loeb, vol. i, p. 92).
2 S. E. Dawson, *The St Lawrence Basin*, p. 50.

more earnest words of Seneca. The famous apologue told by
Prodicus of the choice of Hercules shall end our story. I need
not tell it in full; it must be familiar.[1] Vice—"my friends
call me Happiness, but among those who hate me I am
nicknamed Vice"—a lady rather plump, and as artificially
coloured as a modern girl, and wearing high-heeled shoes,
proposes a life of luxury to the hero. The other lady, robed
in white and in modesty, has other proposals. There is a
contest, and one significant charge that Virtue brings against
Vice is that she buys costly wines, and "runs around in
Summer to find snow" to make her drinks pleasant.

I feel condemned; and yet in Matthew Arnold's letters
I positively find this (15 June, 1861). He is speaking of
Wenham Lake ice—"that is the greatest luxury of modern
times. For threepence one gets enough of it to cool all one
drinks at dinner." There I leave the matter, with a last
medical word from Celsus; Asclepiades,[2] he says, thought
cold water—even very cold water—good; "for my part I
think every man from experiments on himself ought to decide
whether to use hot or cold".[3]

1 Xenophon, *Mem.* ii, 1, 21.
2 Pliny, *N.H.* xxvi, 14 and xxix, 15, gives an interesting account of Asclepiades. He came to Rome in the time of the great Pompey as a teacher
of rhetoric, but found his profession not very remunerative; so he turned
over to medicine, where his gifts helped him to a good "bedside manner"
(*blandiens*). He did not, Pliny implies, know much about medicine, but
he understood his patients, who looked on him as if he had been sent
from heaven. He had five principal rules—abstinence in meat, forbearing
wine, rubbing of the body, walking, and riding in a litter ("we walk
with other men's feet", says Pliny, xxix, 19); and he was clever enough
(*mentis artificio*) to allow his patients—in fact, to prescribe for them—
occasional wine and also cold water; "and, as M. Varro reports, took
pleasure in being called the cold-water Physician" (Philemon Holland).
If what we are told, by Cato and others, is at all true about other physicians
and their methods (cf. Pliny, xxix, 11, the inscription on a tomb *turba
se medicorum perisse*; and xxix, 14, Cato's dictum on the Greek doctors,
jurarunt inter se barbaros necare omnes medicina), one can understand the
popularity of Asclepiades.
3 Celsus, *Medicina*, iv, 26, 4. Cf. p. 138, Cardan's rule.

TEAM OR HERO?

I

THERE are few things so perplexing in ancient Greek life as the significance of the Games. An institution once established needs little explaining; there it is, and it goes on; people accept it as the natural thing; but when one asks how it came to be an institution, that is another matter. The Pythian Games, for instance, were celebrated at Delphi; there was a famous shrine there, of course; but how came the shrine there? The scenery is magnificent—the ring of mountains, the wonderful view, the great spring; but primitive man did not fix the seat of his god with the tourist's eye for scenery. There was an oracle; a gas—or something called πνεῦμα—came up out of the earth, and put people it reached into a condition to prophesy. Waiving altogether the double connotation that *pneuma* carries—physical, meaning wind, breath or even what moderns call a gas, and spiritual, as page after page of the New Testament shows us—the excavator tells us there never was a crack in the earth's surface at Delphi through which *pneuma* in any sense could come, and no earthquake need be invented to have blotted out that crack. Somehow—there we must leave it—somehow the shrine was established; its legend spread and won acceptance; and in course of time shrewd managers started the Games in honour of Apollo at Delphi, as other shrewd persons tried to start other Games for all Greeks in the Greek cities of Southern Italy. What is there left to explain?

That the Italiot Greeks tried their hand at founding Games and offered big money prizes, tells us one or two things. It was in the interests of a place to become a centre of resort. In our own times we have heard of an enterprising railway company in Ireland arranging a theophany of the Virgin at a point on their line, to compete with a pilgrim centre on a rival line; they were foiled by the local priest, who told his congregation that he had heard there was a prospect of one of them beholding the Blessed Virgin, and he would refuse the last sacrament to any one who saw her. But neither in Catholic countries nor in pre-Christian Greece need we assume that the commercial motive was the first in order of time, however much in the process of events commerce gave significance to the Isthmian Games, near Corinth; it is the name of the city rather than that of the games that lets in light.

It may be that the idea of a Truce of God had a real appeal to the small Greek states cut off from one another by so many things—mountains, race, commercial jealousies, desire for corn-lands. We have also to remember that the ancient world had no newspapers, and very few and rudimentary geographies; you could only know about the rest of the world by going to the places or meeting the people. Herodotus cannot have been, clearly was not, the only Greek who travelled "for the sake of inquiry". Races and interest in races must have come in together at a very early period of human history. Commerce, then, travel, intellectual curiosity, and interest in sport combine; and the spot to which each motive brings those moved by it will be crowded.

There was political significance also. Thucydides pauses to tell us of the Olympian triumphs of Alcibiades;[1] the man was not quite intelligible without them, and his interest in chariot races at Olympia had a political element in it; it was a national concern, even international, quite apart from amusement or sport or interest in horses. Sixty years or so earlier the tyrant of Syracuse found a similar appeal in a victory with a chariot at Games in old Greece. Gradually one begins to feel that, just as in the fourth century princes and others saw a value in a "speech" of Isocrates—in modern phrase, a publicity value in a pamphlet by Isocrates, which men would read all over the Greek world, so in the fifth century a resounding chariot victory at Olympia would call the world's attention to a prince of Sicily, and not less if the

1 Thucydides, vi, 16.

first and greatest of living poets could be induced to write a poem about it. It is very few poems in our day, and very few poets, that win the world's attention; and it is worth noting as one of the contrasts between one age and another that Pindar, the least intelligible of Greek poets to many a puzzled generation, was one of the best advocates that a Greek tyrant could engage. Long after Hiero and Pindar were gone, we read how men and women in stray places in Sicily wanted to learn more fully the words and music of the choruses of Euripides; so famous was the poet both for thought and music. There is now no community in the world where anything of the kind would be possible; there is no poet who could hope for such international influence, least of all with odes so intricate as Pindar's. It was a wonderful age; and there in the centre of it was a significant man, singing, as we say—really, writing with extreme care and most amazing inspiration—odes for boxers, running men, horses and chariots; and the great people of the Greek world were at one in recognizing his pre-eminence and its worth to them.

But now his themes—young men, athletes, horses, each and every one of them associated with some great house, preferably a noble house, even if there were families which achieved high position in that world without a divine ancestry. One part of the ode would turn on the legend of the family. The wondrous youth who won the victory at the Games was the scion of a noble stock, with god or hero in the pedigree; and Pindar will break off the story of his immediate victory to tell the family legend of the maiden and the divine lover and the prowess of their godlike child, demi-god as he was and hero himself, destined ancestor of a great line, of which comes this new hero true to the divine type, beautiful to look at, strong of limb, great in endurance—rich, too. Wealth was always an element of happiness—ancient hereditary wealth; and long may it last; long may the hero live in health and wealth and fair renown, never overborne by fate, or democracy, or sickness, or any of the other ills of mortal life. Aristocrat born and bred, he jumped, he ran, he boxed; he won garlands, as his father, brother, uncle and so forth had done, at one festival after another, as a boy and then as a man, a hero indeed.

Here pause, and let us look at another scene. When we were young, we were told about a young hero of another age, strong and noble and beautiful, who rowed in his college boat. It was said that Ouida told the story in one of her novels; though I never saw the novel nor met any one who had read it, Ouida was credited with it. Probably the young man was at Oxford, the most thrilling of all universities, though some spoke of it as Oxford College (as they still do in some parts of the world). The splendid young man rowed in his college boat, and it was remarked by those who watched, and by the story-teller, that he "rowed distinctly faster than anybody else in the boat". We did not hear whether the boat went up or was bumped—probably the latter; and, in any case, if it chanced to have been the Cam on which he was rowing that day, he did not row on the Cam next day; of that we may be certain. That is the significance of rowing. There is no opportunity—or very much less than in other sports, such as cricket or football—for the hero to make an individual exhibition of himself, to win an individual triumph. The Blue will row in the May races in his college boat, but that is a different matter from the University boat; he has to forget the Light Blue victory of last spring, and to row like anybody else with the men actually in this boat; and if he won't or can't, the boat is better without him, though he may be, out and away, the best oar of the lot.

There is the great difference between Greek and English athletics. In Pindar's day the young man won the victory; and, even if the glory covered his father's house and brought renown to the city whence they came, it was an individual achievement. There was no thought of a team in most of Greek athletics. True, there was a torch-race. When Herodotus describes the Persian postal service,[1] "the quickest

1 Herodotus, viii, 98.

thing on earth", he explains that the messengers are stationed at intervals along the great road, and "the first to run [a rider it may be] delivers his charge to the second, the second to the third; and thence it passes on from hand to hand, as in the Greek torch-bearers' race in honour of Hephaestus". Plato uses this race as a metaphor in his *Laws* (776 в), and speaks of families "handing on the torch of life from one generation to another, and worshipping the gods according to law for ever". Where Pindar touches the modern Briton is in his stand for fair play; "wherefore if any of the citizens be friend—yea, even if he be foe—let him not hide good work done for the common weal, and thus do wrong to the word of the old man of the sea [Nereus]. For he bade us praise with full justice and the whole heart even an enemy, when he doeth high deeds of worth."[1] But the poet himself thinks as a rule of no team; his eyes are on the man; he believes in beauty, and recognizes it, he thinks of prowess, of the hereditary heroic character; and perhaps the poets generally are with him. No doubt there is something great in team-work, something big in democracy; but the poets prefer a man; who could write an *epinikian* for a committee? or for a cabinet? You will want an ode for a cabaret next, and perhaps be more likely to get it. "For myself, I have always been royalist", said Goethe; and "strong-winged, imperial Pindar, voice divine", would understand him.

But it remains that the Greek world swung away from the athlete. The chariots of Alcibiades mark roughly the end of an age. Training and professionalism came in; and the better classes contended less and less in the Games. The young Alexander's alleged word was that he would have been willing to run at Olympia, if it had been against kings. Gradually it became clear that, if a man wanted to serve his country, he must not be a professional athlete; it was inconsistent with military service—the athlete had to be for ever training, eating immensely and dieting, he slept heavily, he specialized in one kind of athletics; the soldier had to

1 Pindar, *Pythian*, 9, 93–6.

eat or starve as might be, sleep when and where he could, be ready for anything. What is more, the soldier belonged to some corps, platoon, *lochos*; he had to work in with other men—train, march, starve together, stand together, and, if need be, like the Spartans at Thermopylae, die together. It may be noted in passing that, from an early date, the Spartans sent no athletes to the Games. The athlete ceased to be an aristocrat; he never became a comrade.

There are endless things we still have to learn from the Greeks; in art and thought and letters they are still our masters; but surely in this matter we are a little ahead of them. Plato linked education and play, *paideia* and *paidia*, a pleasant assonance in the Greek; but have not Tom Hughes and Henry Newbolt something to say of worth, which is not in the *Republic*? Did Newbolt consciously think of the torch race in honour of Hephaestus, when he wrote *Vitaï Lampada*?

> This is the word that year by year,
>   While in her place the School is set,
> Every one of her sons must hear,
>   And none that hears it dare forget.
> This they all with a joyful mind
>   Bear through life like a torch in flame,
> And falling fling to the host behind—
>   "Play up! play up! and play the game!"

Abeunt studia in mores, stands the old saying. If you argue that it is this sinking oneself in the team that makes the difference between British Empire and Greek city, the student of ancient history may hesitate a little (students—especially if their subject is ancient history—always hesitate a little, when you generalize); but he may have to agree with you. At any rate we may do well to look into the matter, before we decide.

II

Aristotle, in a well-known passage,[1] tells us that poetry is "a more serious and philosophic thing than history"; it is the function of history to inform us of what Alcibiades did

1 Aristotle, *Poetics*, 9, 3; p. 1451 b.

or suffered. No doubt it is one function of history to tell us such things; but another view is put forward by a great Greek historian.[1] "Who", he asks, "is so worthless or so indolent as not to wish to know by what means, and under what system of polity, the Romans in less than fifty-three years succeeded in bringing nearly the whole inhabited world under their sole government—a thing unique in history?" Men had been saying that kingdoms rose and fell "by chance", that Chance ruled human affairs; and, in the stories of Hellenistic dynasties that succeeded to Alexander's empire or its parts, there were plenty of episodes which would seem to justify their thinking this. So many of the rulers represented nothing but themselves; no principle was involved, no national life; a personal ruler falls by accident into the hands of his personal enemy, and the kingdom—an aggregate of towns and territories with their inhabitants—passes to the captor. "How does fortune banter us!" was the cry of the politician, when Queen Anne suddenly died, and all his schemes, whatever they were, or were to be, were wrecked for ever.

But the larger movements in world-politics—were they all in like manner freaks of Fortune? There were Greeks who said so; it saved in some measure their national vanity; and Polybius himself may have thought so at one time. He began his work, it would seem, with some regard for the view of Demetrius of Phalerum about the rise and fall of Persia and the dominance of Macedon; but he outgrew this. He was a prisoner more or less, not fettered of course, but required to live in Rome for many years, an exile from Greece; and in Rome he came to know the great house of Scipio and its circle, and, what was more, he mastered the secret of Rome, her constitution and her spirit. Thus he came insensibly to modify his conception of Fortune or *Tyche* ($\tau\acute{\nu}\chi\eta$), and at last told his countrymen to seek the explanation of Rome's empire not in the vagaries of Chance, but in the solid qualities of sense and manhood which the Roman consecrated to the state. Empire rests on moral quality, and can only be upheld by

1 Polybius, i, 1.

moral quality; and *Tyche* comes at last to look very like what men call Providence, though *Pronoia* is the Stoic word; and, *Tyche* or *Pronoia*, it was a merciful dispensation that brought the Greeks so decisively and so quickly under Roman control, and ended for ever what was left of Greek self-government. Polybius conceives of history as "a serious and philosophic thing", that explains what happens and makes the world look rational. His theme is a people, a state. Plenty of ups and downs are in his narrative, plenty of the unexpected; but his hero, it has been aptly suggested, is the Roman people, a very different hero from Alcibiades.

On another plane, and confronting larger issues than an Olympian victory or an international football match, we have once more the antithesis of team or hero. The victory of Rome over the whole world was due to the concentred devotion of her people, dedicating character of the highest type to the national good.

Of course the Roman was not the inventor of national ideals. In what is perhaps his noblest ode, Sophocles speaks of Man's achievement.[1] "Many are the wondrous things and none more wonderful than man", man who scours the white and stormy sea, who makes Earth, the oldest of the gods, the immortal and unwearied, submit to his plough, who snares the light-hearted race of birds and captures the beast of the field, tames the horse and yokes the bull—man excellent in wit. "And speech and windswift thought, and all the moods that mould a state, hath he taught himself." Only against death does no contrivance avail him. "Cunning beyond fancy's dream is the fertile skill that brings him now to evil, now to good. When he honours the laws of the land and that justice which he hath sworn by the gods to uphold, proudly stands his city; no city hath he who for his rashness dwells with sin. Never may he share my hearth, never my mind, who doth such things!" A great poet, and a great conception—man's most signal achievement the founding of a people, members one of another, bound together by service and

1 Sophocles, *Antigone*, 332 ff.

loyalty, by justice and the fear of the gods. How came it?
we ask, and ancient thinkers ask—some with their minds
running on the pooling of material interests, some with the
loftier conception that it is Nature that made man a being
for whose perfect life the community, the ordered state, is
inevitable.

Yes! said the sophist, and No![1] Yes, it is the interest of
the many, self-protection against the strong, that frames the
state and holds it together; but do not call it Nature; Nature
has something very different to say. The makers of the laws
are the weaker sort of men, and the more numerous. To
terrorize the stronger sort of folks, they tell them that to
aggrandize themselves is foul and unjust, that it is wrong-
doing. But Nature herself makes it evident that it is right for
the better to have more than the worse, the more powerful
than the weaker. In many and many a way, among men as
among animals, in cities and in races, Nature shows that
justice consists in the stronger ruling over the weaker and
having the advantage. What justice was there in Xerxes
invading Greece, or Darius attacking the Scythians? These
are the men who act according to Nature, yes, by Zeus, and
according to the law of Nature—not the artificial law which
man invents and tries to tame the best and strongest with,
beguiling them from their youth onward with words about
equality and honour and justice. Yes, and, when some man
rises with a nature forceful enough, he shakes off all this
stuff, and treads under foot all our formulas and magic
charms and incantations, and the laws too, every word of
them clean against Nature. Our slave rises in revolt and
shows himself our master; and the light of natural justice
shines forth. As for philosophy, it is a graceful accomplish-
ment, no doubt—up to a certain point—for a man in his
youth, if you like—but it is the ruin of human life. Socrates
had better not carry philosophy too far; it may end in prison
and a death sentence. So Callicles declaims in the *Gorgias*,
in a masterly speech, saying (such is Plato's genius) what

1 See Plato, *Gorgias*, 482–486.

many and many a man would accept as obviously true—
what, indeed, a generation ago Nietzsche said, and what his
disciples are saying, and acting upon, at this very hour. What
other conception of life or right sets the Aryan and his leader
to trample on all Europe? But let us return to ancient
Greece.

So far the poet and the plain man, each with a philosophy
of life thought-out, though Socrates tries to convince Callicles
that he must think further, and that what he has been saying
is not coherent with real thought. Now let us turn to two
other types—the statesman and the frankly unreflective
person.

The funeral speech of Pericles which Thucydides gives us
in his second book, whether Pericles spoke in precisely that
vein over the Athenian dead, or whether (as some suggest)
the speech was recast by Thucydides as an *epitaphios* for
Athens herself—whichever it be, it is famous as an ideal
picture of Democracy. If such a state is ever to be possible,
it must be on the lines of that speech; it must embody the
spirit that animates it. Pericles, then, pictures a concentred
state of highly individual people; every citizen is to be
developed to the highest point his gifts permit, is to be
available for his city's needs and purposes, dedicating brains
and gifts as well as limbs to her, using a keen and practised
intelligence in her service, and finally passionately in love
with Athens. "Lovers of the beautiful, but simple in our
tastes, we cultivate the mind without loss of manliness."
Athens is thus, he says, the education of Hellas; and the
individual Athenian in his own person seems to have the
power of adapting himself to the most varied forms of action
with the utmost versatility and grace. None of the men,
whose death he commemorates, were enervated by wealth;
none hesitated to resign the pleasures of life. They resigned
to hope their unknown chance of happiness; they fled dis-
honour, but on the battlefield they stood fast, and at the
height of their fortune they passed from the scene of their
glory. They were worthy of Athens.

The emphasis here is divided, is twofold—it falls on the city, and upon the individual Athenian.[1] Sixty or so years later we have another picture of what that individual Athenian could become. Plato would have us believe that the great spirit of Athenian Democracy was no more; in his dialogues you meet phrases, not to be taken too literally, which suggest that it never had quite existed, or that it had been passing away since the battle of Marathon, a victory more noble than Salamis. Of course it was not Plato's intention that everything he makes Socrates say is to be taken literally; Socrates was famous for his "irony", his way of saying what he did not quite mean to suggest what he did mean, a habit which plain people found exasperating. In the *Republic*,[2] then, we have a picture of the Democratic Man. The individual Athenian had been the theme of Pericles; no one could be more individual than the man Plato so mordantly sketches. He is the child of impulse—of Nature, some might say, but that involves discussion. The child of impulse, he thinks nothing out, he has no fixed principles, he does not see life steadily or see it whole. His guide in life is inclination. His mind is itself a democracy, a rabble of appetites and notions; and he is at the disposal of the pleasure, of the fancy, that comes first, till he tires of it; and then he tries another. Now he is all for drink and flute-music; now for total abstinence and the endeavour to become thin; gymnastics, idleness, philosophy (imagine it!), politics; he may decide to be a warrior or refuse to fight, choosing peace when his city is at war; anything, everything, as long as he is not tied to it; and this negation of law and order is his idea of freedom and is very sweet—insolence you may call it, anarchy, impudence, in bright array and garlanded, all decorated with great names that do not belong to them, liberty, magnificence, courage. And people will emulate him and copy him; and you get a proper democracy, whose

[1] Cf. the judgment of Pausanias, for what it is worth, centuries later. None ever throve, he says (iv, 35, 5), under democracy except the Athenians; *they* had sense and were law-abiding.

[2] Plato, *Rep.* viii, 559–62.

cup-bearers ply it with over-draughts of the strong wine of
freedom; and the end of it is tyranny.

It is, wrote James Adam, "one of the most royal and
magnificent pieces of writing in the whole range of literature",
though, he adds, "doubtless somewhat exaggerated, as
usual". Exaggerated, not false; provocative and meant to
be so. "The worst of me", said Mark Twain plaintively, "is
that I exaggerate so; it is the only way I can approximate to
the truth."[1] The type is familiar, everything by turns and
nothing long; and an electorate made of such individuals—
Little wonder that Plato swings away to another conception
of the state; and he had a model in Sparta. The Spartans did
not invite strangers to make their homes in Sparta as the
Athenians welcomed resident aliens to Athens; ξενηλασίαι
were their rejoinder to the alien, a peremptory expulsion.
So their institutions were not well known outside, but became
the subject of legend; and many people thought the legend
confirmed by Sparta's victory in the Peloponnesian war. This
was perhaps shallow thinking; for Lysander was not a typical
Spartan product, and Cyrus was a prince and a Persian;
and Athens certainly contributed to her own downfall.
However, a closely organized state was in the ascendant for
ten years, all-powerful as Nazi Germany and little less
ruthless; and the moral was that a thought-out form of
government was better than a day-to-day improvisation.[2]
Questions are always being begged in practical politics, and
in political philosophy as commonly pursued. So Plato works
out a new type of government, where everything is prescribed,
and "guardians" (blessed word!) watch over state and
individual. These guardians are the imagination of a man of
genius, who had no experience of a civil service or a board
of education; and the ideal state would have been intolerably
like Nazi Germany or Jesuit Paraguay; even the children's

1 Cf. D. R. Dudley, *History of Cynicism*, p. 31. Diogenes compared himself
with the trainers of choruses "who pitch the note too high that the rest
may get the right one"; Diogenes Laertius, vi, 35.
2 Another moral may be drawn by those who study Sparta's government
of the world—a moral with more hope in it for to-day.

games were to be unalterable, and everything else clamped
and cramped.

Broad and long, however, it is evident that a state must
rest on some philosophy of life, rather than on the artist's
outlook. Jane Austen's antithesis of sense and sensibility
returns to the mind; the state requires sense, forethought,
system. But that "ancient quarrel" which Plato found
between philosophy and poetry is found here also; temperament is against temperament; and system means revolt—
not always effectual bloodshed, though that may follow
excess of system; but we remember French "despotism
tempered by epigrams". The hatred of Napoleon and others
for Tacitus as the adherent of the epigrams against the despot
deserves consideration.[1]

But there was reaction. "Nature" had been expelled with
a pitch-fork, but she came back. And what was Nature?
Trained by the sophists, men made a sharp antithesis between
Nature and Custom—νόμος, custom or law or both, the
device of men. The familiar iambic line puts it abruptly and
distinctly:

ἡ φύσις ἐβούλεθ' ᾗ νόμων οὐδὲν μέλει—

'Twas Nature's choice; she heeds not man-made laws.

The Cynic philosopher was content to be compared with the
dog;[2] "man walks with beasts, and so he always will". Let
us grant—let us hope—that a great many of the stories about
Diogenes the Cynic are inventions, those disgusting anecdotes
that we read in Diogenes Laertius about his wanton outrages
on convention and decency, in conduct and language, all
committed with a purpose of display, exhibitionism to advocate a philosophy.[3] Let us hope so; but behind such a mass
of tales there must be a tradition. E. A. Freeman's principle
is valid that a false anecdote may be good evidence—not to
fact but to character, or it could not gain currency. But
Nature is not to be defined so simply; the Cynic may compare

1 Cf. Boissier, *Tacite*, ch. iii, § 1, p. 112.
2 Cf. Diogenes Laertius, vi, 33, 60.
3 Cf. D. R. Dudley, *History of Cynicism*, pp. 29, 30.

himself with the dog, but the dog does not make the comparison. The dog has neither the memory nor the mind that have made human morals; so the *nature* of the one creature will be different from that of the other; the "virtue" (*areté*) of the one from the other's. There will be endless differences over "Nature". The Stoic conception of Nature was very different from the Cynic's; the *cosmos* filled the place in his mind that the dog did in the mind of the Cynic. The contrast can be brought out by comparing "those unwritten laws, the breaking of which brings admitted shame"—a great phrase in Pericles' speech—with the ideal of "the pleasure of the moment" (ἡδονὴ μονόχρονος) advocated by Aristippus; which is Nature? Even Athenaeus has a retort to those who say that pleasure and the passion for it are implanted in us by Nature; "so is fear", he said; and the Stoic phrasing of this is familiar in Horace's *Epistles* if nowhere else. Epicurus knew no pleasure that the body did not give, extending the body to include ear and eye, which really come very near the mind. What is Nature? Professor Earp remarks that the Greeks had no word for "unselfishness";[1] perhaps not. It was at a late date in human history that the Stoic coined the word "conscience", but the thing was there, in one form or other, from the time when man first began to reflect; and whatever lack of a term there was for unselfishness, it was there from the hour of the birth of the first human baby. Is selfishness natural? We are obliged to say that it is. But, if we linger a little over the Stoic conception of Nature, we shall have to rejoin, So is unselfishness; and as truly, though less obviously, so is the service of the state. The state is a creation of Nature, and Nature inspires the devotion that saves it.

1 F. R. Earp, *The Way of the Greeks*, p. 218. Plutarch appears to use the adjective ἀφίλαυτος, and Shelley in a letter makes a noun of it.

III

One great feature of the legislative work of Solon was his frank liberation of the individual. Ancient laws, or usages, as to inheritance were relaxed. In reason a man might, if he had no legitimate sons, leave his money where he would; it should no longer go perforce to his brother's sons, who might be as hateful to him as their mother; it was therefore likely that he would be keener to make money, if they were not to have the spending of it; and Athens would surely profit by the free and glad application of his brains to business. Solon, who understood Aegaean and Black Sea commerce, in the same spirit of freedom, altered the laws about money-lending and bottomry; the parties concerned should decide on a view of conditions what was a fair rate of interest. There was the season of the year to be considered, the length of the voyage, the position as to war and peace on the sea, or in this or that land that might be visited and skirted; the state and age of the ship were relevant, the record of the captain, a dozen things; how could a legislator enact rates of interest aright for all time and all conditions? Let the business people hammer it out. Furthermore Solon threw open Athens to capable immigrants. This is easily said; but there has been very little study of immigrants as a class; they do not universally court inquiry; but impressions gathered in the new world suggest that, since men left the old countries to settle in North America, the man who thought over emigration and did emigrate has normally been a man of some imagination and enterprise, and very frequently has proved of some real capacity. It is reasonable to suppose that such facts did not escape Solon, and that he knew what sort of people he was inviting to Athens. At all events they came, and they helped to make that great age which we know as the fifth century. When we speak of Greece, nine times out of ten we are thinking of Athens, not of Aetolia, just as in speaking of America we hardly mean Guatemala unless we say so. Most of Greek literature and history is in one way or another conditioned by Athens—that is, by the state where there was most individual freedom, and (to use a modern phrase) most individuality. But the Frenchman was not far astray who coined the phrase "the defects of his qualities".

In writing of Erasmus,[1] Froude urged that "there is no kind of person more difficult to provide for than a man of genius. He will not work in harness, he will not undertake work which he does not like; his silent theory about himself is that he must be left to do as he pleases...", and so forth. Froude was the intimate friend and biographer of Carlyle; and we may conclude that it was with some experience of the difficulty of genius that he wrote. Carlyle himself wrote in much the same vein about Dante.

The man of genius, poet or painter, does not see things as the common man does; he misses the obvious and loses his way—a not unlikely event when every bush is afire with God; the common man knows that the bush is quite normal, nothing to notice. They live in different worlds and speak different languages. "It is less difficult perhaps", wrote La Bruyère, "for the rare genius to foregather with what is noble and sublime than to avoid all sorts of blunders." Genius isolates a man; a humourist has said that it is unfortunate to be a genius, for it means that all the clever people will hate you. Where poetry is concerned, Plato says that the poet can do nothing till the god is in him and his own mind out of him; the poetry of the man of sense is knocked out by the poetry of the madman. Σωφρονεῖν is his word, sense, sanity, a sound realization of things—the very faculty that gives a man a high place in the practical world. But that world will not sing his songs, no, nor read them. The poet is of a peculiar build—is a personality, says Goethe—is a great soul, says Longinus—is born the way he is and cannot be manufactured by any training, says Pindar; but we need not repeat the familiar words here. The criticism he incurs from the commonplace rarely reconciles him to the mind and thought of the average man; and he may revolt into all sorts of

---

1 *Life and Letters of Erasmus*, Lecture 3, p. 51.

irrelevance, flouting common standards which have no obvious connexion with his art. Browning shows us something of the sort in his *Fra Lippo*. The open eye and the candid nature make a great endowment; but with them very often goes a blank inability to understand slower temperaments, which not infrequently develops into a certain suspicion of all the settled convictions of mankind.

In that delightful book *The Comments of Bagshot*, we have two suggestions that bear on this. The trouble, said Bagshot, about the artistic temperament is that there is so often so much temperament and so little art. Elsewhere, more suggestively, he says of the same temperament that it means an unstable personality, moving about in many worlds and firmly rooted in none. Add a word from William Wordsworth—"moving about in worlds not realized"; and the difficulties raised by the man of genius are nearly summed up. He will not fit in; he will not accept traditional standards; he does not see the obvious, and he is apt only imperfectly to recognize what he does see; there is a want of focus; and he revolts. Often it is a foolish revolt. To achieve anything in art, said Goethe, one needs a good head and a good inheritance. Art after all—let me borrow Miss Welsford's words[1]—"needs conventions, formulae, accepted traditions of shapeliness, and these it must derive from a social or religious ritual, or from the practice of the ancients". Culture, according to Matthew Arnold, meant knowledge of the best that has been said—an understanding, that is, of the best thinking of mankind. To be ignorant of the past, said Cicero, is to remain a child.[2] And, further, Art is never really independent of the influence of the community, however unconscious of that influence the artist may be. So he revolts, and pursues mannerisms and private judgments and half-views, and is frightfully crude and impossible and inspired; and by and by he sees more, and either loses his first vision, or sees the world and truth and the things that matter in a new and yet more inspiring way. Co-operation

1 Enid Welsford, *The Fool*, p. 248.   2 Cicero, *Orator*, 34, 120.

is one law of Art, never without Independence. Sacrifice either and the Art is ruined. It depends on a miraculous harmony between Law and Liberty. What Law? Plato, in his book *The Laws*, wants the poets to be amenable to the laws of the magistrates, to write the hymns specified by the authorities. Of course the poet will not hear of that. Then can it be the Law of Nature, if we may borrow Stoic language? What else could it be? But Nature does not reveal her laws to every casual passer-by; and the artist is apt to be impatient. Yet, as a great Frenchman said, Time does not care to preserve work in which it has had no share.

It is not surprising, then, to hear it said that God gives us the genius, but, thank God! not too often. That saying does not seem very grateful, when one reflects that the progress of the community again and again has depended on the rebel genius, on the man who did his own seeing and his own thinking and would not submit to the community. But such a man often needs to be dead before the average people will forgive him; and they may owe him more than they will ever recognize. We have come, it would seem, a long way from the splendid athlete of Pindar and the valuable footballer of Britain; but it is still the same issue—the group or the great man. We have one more stage of further travel.

IV

In or about the year A.D. 111 the Emperor Trajan received a letter from Pliny the Younger, his representative in Bithynia.[1] It was Pliny's regular custom, as he says, to consult the Emperor when in doubt, as the correspondence suggests that he frequently was. This time it was about a group of people denounced to him by some anonymous accuser as Christians. He had never been present at the trial of Christians; so he was not clear as to procedure, or as to any allowance that should be made to old or young. The accused, or most of them, admitted that they were Christians;

1 Pliny, *Epp.* x, 96.

if they denied it, he let them go; some confessed that they had once been, but had ceased to be Christian—one of them as long ago as twenty years. So far as Pliny could learn, there was nothing against them but their profession; they were moral and well-behaved, and honest; the scandals about their common meal were apparently unfounded; what was eaten was everyday food and quite harmless. He found there was nothing to be held against them but superstition, bad and boundless (*pravam immodicam*). Some, upon their persistent avowal of their faith, he had ordered for execution. The trouble could be stopped, he thought; indeed, since he took action, people were going to the temples again which had been all but abandoned, ceremonies were being performed after intermission, and fodder for sacrificial victims found a market.

Trajan replied that Pliny's procedure had been correct, and that no very definite rule of action could be laid down. No anonymous charges were to be considered. Christians were not to be sought out; but, if properly accused and convicted, they were to be punished, unless they would recant and worship our gods. That had been a test applied by Pliny; images of the gods and the Emperor's statue were offered for worship, and he had required them to curse Christ.

At the end of the century Tertullian, a greater man than Englishmen are apt to suppose, dealt with this rescript of Trajan's to Pliny, with great contempt for the conception of law implied. It was a perfect tangle. Christians are not to be sought out; that means they are innocent; they are to be punished, which means they are guilty. The Emperor spares and rages at once. If they are to be condemned, why not hunt them down, as bandits and traitors and so forth are hunted down; if they are not to be hunted down, why not acquit them? And if a person accused denies that he is a Christian, he is to be acquitted; no other accused person is acquitted on a mere denial of the charge. Christians are tortured—not to make them confess, as other criminals are, but to force them to deny. Trajan, in our English phrase, was resolved to let sleeping dogs lie, but otherwise to maintain Imperial authority; there was to be no freedom for individuals to repudiate the state at the altars.

As we look back through ancient history, we find that in old Athenian days it was a matter of choice with a man whether he were initiated into the Eleusinian or any other mysteries. He was so far free; but to repudiate the religion of the state was a very different thing from reluctance to be initiated in what we might call an extra cult. There is a disruptive force in a new idea; but an extra cult is not a new idea. Anaxagoras had to fly Athens; it was said, to avoid prosecution for some offence against the national religion—not such an offence as the mutilation of sacred images charged against Alcibiades, but because of his teaching. Socrates was condemned to drink hemlock, for corrupting the youth—a vague enough charge, and probably honestly believed by the popular court that condemned him; it was not the kind of obviously faked accusation familiar in other ages and other courts, designed to cover mere differences of opinion. But in general such cases did not arise, until the Romans were confronted with the Jews; we may for the moment ignore the short attempt of Antiochus Epiphanes to Hellenize the Jews, significant as it is in the history of Judaism. There was no doing anything with the Jews; so the Roman government decided to allow Judaism as a national religion and to let it alone, with a tax on every Jew after the destruction of the Temple—a *vectigalis libertas*.

But the Christian was not covered by a national immunity, conceded by the government. He had no nation behind him; he and his group were a new kind of people, a third race, not perhaps likely to endure. Tacitus, at all events, writes of the sect and its founder in the past tense;[1] his *Annals* seemed likely to outlast the superstition. "Hatred of mankind" was charged against the sect, and defiance of the government, which every subject was morally bound to obey. But they

1 Tacitus, *Annals*, xv, 44.

were obstinate. Marcus Aurelius, in his diary, bids himself be firm, not obstinate like the Christians for the mere sake of opposition (μὴ κατὰ ψιλὴν παράταξιν, xi, 4). So the persecution went on; but it was not the work of religious bigotry, rather of officialism offended by independence and egged on (again and again) by local quarrels and jealousies, by Jews and others. Possibly Pliny's reference to fodder for victims gives a clue to the source of the anonymous accusation in some group of dealers; for later it was a regular charge against the Christians that they were "unprofitable" to local business.

There were Christian defences written and read, the most brilliant the *Apology* of Tertullian, the most charming (for what Gilbert Murray has called its "antiseptic quality") the *Letter to Diognetus*. The gist of all can be given in a sentence of Tertullian—*non religionis est cogere religionem*. It recalls, to a Cambridge man, the rejoinder made by Connop Thirlwall, when the Master of Trinity, Christopher Wordsworth, announced his principle: "Better compulsory religion than none". Thirlwall said the distinction was so fine that he could not draw it. It was not till the fourth century that the issue was settled, after several furious but unavailing attempts to stamp out the church. Constantine, in his Edict of Milan in 313, granted to Christians, and to others, full freedom to follow whatever religion they thought best. The individual had won, for the time, the battle of independent thinking against the sovereign state. It has had to be re-fought often enough since then, and the issue is still a living one in Europe and America, and where Japan rules.

But meanwhile the Christian community had had the same trouble to face within its bounds. What was the Christian religion? These new "prophets", inspired, they said, by the Holy Spirit, had strange things to say, that perplexed honest minds; and, in reaction, a new emphasis was laid on episcopacy; the bishop was to be a safeguard against the "prophet". Prophesying died, says a modern historian, when the Catholic church arose. The old quarrel between church and state was transformed, and became one between orthodoxy and heresy. There is much to be said for Dean Inge's dictum that the genius of Christianity is to be recognized chiefly in its heretics. St Paul had said something of the kind: "Where the Spirit of the Lord is, there is Liberty".

It is the old antithesis with which we started; and the pioneers of Christian freedom include Solon and Pericles, each recognizing in the independent Athenian, with all his gifts of insight and judgment developed to the highest point, the truest asset of Athens. The same view has been taken of the Christian gospel; its purpose is not to standardize men but to make them—to develop them into themselves, their ideal selves which they would never achieve without it, to liberate the human soul, the human faculty, for its fullest development. "I came not to destroy but to develop", is a possible translation of the Founder's words.

Yes, but where are we after all? Is the team or the hero to claim our allegiance? the individual or the group? the rebel or the government? the heretic or the church? Life is never so easy as a choice of that kind; there is no rule to be used without exception, if we may quote Trajan again. What then? There is the caustic old maxim of Cambridge: "Whatsoever thy hand findeth to do, remember that other people think differently"—a rule not so flippant as it looks. But it has been put more nobly by Luther in his *Freedom of the Christian Man*—"A Christian man is the most free lord of all and subject to none; a Christian man is the most dutiful servant of all, and subject to every one." Further than that it is not easy to go; but after all, easy decisions do not necessarily make for manhood; bigots have much simpler rules than thinkers.

HOMER AND HIS READERS

I

HOMER—the name to Greeks meant the poet of the *Iliad* and the *Odyssey*, though some few vaguely wondered whether the two poems were by different authors, and others attributed to the poet other epics and dubious miscellanea and some notable poems still known as the Homeric hymns. About the poet himself they knew next to nothing. "Seven Grecian cities", says the famous epigram, but they were not always the same seven that "fought for Homer dead". Thucydides quotes as authentic the lines from the *Hymn to Apollo*, which are quite definite, in which the poet addresses the women of Delos:

Remember, whenever a stranger and wanderer over earth
Comes hither and asks of you, "What minstrel is most of
    worth
"Of all that sail to Delos? Whose songs have sweetest fall?"
Then ye shall make this answer to his question, one and all:
"A blind man. Far in Chios he dwells 'twixt crag and sea,
"And *his* songs are the sweetest for all the years to be." [1]

So there we have the figure which inspired the sculptor to make one of the noblest heads that have come down to us from antiquity—

> The blind old man of Scio's rocky isle. [2]

But a good many would have asked how he came to be called Melesigenes, if he did not come from Smyrna; [3] the "bard of Avon" seems to imply Stratford, and Meles was the Avon of Smyrna.

But wherever he was born he did not stay there. He lived a life of wandering, they said, in poverty, procuring by his

---

1 Thucydides, iii, 104; *Hymn to Apollo*, 167. The version is that of Mr F. L. Lucas.
2 Byron, *Bride of Abydos*, ii, 2.
3 Cf. Plutarch, *Sertorius*, 1, says Smyrna or Ios, one of them his birthplace, the other the place of his death.

songs just enough to keep him alive—one more sign of his
courage and high spirit—a great poet, who, unlike all others
who write prose or poem, never mentions his own name; he
is more like the prophets of the gods who speak unseen from
the darkness of the shrine.[1] The thought haunts Dio
Chrysostom—of the great poet a beggar and labelled mad[2]—
yes, a poet and in his way a philosopher, content ever to be
abroad, to pick up five and twenty drachmas by begging for
it rather than live in his own country at home.[3] The Platonic
Socrates puts another colour on all this; it was characteristic
of Socrates, wrote Benjamin Jowett, to mix up sense and
nonsense so that the listener was hard put to it to draw the
line between them. If Homer, then, Socrates says, had really
been able to educate and improve mankind, if he had really
possessed knowledge, are we to believe that his contemporaries
would have allowed him to beg his way as a rhapsode; would
they not have been as loath to let him go as gold and kept
him perforce at home?[4] A later age left us a story of a contest
in song between Homer and Hesiod; a story that rested
somehow on old legend and ignored the possible two-
hundred-year interval between the poets. Montalembert
managed to contrive a meeting between St Patrick and
Ossian.

But for our present purpose we may take a hint from the
traveller Pausanias.[5] "I have very carefully investigated",
he says, "the dates of Hesiod and Homer; but I do not like
to state my results, knowing as I do the carping disposition
of some people, especially of the professors of poetry, at the
present day." No, he says at a later point, "I have heard all
this and read the oracles, but I express no view of my own
as to the native land or age of Homer." And to his prudence
let us add the orthodoxy of Strabo, the geographer, a great
reader and a thorough-going admirer of Homer, who will

---

[1] Dio Chrysostom, *Or.* 36 (=53; *de Homero*), 9.
[2] Dio Chrysostom, *Or.* 11, 16.   [3] Dio Chrysostom, *Or.* 30, 5.
[4] Plato, *Rep.* x, 600.
[5] Pausanias, ix, 30, 3; x, 24, 3. In ii, 33, 3, he concedes Homer's blindness
and wandering life.

not allude to the Homeric hymns or anything not canonical. Nor need we, for our present purpose, linger to dispute who were the Homeridae of Chios; they have a modern advocate of great learning and great powers of faith;[1] but whether they were rhapsodes, or a guild of poets, or descendants of Homer himself, is for us not very relevant. Dundee knows "the sons of the piper"—"an' wasna he a roguie, the piper o' Dundee?" but the last thing you would assert of that anonymous genius would be that he was the ancestor of all those sons. Nor again need we discuss the part alleged to have been played by Pisistratus in securing us the *Iliad* and the *Odyssey*.[2] One may have admiration for that brilliant ruler without bestowing on him the poetic genius to make such poems of scattered "lays" which he assembled from unknown quarters. It is arguable that all he did (and, if he did it, it was a considerable service to mankind) was to secure a sound text of the poems; but perhaps he did not even do so much. We may leave him.

Homer, then, and the *Iliad* and the *Odyssey*—coming to us as it were "out of the dimness of the shrine", the poet unseen and unknown, the poems beyond mortal reach or compass. Wolf, of course, and the generations that so ardently imitated him—they come long after the period that limits our present range; and the words of Goethe are more relevant—"Wolf has demolished Homer, but he has not been able to injure the poem; for this poem has a miraculous power like the heroes of Walhalla, who hew one another to pieces in the morning but sit down to dinner with whole limbs at noon." Let his quip suffice. Since my undergraduate days, it seems to me, interest has slackened in Achilleids and insertions; the whole conception of cobbling up epics grows quaint; there is more realization that for great poetry a great poet is needed, and is more probable than a large committee. In short, to quote Goethe again,[3] "to *do* something you must *be* something"; or, if Goethe, like Wolf, is outside our period,

1 T. W. Allen, *Homer, Origin, and Transmission.*
2 Pausanias, vii, 26, 3.   3 Goethe to Eckermann, 1 February 1827.

let us quote Longinus[1]—"the real thing in literature [ὕψος is his simpler and stronger word] is the echo of a great soul"— and that no committee ever had.

The ancient world, then, believed in Homer, and, what was more, it read him, loved him, and learnt him by heart— "the only poetry that I see to be truly noble and splendid and royal, fit for one destined to rule over men". These are not to be supposed the actual words of the historic Alexander; posterity was for ever putting words in his mouth and calling it history; but Dio Chrysostom here represents what was in truth the feeling of the king about the poet, as we shall see, and what countless myriads of lesser readers felt. "Nobility" was one of Matthew Arnold's "marks" of the Homeric genius. However wrong Achilles may be at times in word or act, he is always on a high level—a great character, man at his highest, right or wrong, a hero. Nor is he the only one; in Hector we have as true a picture of patriot, general, husband and father; Priam, too, is noble. There is a grandeur about them, these heroes of the *Iliad*, which gives a new interpretation to humanity. They show us what our king may be. It was a criticism levelled at Tennyson, that, setting out to show the same thing again, he made his King Arthur, *flos regum Arthurus*, a "prig". That may be so; but no one would say any such thing of Homer's heroes. They are clear-cut, intensely human—goddess-born, if you like, but real human nature. No wonder the Greeks studied them for growth in character, as we shall see; but that is not all. "Poetry", said Aristotle[2] (we shall return to this) "is a more serious, a more philosophic, thing than history." The *Iliad* is no allegory like the *Faerie Queene*; but, as Wordsworth said about *The Jolly Beggars*, even if there is no moral purpose, a moral effect is not excluded. There is no moralizing in Homer, or next to none; but great questions of human life and conduct, of man's relations with man and with God, questions of prayer and destiny, rise in the reader's mind. It is not the least like Lucretius', a philosophic poem, but

---

1 Longinus, 9, 2.   2 Aristotle, *Poetics*, 9, 3; p. 1451 b.

it wakens a profounder philosophy. And, with all, it is a story, magnificently told. The world had no such stories again till, after two millenniums at least, Cervantes told the adventures of the Don and the man. Next after him came *Robinson Crusoe*; and then we pass into a lower class of narration. Some one has called the *Odyssey* "*die älteste Robinsonade*"; and Sainte-Beuve lingers over the stag-killing on Circe's isle, as Odysseus tells it, "all in the style of Robinson Crusoe".[1] So it is; there is the same art; we watch our hero face to face with a problem, we see him consider ways of solving it, and then he achieves it; and all the time it is our problem, our story. So with the *Odyssey* generally; we are always watching a man and no ordinary one. In *Don Quixote*, the knight errant has only to speak, or, most of the time, the squire, and we cannot help listening; somehow the inserted stories do not grip in the same way, but the two great characters hold us; and, the better we know them, the more they hold us. Homer inserts no "Curious Impertinent"; and great as are Cervantes and Defoe in their masterpieces, Homer remains the chief and prince of all story-tellers. To this point we must return.

But, asked serious people in antiquity, is what he gives you History? A simple question, till you realize that there are many conceptions of History. Was he, ask some of the moderns, contemporary with the men he describes? Paul Louis Courier suggested that Homer had "made war"—"savage war"—and might have been secretary to Agamemnon. Napoleon also emphasized "the life-like character of the military operations". But the scholars wonder at times whether, so to put it, Homer was, like a modern, bringing genius to bear on precise erudition. But the ancients were blunter. Homer indeed, says Thucydides,[2] lived long after the Trojan war, and he described Agamemnon as "king of many islands and of all Argos", which implies, he continues, that he possessed a considerable navy, or he could only have ruled over adjacent islands. Homer was a

1 *Étude sur Virgile*, p. 243.　　2 Thucydides, i, 3; i, 9–11.

poet, "and may therefore be expected to exaggerate"; but his data imply a smaller expedition than you might think, the invading forces not very numerous and great difficulties with money and commissariat, the inevitable dispersion of their troops in pillaging forays, and the maintenance of Troy's defences for ten years. Herodotus was more critical; he learnt of variations in the epic story, and concluded that Homer took the variant that best suited his poetic purposes.[1]

A later age had graver doubts. Chaucer tells us

> But yet I gan full well espy,
> Betwix hem was a little envy.
> One said that Homer madè lies,
> Feigning in his poetries,
> And was to Greekes favouráble;
> Therefore held he it but fable.[2]

The middle ages relied for the history of the Trojan war on two authors, not so well-known in antiquity—Dares, who supplied Chaucer and later poets with the tale of Troilus and Cressida, a writer of the Trojan party, and Dictys of Crete. Dictys, like a good many ancient worthies—Enoch, Esdras and Numa Pompilius—did more for posterity than for his contemporaries. He kept a diary of the Trojan war, a diary in which gods had not the significance that Homer gave them, and women had more. He wrote in Phoenician characters, and, like the other writers just named, he did not publish his work, but had it buried with him. In Nero's reign an earthquake in Crete rent his tomb open and gave back his diary to mankind. In other words the book was forged in Nero's reign, at the earliest. He seems to have been known in the second century A.D. and to the Byzantines; but he had only survived in Latin, till in 1907 the world of letters was surprised by the discovery of a papyrus fragment in Greek, of about the third century. It is all strange enough—this discrediting of Homer. But stranger still, a great Oxford scholar would have us believe that Dictys

---

1 Herodotus, ii, 116. Cf. T. W. Allen, *Homer, Origin*, etc., pp. 131, 171.
2 *House of Fame*, 1475. Cf. Lounsbury, *Studies in Chaucer*, ii, 307–308, who discusses Dictys.

represents an older tradition than Homer himself, and that
the poet took Shakespeare's freedom in handling his authorities, like Thackeray writing *Esmond* and bringing the
Pretender to London at the moment of Queen Anne's death
and letting him miss the moment by his unnecessary dash
into the country after Beatrice Esmond. What stands is the
fact that somebody had the fancy and the ingenuity in the
first century A.D. to invent an entirely new story of Troy, as
clear of gods as Lucan's *Pharsalia*.

So there was some doubt or perplexity about Homer being
a reliable historian. The matter is sensibly and pleasantly
discussed by Strabo in an early section of his book;[1] myth
has its uses.

So Homer took the Trojan war, which really happened
(γεγονότα), and decked it out with myths, and the wanderings
of Odysseus in the same way; for to hang an empty story of
marvels (κενὴν τερατολογίαν) on something wholly untrue
was not Homer's way.... This is what he means when he
says that Odysseus "told many lies in the likeness of truth",
not *all* but *many*.... He took then the foundation of his story
(τὰς ἀρχάς) from History.

And he quotes a shrewd aphorism of Polybius—"to invent
everything is neither convincing nor Homeric". Goethe is
with these Greek critics—"What would be the use of poets
if they only repeated the record of the historian?...The
Greeks were so great that they regarded fidelity to historic
facts less than the treatment of them by the poets."[2] Isocrates
praised Homer for his skill in combining delightful fiction and
sound teaching;[3] it was a recognition of man's real nature;
and characteristically he expressed some emphatic contempt
for the discussions on Homer by sophists of his day.[4]

There were still more questions about the Geography of
Homer—those islands of the Cyclops and Calypso, where
were we to look for them? In Sicily and its neighbourhood,

1 Strabo, i, C. 18–20; citing Polybius in C. 25.
2 *Conversations with Eckermann*, 31 January 1827 (Engl. tr. i, 352).
3 Isocrates, *ad Nicoclem*, 48.
4 Isocrates, *Panath*. 18. See Atkins, *Literary Criticism in Antiquity*, i, 131.

or far away in Ocean? Eratosthenes caustically opined that you will discover where Odysseus wandered, when you discover the cobbler who stitched the bag in which Aeolus tied up the winds.[1] It was against this that Polybius made the protest already quoted. Modern travellers bring a further indictment against Homer's Geography; how defective was his knowledge of Greece itself! W. G. Clark, the Cambridge Public Orator, travelled through the Peloponnese in 1856, and roundly declared that there never was a road by which Telemachus could drive across it in two days.

A curious parallel comes from another quarter. Sir Raymond Beazley, in his *Dawn of Modern Geography*[2] (a most enlightening and engaging book), speaks of "the essential truthfulness" of the Voyages of Sindbad the Sailor, which had been recognized in the eighteenth century by the Englishman Richard Hole, who called the Sindbad tales "the Arabian Odyssey". The tales are based, Sir Raymond tells us, on books of Moslem travels, with borrowings from Greek poetry, Indian tales and Persian traditions. Fiction plays a part in the attribution of all the adventures to one man of amazing good fortune; but, he says, few of the incidents, even the most surprising, cannot be shown to be founded on fact. The listener in bazaar or coffee-house wanted to hear marvels; the Geography was of minor importance to him— that is the concern of the modern reader. All the voyages are to points in the Indian Ocean; which are not always recognizable to the English reader, unless for instance he thinks of Ceylon as Sarandeeb. E. W. Lane, in his first edition of the tales,[3] says much the same; there are abundant coincidences between the tales and the scientific works of the Arabs, and it is less likely that the geographer borrowed from the teller of tales than the other way. Similarly, Sir John Mandeville is far from being a complete liar, as any one will see who compares him with Odoric in the volume of the Library of English Classics which gives us both, though he

1 Strabo, C. 24.   2 C. R. Beazley, *Dawn*, i, 438–40.
3 Lane, *Arabian Nights*, iii, 80.

(and here one thinks of Odysseus) turns most countries into islands—Cathay and Tibet among them.

After all this, it may seem of less interest to speak of the Greek scholars mostly at Alexandria, who dealt with Homer, studied his language, "purified" his text, "athetized" doubtful lines on various grounds—e.g. the indelicacy of Nausicaa thinking or saying to herself that a husband like Odysseus would be very attractive—an unmaidenly remark. Aristarchus struck out a canon of the greatest importance in the interpretation of poetry; the final court of appeal in the interpretation of a poet is the poet himself—the concordance, in fact, and not the dictionary. But there were those who tired of minutiae, and with the ribald comment on the grammarians launched by Herodicus, we may end this section.

> Pupils of Aristarchus! flee
> Over the broad back of the sea!
> More timid than the tawny doe,
> Out with you all, from Hellas go!
> Buzzers in corners, all whose mind
> To monosyllables is confined—
> σφῶϊν and σφίν,
> And μὶν and νίν;
> Go, all together,
> And meet bad weather!
> But for Herodicus, may Greece
> And God's own Babylon dwell in peace![1]

II

We may let the "monosyllabists" go, even if it is a little ungrateful, and turn to the interests of more ordinary people. Homer, then, may be described as the Plain Man's Guide; that is at least one of his functions, and a very important one. Philosophers and grammarians dealt with him after their own minds, and (to judge by later ages) were doubtless convinced of the value of their opinions; and then we find Aristotle announcing his amazing belief that "the general public"—

1 Quoted by Athenaeus, 222 a.

or, if you prefer his exact and more vulgar expression, *hoi polloi*; he says no less—"the general public is a better judge of the works of music and of the works of the poets".[1] Spain and England offer some confirmation; for it was the "general reader", and a lowly kind at that, which imposed *Don Quixote* and *The Pilgrim's Progress* on the literature of their countries and of the world. Plato bears testimony to the hold that Homer had gained on ordinary people;[2] "we meet", he says, "the eulogists of Homer, declaring that this poet has been the educator (πεπαίδευκεν) of Hellas, that he is profitable for the management and administration of human things, and that you should take him up and get to know him, and regulate your whole life according to this poet"; and, he continues, "we may love and honour the intentions of these excellent people, excellent as far as their lights extend" (ὡς ὄντας βελτίστους εἰς ὅσον δύνανται). His praise has an edge about it, and we shall shortly see what he thinks; but meanwhile there is plenty of evidence as to the current opinion of Homer.

We find perhaps the most delightful illustration of this in Xenophon's *Symposium*.[3] Socrates is suggesting that each guest shall tell what he considers the most valuable knowledge in his possession. Niceratus, the son, as we learn, of the luckless general Nicias, when it comes to his turn, says: "My father was anxious that I should be a good man, so he made me learn all the works of Homer; and I could recite you now by heart the whole of the *Iliad* and the *Odyssey*." Later on he endorses his father's view—"you know, I am sure, that Homer, the wisest of men, has written (πεποίηκε, has made his poetry) about practically everything pertaining to man". But in the meantime, Antisthenes the Cynic snaps sharply back at him; "has it escaped you that all the rhapsodes, too, know these poems?" "How should it, when I listen to them nearly every day?" "Then," says the Cynic, "do you know

1 Aristotle, *Politics*, iii, 6; p. 1281 b.
2 Plato, *Rep.* x, 606 E. Jowett's translation, but twice restoring the words "this poet", which surely count.
3 Xenophon, *Symposium*, iii, 5, 6; iv, 6.

any sillier tribe than rhapsodes?" "No, by Zeus," says the
young man, "I don't think I do." Niceratus urges the value
of Homer (and of his students) to the man who would be a
general or a politician or a householder—look at his heroes!—
and he himself has learned from him. "Oh!" says Antisthenes, "then you know how to be a king" with Agamemnon
before your eyes, "goodly king and spearman strong"?[1] Yes,
he says, and there is chariot driving, too; and (he must have
had some sense of humour or been very simple) he recalls
how Homer, dealing with other aspects of life, speaks of an
onion as a relish for drink.[2] One has a haunting suspicion that
Antisthenes—or perhaps it was Xenophon—has been reading
Plato's attack on Homer.

Another young friend of Socrates was interested in Homer.
Alcibiades, "getting past boyhood", we read, accosted a
schoolteacher (γραμματοδιδασκάλῳ), and asked him for a book
of Homer. The man said he had nothing of Homer's, and
Alcibiades hit him with his fist and went off. Another teacher
had a Homer which he had corrected himself. "Oh! and
you are teaching boys their letters, when you can correct
Homer? Oughtn't you to be teaching young men?"[3]

Aristophanes also contributes to our story. The writers of
comedy did not, one assumes, always intend to be taken
seriously as historians, despite some grave scholars. Even
when he is giving his audience exactly what they will believe,
one suspects his intentions. In the *Clouds*, for instance, the
Δίκαιος Λόγος (the Right Way of Life, or however you
translate it) is so very righteous, so very conformable to
mid-Victorian ways, that one begins to wonder whether
Aristophanes was not laughing just a little at him as well as
at his up-to-date and degenerate rival. So, when in the
Frogs he urges that the great real value of poets is their
practical use in teaching useful arts—what to-day (though
the arts are less exalted) we call vocational training, no doubt
he counted on agreement on the part of his listeners; but did

---

1 *Iliad*, iii, 179.   2 *Iliad*, xi, 630.
3 Plutarch, *Alcibiades*, 7.

he not also laugh once more—a little? This at any rate is what he says:

And just consider, how all along
From the very first they have wrought you good, the noble bards, the masters of song.
First, Orpheus taught you religious rites and from bloody murder to stay your hands:
Musaeus healing and oracle lore; and Hesiod all the culture of lands,
The time to gather, the time to plough. And gat not Homer his glory divine
By singing of valour and honour and right, and the sheen of the battle-extended line,
The ranging of troops, and the arming of men?[1]

It reminds us of Niceratus and his notion of learning strategy from Homer. But of course a comic poet needs to be checked. There is nothing comic, no shred of humour, about Pausanias, who tells us six hundred years later how the Messenians took a stratagem from Homer, who has other pieces of strategy, and indeed "ideas that have proved useful to mankind in all manner of ways".[2] Aeschines, also, may be trusted with the commonplace. "Hesiod the poet", he says,[3] "has a good observation on those matters. He says it somewhere, when he is educating [παιδεύων again] the masses and advising cities not to tolerate bad demagogues. I will quote the lines; for I suppose it is for this we learn the maxims of the poets when we are children, that, when we are men, we may use them."

Long after Aeschines, and not addressing a popular audience, Horace tells a friend that he has been reading Homer and finding great moral lessons in him[4]—

Better than all the logic of the sage,
Than Crantor's precepts or Chrysippus' page...
His glowing pencil paints what mischief springs
From the mad broils of nations and of kings....

1 Aristophanes, *Frogs*, 1030–6 (B. B. Rogers's translation).
2 Pausanias, iv, 28, 7.　　　　　3 Aeschines, *in Ctes.* 134–5.
4 Horace, *Epistles*, i, 2; version of Francis Howes (1845).

> . . . To pride and passion each holds true;
> And while the monarchs rave, the people rue.
> By envy, faction, lust and fraud they sin
> Alike without Troy's bulwarks and within.

And then he turns to the *Odyssey* and finds a hero indeed, who

> Saw various realms and well their manners weighed. . . .
> Firm in adversity, in peril brave,
> And buoyant upon Fortune's roughest wave,

—so unlike his companions, whom Circe bewitched, and "the spruce fribbles of Alcinous' court".

But does Homer really teach all these wonderful things? There is the rhapsode Ion, in Plato's dialogue that bears his name—Ion the perfect presentment of the artistic temperament, contemplating with pride his own reactions, and taking himself very seriously, a specialist in Homer, both as reciter and commentator. "I lose attention and go to sleep and have absolutely no ideas, when any one speaks of any other poet; but when Homer is mentioned, I wake up at once, and am all attention, and have plenty to say." Socrates plays gently with him; he must have a splendid life; he must share the inspiration of the poet, when he can communicate it as he does—his eyes full of tears, his hair on end, himself entirely carried out of himself, and his listeners wrought up to share every emotion. Wonderful! and he can comment, and do it well on everything in Homer—chariot-driving? really? and generalship? and why doesn't Athens engage him as a general, then? A foreigner? Ah! well, they have before now engaged foreigners. But, to conclude, if his art is not really art, but inspiration, still Socrates won't say that Ion has been playing Proteus, twisting and turning and slipping away from the issue—but which would he prefer, to be thought dishonest or inspired? A great difference between them, Ion rejoins, and inspiration is the far nobler alternative. Altogether, there are few pieces of Greek prose so amusing or (as everybody but Ion would feel) so devastating; but the artistic temperament has rarely much range in humour, and some natures are protected against irony.

But it was not only the rhapsode who incurred Plato's
criticism; he was only a link in the chain. As when a series
of rings magnetized hold up each the one below it, the poet
hangs directly upon the Muse, the rhapsode ("like you, Ion")
hangs from the poet, and the listeners from the rhapsode, the
magnetic force being inspiration.[1] Now there is, as Plato
says, an ancient quarrel between Poetry and Philosophy[2]—
a dictum to which we must return. Plato, faced with the
choice between them, stands for Philosophy; and, as is
familiar, when he frames his ideal state, he lays it down that
Poetry and poets will not be admitted. If a poet gets in, his
great gifts will be respectfully recognized, he will be crowned,
and, with supreme courtesy, he will be put over the frontier[3]—
unless—Well, there will have to be hymns for the gods, and
poets will be required to make them, but they will be limited
to hymns and will make them under the control of the
magistrates.[4] So much for inspiration. Homer, whom they
credit with knowing all arts, who is the teacher and exemplar
of all the poets, especially the dramatists,[5] incurs every kind
of censure. It had not always been so; Plato had been caught
as a boy; "a certain love and reverence that I have felt for
Homer from boyhood hampers me, but I will speak out."
And he does. As to the poets, and Homer in particular,
understanding all arts,[6] they frankly do not; a poet is apt to
be the last person to understand his own poetry; Socrates
found "there was hardly a soul present who would not have
talked better about their poetry than the poets did themselves."[7] Poetry is a kind of Rhetoric, and Rhetoric is own
sister to cookery and such arts. Besides Homer does not show
us a high type of character, the type we would wish the young
men to copy; think how Achilles surrenders to the agony of
sorrow, pouring ashes on his head and wailing, how Priam
rolls in the dirt, how Homer will have it that Zeus himself
laments for Sarpedon.[8] Nor ought the "guardians" of the

1 Plato, *Ion*, 535 E, 536.   2 Plato, *Rep*. x, 607 B.   3 Plato, *Rep*. iii, 398.
4 Plato, *Laws*, ii, 660 A.   5 Plato, *Rep*. x, 607 A.   6 Plato, *Rep*. x, 598.
7 Plato, *Apology*, 22.   8 Plato, *Rep*. iii, 388.

ideal city to be given to laughter, or to lying, to vulgar abuse,
like the taunts levelled by Achilles at Agamemnon ("O heavy
with wine, who hast the eyes of a dog and the heart of a
stag") and so forth.[1] To Plato's criticism of Homer's gods
we return later.

Others pursued this line of attack. Timaeus, the armchair
historian, would have it that the way in which Homer lingers
over meals suggests he was a bit of a glutton.[2] To this
Athenaeus, in his *Gastronomers*—and there is no greater
authority on the delights of the table—makes a vigorous
reply. Glutton? Always roast meat, never an entrée, never
a honey cake, fish only on an emergency, no fowl, nothing
but the food that builds strength.[3] Outstanding among those
who abused Homer was the famous Zoilus, whose name
became a by-word, though he did not say anything much
worse than what Plato had said long before. *Malo errare cum
Platone* than with Zoilus. The errors of genius are errors, of
course, but they can stimulate and suggest.

Another line of attack is mentioned by Plutarch.[4] People
(*hoi polloi* again) will not believe that behind some great and
surprising deed is inspiration, as Homer says time and again—
"into his mind the grey-eyed goddess Athene put it"—such
impossible exploits and incredible tales as he describes make
it difficult to believe in a man's reasoning power affecting
his choice of action. But that, says Plutarch, is unfair. Homer
shows us his heroes thinking, divided in mind, often enough
in ordinary matters; on great occasions the god does not take
away, he rather prompts, a man's choice of action; he does
not create impulses (ὁρμάς) but conceptions (φαντασίας)
which lead to impulses; the man's will is set in motion, and
courage and hope are given. How else, he asks, could gods
act—unless you are to cut the divine clean out of our actions?

After all the debates (though perhaps they were happy
enough not to have heard of them) simple people held on to

1 Plato, *Rep.* iii, 388–90.   2 Polybius, xii, 24.
3 Athenaeus, i, 8 e–10 d; so too Plato, *Rep.* iii, 404.
4 Plutarch, *Coriolanus*, 32.

Homer. Let us recall the sentence we began with from Aristotle about *hoi polloi* as judges of literature. Two pictures are given us, charming pictures, from the very outskirts of the Greek world. Dio Chrysostom found it necessary, or at least convenient, to be out of sight for a while, in Domitian's reign. He went to Olbia on the Borysthenes (the Dnieper), on the North shore of the Black Sea, an old Greek community in the wilds, on the defensive amid barbarian Scythians.[1] He found the people enthusiasts for Homer, the poet of war and the poet of Achilles, who has a temple in the North. They will listen to nothing on behalf of any other poet; and you might say that pretty well all of them have the *Iliad* by heart. To tease a young friend of eighteen, Dio asked him whether he thought Homer the better or Phocylides. The youngster laughed; why, he didn't even know the other poet's name, and he didn't think anybody else there did either. "We don't count any one a poet but Homer." "And you don't know Phocylides! And he was one of the famous poets." Would it not be well to sample him, as you would the wine, say, of some new-come merchant? a little sample? for he does not write thousands of lines about a single battle, as your poet does; no, two or three lines at a time, and he puts his name to every thought—not like Homer who never mentions himself. For instance—about Achilles—but it won't do. The boy won't have it: "Stranger," he says, "we love you and greatly regard you; otherwise no Borysthenite would have tolerated you talking like that against Homer and Achilles."

Synesius of Cyrene, about A.D. 410, was an avowed admirer of Dio, and imitated Dio's *Praise of Hair* with a corresponding *Praise of Baldness*; and I have often wondered whether his description of the people in the back parts of his North African colony was not suggested by Dio's account of his Black Sea hosts. He lives away to the South "the last of the Cyrenians", and his neighbours are like the people Odysseus had to find who did not know what an oar was, though they

1 Dio Chrysostom, *Or.* xxxvi, *Borystheniticos.*

do know salt, sal Ammoniac, in fact, from Siwah. The tax-collectors remind them of the Emperor, but they are not all quite sure who he is—Agamemnon, son of Atreus, perhaps, who went to Troy; that is the king's name we have heard from childhood. And the good cowherds talk about his friend Odysseus, a bald man, and a rare hand to deal with affairs and find a way in difficulties. Don't they laugh when they tell about him, supposing it was only last year the Cyclops was blinded, and how the old fellow (τὸ γερόντιον) was dragged out under the ram, while the scoundrel (τὸ κάθαρμα) sat at the door and fancied the leader of the flock came last not because of the load he carried, but from sympathy with his master. Elsewhere Synesius tells of a voyage he made which had moments of danger, when a line of Homer rang in his mind—

Ajax drank of the salt sea wave and utterly perished—

it is not in our Homer quite like that; no matter, he avowedly had bad texts among his books (a bad text, he said, stimulates the mind to correct it); but did it mean that Homer thought death by drowning extinguished the soul?[1]

Perhaps it will not be amiss to add to our list of the un-sophisticated readers of Homer the great Alexander, himself a descendant of Achilles and of Andromache. He was a "lover of reading", we are told, and read Homer throughout his campaigns all over Asia.[2] We are even told of a special box, found among the spoils of Darius, which he took as his portion; it was so exactly suited to carry his Homer. It chimes in well with all we know of that great and simple nature—the two adjectives seem to spell genius—that the greatest and simplest of poets should so deeply appeal to him. Caesar, too, was a "lover of Alexander", and himself a descendant of Iulus and the Trojans, of Venus and Anchises (theme of the Homeric hymn); and he, like Alexander, found a special pleasure and interest in visiting Troy.[3]

1 Synesius, *Epistle*, 4.   2 Plutarch, *Alexander*, 8; 26, 1; Strabo, C. 593.
3 Strabo, C. 594.

III

In a much discussed passage Herodotus states his belief that Homer and Hesiod shaped the religion of the Greeks, or, more literally, "made a Theogony" for the Greeks.[1] He has been discussing Egyptian contributions to the Greek pantheon with chronological data to show the immense antiquity of Egypt's gods. Homer and Hesiod lived, he supposes, four hundred years before his own time, and he adds "and not more", which suggests that other people gave them an earlier date; but he holds that Greek knowledge of the gods dates "from yesterday and the day before"; and Homer and Hesiod "made the Theogony and gave the gods their several names, divided among them their honours and their arts, and declared their outward forms".

The anthropologists protest. Greek religion must have been in existence long before Homer, and it contained elements—beliefs, rites, practices—of which Homer says nothing. Great areas of Greek religion he leaves ignored. Even a cursory reading of Pausanias, ten centuries according to Herodotus later than Homer, reveals masses of traditions, cults and superstitions, which it is agreed to call primitive. But some caution is needed. The modern Protestant—or the anthropologist, for that matter—finds in Italy, Spain and Mexico abundance of ideas and usages of which no trace is to be found in the New Testament; they certainly do not belong to primitive Christianity, whatever their source. Perhaps the difficulty lies in the word "Greek", but I do not propose to digress to the Pelasgians or any other races who may have contributed ideas, as Herodotus says the Egyptians did. The fact is that we do not know exactly what "Greek religion", if the vague expression may be allowed, was before Homer, nor what tribes or races added their beliefs at one period or another. Blood and race do not strictly determine beliefs, and superstitions are careless of frontiers. Even where we find a suggestion of Homer in a Greek cult, questions may

1 Herodotus, ii, 53.

arise. At Chaeronea in Boeotia the god most honoured,
Pausanias tells us, was the sceptre of Agamemnon; they call
it a spear, and explain how it came to them; there is no
temple, but every day a table is set beside it covered with all
sorts of flesh and cakes. There is no difficulty in accepting his
statement that these sacrifices were offered to a spear; but
who shall say when or by whom the interesting suggestion was
first made that linked the thing to Homer? Sometimes it is
possible to learn such things—as, for example, the date of
the arrival of St Joseph of Arimathaea at Glastonbury, which
from Dean Armitage Robinson's researches appears to have
been well after the Norman conquest; but there he is for
ever with his thorn.

Herodotus is not really very illuminating as to the origins
of the Greek race; he has many suggestions, but they are not
readily intelligible to a modern student of race and history—
not reducible, that is, to what we can think and understand.
But everybody in his day knew who the Greeks were and
what they were, just as to-day everybody knows who and
what the English are—one thinks of the botanists and the
"garden origin" they assign to some well-established plants.
"The Greek race", says Herodotus,[1] "is of one blood and
one speech; it has temples of the gods in common, common
sacrifices, and ways of like kind." And Homer gave them
that religion. Taken in his own sense, Herodotus is more right
than the anthropologists. A Greek race developed, emerged,
was recognized, and the common religion, as distinguished
from local cults, was created by Homer.

That Homer could have looked on himself as either the
founder or the reformer of a religion, is unthinkable. He was
not a Luther nor a Mohammed. He was a poet with a story
to tell; and, like other poets, he took what he wanted, and
gave it the form that suited his purpose—a form not too far
from what his listeners would count right and tolerable; so
far he may be taken to represent them. But a supreme poet
is a creator, not a reporter. He remade the gods of Olympus.

[1] Herodotus, viii, 144.

Whatever they were before he made his *Iliad* and *Odyssey*, ever after they were what he drew in his poems. Everybody knew the poems, and it was impossible for a man who had the poems in his heart—or even by heart—to think of the gods as different from Homer's portrayal. Down from the heights of Olympus in wrath comes Apollo, and the arrows rattle in his quiver as he comes. Homer, you might say, made the Apollo Belvedere, gave him his "outward form"; and Hephaestus limps for ever.

But a great poet has many thoughts, and, like other great thinkers and writers, he does not stay to organize them all. His story he organizes, magnificently; but the incidental thoughts will scarcely fit into a system.[1] What is the relation between Zeus and Fate, between *Aisa* and the "plan of Zeus"? How are prayers and Fate to be combined? Why must Zeus weigh the fates of warriors in the scales? Why should Zeus blame Aegisthus for the seduction of Clytemnestra, when the morals of gods, and his own, are so dubious? Does omnipotence excuse conduct—or is it omnipotence? Homer is not careful to answer, nor to ask, such questions. Again, how much do gods know? No, they are not omniscient; divine plans can be made when Poseidon's back is turned; the Sun has to tell Hephaestus of Ares and Aphrodite. One great picture of the *Iliad* is the pomp of Poseidon, driving magnificently over the sea.[2] But Hera's progress is different. She sped from the hills of Ida to high Olympus, "and even as when the mind of a man darts speedily, of one that hath travelled over far lands, and he considers in his wise heart 'Would that I were here or there', and he bethinks him of many things, so swiftly fled the lady Hera in her eagerness".[3] As a religious system Homer's Olympus will not do; yet it *did*—it was accepted all over the Greek world, supplemented by local cults, no doubt, but it became and remained the dominant framework of Greek thought about the gods. The

---

1 One might compare Horace's Ode *O diva gratum* (*Odes*, i, 35), in which Fate, fortune and altars, hope and faith, are in delightful confusion.
2 *Iliad*, xiii, 23–31. 3 *Iliad*, xv, 80.

Greek thinkers assailed it, did their best for it, interpreted it, and so forth; and when the Christian Church had to defend itself against the pagan world, there was the Olympus of Homer high over all—and alongside were the philosophers supplying munitions to the conquering Church, not its strongest weapons by any means, but an ample store of criticism by certain of your own philosophers. Homer was a fatal ally.

> Homer and Hesiod put upon the gods
> All that is shame and blame among mankind—

So said Xenophanes,[1] an author whom Clement of Alexandria knew in some form or other and quoted[2]—

> One god there is, 'mid gods and men the greatest,
> Not like in frame to mortals, nor in thought.

If cows and lions had had hands, he said, and carved gods, it would have been in their own likeness; and there were *black* gods in Africa and red-haired gods in Thrace;—so much for anthropomorphic gods and gods with men's passions. Heraclitus was perhaps even more contemptuous: "Polymathy does not teach the mind, or it would have taught Hesiod and Pythagoras" and others; and as for Homer, he ought to have been turned off the course and whipped.

But Homer had little to fear from the conscientious stanzas of Xenophanes; in Plato he had a foeman of his own dimensions. For Plato the training of the young was all-important, and he had different views from the father of Niceratus; there was to be no Homer for children, nor Hesiod either. Nothing was to be told to children of quarrels in heaven or battles of giants, of Hera bound by Hephaestus, or Hephaestus sent flying headlong to earth by Zeus.[3] No, "God must always be represented *as He is*, whatever the sort of poetry we write, epic, hymn or tragedy".[4] God does not prompt to lies or to strife, nor change His shape or take

---

1 Xenophanes (Diels), fr. 11.   2 Clem. Alex. *Strom.* v, 601 c; vii, 711 b.
3 Plato, *Rep.* ii, 378.   4 Plato, *Rep.* ii, 379 A.

disguise; He is no wizard and cannot lie; the gifts of men will
not change His mind or deflect His purpose;[1] He is "perfectly simple and true both in word and deed".[2] Homer's
stories shall not be defended as allegories; allegorical or not,
they shall not be taught to the young.[3]

The later philosophers did nothing to re-establish Homer.
Of course the Epicureans had little but contempt for his
pictures of the gods, and the Stoics defended them by
allegorizing them. Demeter became grain or bread; but
nobody, says the critic in Cicero's *de Natura Deorum*, could
imagine himself to be eating God. Plutarch is the enemy of
the Stoics, who turn gods into things which will melt like tin,
when their final conflagration of the universe comes. "Homer
would certainly be impious if he were not allegorical", said
a first-century Stoic; and even Plutarch can make use of
allegory to apologize—not for Homer—but for obscene
images of the gods, as familiar in that world as in India
to-day.

Later again the Neo-Platonists used allegory more boldly,
not with the mean triviality that made Demeter into grain.
Porphyry wrote an exposition of the Cave of the Nymphs in
which Odysseus, aided by Athene, hid the gifts he had
received from the Phaeacians. The cave became a parable
of the universe; but to the ordinary reader who enjoys Homer's
story it is not exactly obvious why Homer should have seized
that moment for an elaborate allegory, which nobody would
unravel for a thousand years. Macrobius and others explain
another passage more engagingly. In the eighth book of the
Iliad Zeus addresses the gods, with a strong menace; and, if
they doubt of it,

go to now, ye gods, make trial that ye all may know. Fasten
ye a rope of gold from heaven, and all ye gods lay hold
thereof, and all goddesses; yet could ye not drag from heaven
to earth Zeus, counsellor supreme, not though ye toiled sore.
But once I likewise were minded to draw with all my heart,

1 Plato, *Rep*. iii, 390.   2 Plato, *Rep*. ii, 382 E.
3 Plato, *Rep*. ii, 378 D.

then should I draw you up with very earth and sea withal.
Thereafter would I bind the rope about a pinnacle of
Olympus, and so should all those things be hung in air. By
so much am I beyond gods and beyond men.[1]

So spake Zeus, and the gods were silent. A forceful if rather
naive picture of omnipotence. Not that exclusively, for the
golden rope is that chain of "being" that goes through all
existence, from God beyond our sight and knowledge, through
each created order down to the lowest, a linking of all things
with God, if yet they "are" less and less as more remote
from their source.

Yet, as in our last section, where we dealt with the plain
man and Homer, and found the simplest of great natures,
Alexánder the Great, a life-long lover of Homer drawing
inspiration from the copy he took across Asia, so here in the
sphere of religion a man of genius went to Homer for his
supreme conception of God, and found it and gave it in its
majesty to the Greek world. It fell to Pheidias to make the
statue of Zeus at Olympia. What model could he find? And
he said he would use three lines of Homer—

Zeus spake, and speaking his dark brows inclined:
The ambrosial locks from that immortal head
Streamed, and he made the great Olympus shake.[2]

Antiquity was unanimous about his great creation; that
statue came nearer what Zeus would be like than anything
else—beauty, grandeur, yes, and more. Dio Chrysostom
wrote that a man heavy-laden, who had drained the cup of
misfortune and sorrow, if he were to stand and gaze at this
statue, would forget the heavy and the weary weight of all
this unintelligible world. Twenty years ago a sculptured head
was found among the ruins of a church at Jerash in Palestine;
whose was it? Was it Asclepios, as some said, or could it be
Christ himself? It was clearly modelled after Pheidias' Zeus,
modelled, that is to say, on Homer's lines; and, if there is to
be a statue of Christ, there is no better portrayal of him.

1 *Iliad*, viii, 18–27, Walter Leaf's translation; Macrobius, *Dream of Scipio*,
   i, 14, 15.   2 *Iliad*, i, 528–30.

IV

Even the greatest poets, as we have seen, have their critics, and we read that Virgil had detractors and parodists; he deviated from History—notably, we are told, by a century or two in Dido's case—and, above all, he took a great deal from Homer. Asconius Pedianus wrote a book in his defence, and quoted what Virgil said for himself; "why did not his critics attempt the same kind of theft? but they would find it easier to wrest his club from Hercules than a line from Homer".[1] What Virgil owed to Homer was something more than occasional translated lines—an impulse and an inspiration. "The purest originality", says an English writer on Wordsworth, "has parentage and ancestry; and that influence does not turn first-hand into second-hand work."[2] Virgil is not read because he owes lines and even ideas to Homer, but because he is Virgil. Yet Plato is right in describing Homer as the teacher and guide of the poets. Aeschylus is quoted as saying that his dramas were *temachê* from the great banquets of Homer[3]—"slices", most people have translated it, though we are now told it means dishes uncut and reserved for another banquet. Whatever he meant —and whatever Plato meant whether referring to religious ideas, moral standards or poetic inspiration—Homer was a supreme influence on all Greek literature. A catalogue even of the lines and passages men quoted from him through the centuries would make an enormous volume.

It was much debated whether a poet's function was *psychagogia* or teaching. *Psychagogia*, literally "influence on the soul", was a word with some magical associations, which we need not pursue; it suggested charm, appeal, bewitchment, a ministry to enjoyment—the "pleasure that is a philtre leading to learning".[4] Children love tales, and so do men;

1 Suetonius, *Vita Vergilii*, 46.
2 D. W. Rannie, *Wordsworth and his Circle*, p. 262.
3 Athenaeus, viii, 347E.
4 On this whole question see Strabo, C. 19, 21, 27.

philosophy is for the few, but poetry is more useful for the people (δημωφελεστέρα) and can fill the theatres; and of no one is this more true than of Homer; and, as we have already seen, he mingled myth with truth. So Strabo; but, long before him, Pindar had written of Homer's art: "Now I have suspicion that the fame of Odysseus is become greater than his toils, through the sweet lays that Homer sang; for over the feigning of his winged craft abideth somewhat of majesty; and the excellence of his skill (σοφία) persuadeth us to his fables unaware."[1] It is very odd to find Professor Bury (in his youth) maintaining on the evidence of this passage that "Homer affords an example of the power of 'sweet verses' misused. Pindar was a countryman of Hesiod, and he did not forget the mythical contest between Hesiod and Homer; he conceived the poet of the *Odyssey* as a sort of 'sophist', one who deceives his readers by cunning words, the friend of the crafty Odysseus."

This reference to Hesiod recalls what the poet of the *Theogony* tells us, whether he refers to himself in the third person or, more probably, to Hesiod as somebody else.[2] The Muses "on a time taught Hesiod noble (καλήν) song as he pastured his lambs under holy Helicon; and this word first the goddesses spake unto me, the Muses of Olympus, daughters of aegis-bearing Zeus: 'Shepherds of the wilderness, wretched things of shame, mere bellies, we know how to speak many false things as though they were true, and we know, when we will, to utter true things'"; and then they gave him a rod, a wand of sturdy olive,[3] and breathed into him a divine voice to sing of the race of the blessed gods, and of the Muses themselves; "but why", he concludes, "all this about an oak or a stone?" There are tangles enough in this; but who was it who sang lies that look like truth? Is this a blunt Boeotian way of saying what Pindar said? But surely Professor Bury misjudges Pindar as critic; surely Pindar is

1 Pindar, *Nem.* vii, 20–23. Grote had said earlier something of the same sort as Bury.
2 *Theogony,* 22–35.   3 *Theogony,* 22–35.

not condemning Homer for sophistries, but suggesting, as he does elsewhere so explicitly, that there are ways to escape oblivion. The poet who told the tyrant Hiero "not to grow tired of paying" had not Plato's anger against inspired poets and their work. No one could put the case for inspiration with more spirit.

Homer was before him—Homer who never speaks of Homer, but who invokes the Muse, and who shows us Phemios in the *Odyssey* pleading to have his life spared—"I am self-taught (αὐτοδίδακτος)", says Phemios, "and God has breathed into my heart songs of all kinds."[1] He did not need a teacher, and Pindar says the same thing; poetry is a gift of Nature, not to be acquired, not to be taught. Thus:

> 'Neath my bended arm, in my quiver lies
>   Full many an arrow swift to speed,
> And each with a voice, with a word, for the wise,
>   Though one to interpret the many need.
> HE is the Poet whom Nature inspires!
>   But they who have *learned*, though afar be heard
> The noise of their tongues, as of jackdaw quires,
>   In vain would they rival Jove's sacred bird.[2]

And again:

> Best ever the gift by Nature given!
> Though many a man to learn hath striven,
>   To get him virtues to raise him high,
> Yet, if God hath not willed to give the wight
> The boon he desires, 'twere wise and right
>   To let what he doth in silence die.[3]

Here we may revert to Plato's complaint about the poets, that they are not amenable to ordinary rules—or, we may put it in the words of Herodotus about tyrants, they are "outside the ordinary thoughts".[4] A poet, says Socrates to Ion,[5] "is a light and winged and holy thing, and he cannot

---

1 *Odyssey*, xxii, 347.
2 Pindar, *Olympians*, ii, 83–8 (=91–7 Gildersleeve).
3 Pindar, *Olympians*, ix, 107.   4 Herodotus, iii, 80.
5 Plato, *Ion*, 534, B, C.

make poetry (ποιεῖν) until the god is within him and his wits
are out of him (ἔνθεός τε γένηται καὶ ἔκφρων) and his mind
is no longer in him; and until he has reached that state no
man is able to make poetry or to give oracles...they are
inspired to utter that, and only that, to which the Muse
impels them", dithyrambs, epics, or whatever it be, and not
another kind. He cites Tynnichos of Chalcis who wrote the
best of all paeans, the worst of poets one supreme song—
which must prove it God's gift. Again in the *Phaedrus*, we are
told of a third kind of madness, a madness from the Muses,
a "possession" which enters into a delicate and virgin soul,
stirs it up to a bacchic frenzy, in songs and the other kinds
of poetry, with those adorning the myriad actions of the
ancients for the education of posterity. "But he who, with no
touch of the madness of the Muses comes to the doors of
Poesy and thinks that art after all will make him a sufficient
poet, he achieves nothing [or fails of initiation, ἀτελής] and
the poetry of the sane is extinguished (ἠφανίσθη) by the poetry
of the madmen."[1] He gives the same account of it as Pindar,
but with a different inflexion of voice, a touch of irony rather
than pure admiration.

Nature, says Pindar, inspires the poet; and Nature, adds
Aristotle,[2] Nature herself teaches him to choose the proper
measure; and for a poem on a great scale it is heroic verse,
the metre of Homer. And Nature showed Homer a good
many more of the secrets of great poetry. Poets have written
Herakleids, and *Theseids*, and the like, diffuse affairs, full of
unnecessary incidents and so on. "But these incidents
belonged to the life of Herakles!" Yes, but not to this poem
about him; they destroy the unity of the piece. "But Homer,
as in all else he is of surpassing merit, here too, whether by
art or nature [Nature again!], seems happily to have discerned
the truth." He did not put all Odysseus' adventures into
the *Odyssey*, but he made it centre round an action, which
"in our sense of the word" is *one*. The plot must turn—and
in the *Odyssey* it does turn—on *one* action, and that a complete

1 Plato, *Phaedrus*, 245 A.   2 Aristotle, *Poetics*, 24; p. 1460 a.

whole, with its incidents so closely connected that the transposal or withdrawal of any one of them will disjoin and dislocate the whole. An incident that may be included or left out without making any perceptible difference is no real part of the whole.[1] Each episode must be "necessary or probable"; it is no use saying that such and such a thing has actually occurred; he dismisses that idea with the epigrammatic suggestion that some actual events are also probable—i.e. fit in with the poetic truth of the piece. Further, in reply to Xenophanes (and, no doubt, to Plato), the question is not whether such and such an action or word is morally right or wrong, but we must consider by whom it is done or said.[2] There again Homer is unique in understanding his own place in it all; for "the poet should speak as little as possible in his own person, for that is not what makes him an 'imitator'. Other poets are perpetually coming forward in person, and say but little, and that only here and there, as 'imitators'; but Homer after a brief preface brings in forthwith a man, a woman, or some other character —no one of them characterless but each with distinctive characteristics."[3] Thus Homer does not describe his heroes to us; Priam describes them to Helen, as he and she stand together on the wall of Troy and look out over the Greek army, and he describes them to her so that she may tell him their names.[4] Odysseus, we learn, is rather long in the body and short in the legs. "You must do some degree of violence to yourself *to get out of the idea*" Goethe said—to turn your conception into a person. Like Shakespeare, Homer stands aside; you can only reach his real interests by studying the men and women he describes and their particular interests, and moreover his similes from nature and from the trades of men.

Other readers note other features. Theophrastus is quoted

1 *Poetics*, 8; p. 1451 a.
2 *Poetics*, 25; pp. 1460b, 1461 a. Cf. Athenaeus, v, 178d, οὐ γὰρ εἴ τι λέγεται παρ' Ὁμήρῳ, τοῦθ' Ὅμηρος λέγει.
3 *Poetics*, 24; p. 1460 a.
4 Cf. *Iliad*, iii, 161 ff.; and Lessing, *Laocoon*, chs. 16, 18.

as saying that some things should be left to the reader to supply himself; in that way you take him into partnership, he sees things for himself when you are not too long-winded, and so he has a friendlier feeling for you.[1] Whether this was said specifically of Homer or not, it is relevant. Servius said the same thing of Virgil—*artis poeticae est non omnia dicere.* Plutarch felt the power and grace of Homer, but remarked how easily (εὐχερῶς καὶ ῥᾳδίως), with how light a hand, he secured his effects.[2]

Dionysius of Halicarnassus, a Greek long resident in Rome—"ce bon Denys" as Sainte-Beuve called him—dealt with Homer and other poets in a considerable essay on literary composition. The sum and substance is this, he says; it is due to the interweaving of letters that the quality (δύναμις) of syllables is so various; to the combination of syllables that the nature of words has such diversity; to the harmonies of words that speech has so many forms. Thus inevitably style is beautiful where words are beautiful, and their beauty depends on that of syllables and letters; their affinities charm the ear and make language charming. It all goes back to Nature.[3] Homer, "many-voiced above all poets", is exquisite in his sensitiveness to the harmony of letters.[4] English readers may recall how Oliver Wendell Holmes in *The Poet at the Breakfast Table* quotes the line

αἴγλη παμφανόωσα δι' αἰθέρος οὐρανὸν ἷκε;[5]

it has, he says, nearly every consonantal and vowel sound in the language; and he pictures Homer's delight as he thundered out the ringing syllables. Dionysius gives us his views on the qualities of the letters; λ is pleasant to hear; ρ has a rough quality and is the noblest of its class; σ lacks grace and pleasantness; and so forth. We need not pursue these curiosities. But a passage rather too long to quote calls our attention to a stirring episode, though, as he says, it is made

1 ap. Demetr. *de Eloc.* 222.   2 Plutarch, *Timoleon*, 36, 2.
3 Dion. Hal. *de Comp.* 16.   4 Dion. Hal. *de Comp.* 16.
5 *Iliad*, ii, 458.

up of trifling and everyday matters, yet "rendered more than
well".[1] It is the appearance of Telemachus at the swineherd's
hut on his return from the Peloponnese, safe and sound. His
father catches the sound of steps of someone coming and
notes that the dogs do not assail the newcomer as they had
assailed himself; a friend, then? Not yet was his word (to
Eumaeus) spoken, when his dear son stood in the door; and
Eumaeus sprang up and kissed him on the head and both
his beautiful eyes and his hands. Everybody, says Dionysius,
would bear witness that there is enchantment in this passage
(ἐπάγεται καὶ κηλεῖ), that it would rank second to no poetry
of the sweetest; and why? Not through the choice of words;
for the words, he says, are obvious enough, such words as any
one might use, farmer or sailor, who was no specialist in
speech; and he puts it down to the "composition" (σύνθεσιν).
A modern would agree that the narrative is plain but, as
Arnold would urge, rapid and noble; he would, I think, go
further and find some part of the appeal in the swift mind of
Odysseus.

Nature—we keep coming back to Nature—is the source
and teacher, the inspirer; Nature suggests these harmonies
of letter and syllable, and the greater things into which they
are woven (πέπλεκται). We cannot think of Homer hunting
the letter, but with him as with other great poets the music
seems to come of itself; call it ear or call it instinct, or call it
with Pindar φυή, he does the right thing almost uncon-
sciously; or if not, he cannot leave the thing till it comes
right. Once again, we think of Goethe's "To do something
you must be something". Longinus had said it in his own
way first: "The sublime is the echo of a great soul" (ὕψος
μεγαλοφροσύνης ἀπήχημα); and he illustrated it not with any
combination of consonants but with the great conception of
the meeting of Odysseus and Ajax in the world of the dead,
when Ajax saw his rival of old days and turned away without
a word—"a great thing and nobler than any speech".[2] "The
ninth chapter [of Longinus]", wrote Gibbon, "is one of the

1 Dion. Hal. *de Comp.* 3.   2 Longinus, 9, 2.

finest monuments of antiquity." The judgment of Longinus
is confirmed by Virgil; Dido in the shades

> *Illa solo fixos oculos aversa tenebat.* (*Aen.* vi, 450–474.)

Again and again Nature has been invoked in this long story;
Nature inspires the poet—yes, but also the listeners, adds
Longinus, and it is amazingly true. "It is a fact of Nature
that our soul is raised by the true sublime, and, in a proud
swing upwards, is filled with joy and exultation, as though
it had itself produced what it has heard."[1] He recognizes,
with Dionysius, the appeal of beautiful words: "they are in
truth the light of the mind".[2] One more passage, which may
well have been prompted by the thought of Homer—"That
is the really great which will bear repeated examination,
which it is difficult or, rather, impossible to resist, and the
memory of which is strong and indelible"—no washing it
out of the mind.[3] In short, there is no resisting Nature, no
bettering Nature, no forgetting Nature.

Now let us go back to Plato—"There is an ancient quarrel
between Philosophy and Poetry."[4] The poet does not understand what is happening to him, nor how he has produced
his poem; and sometimes, like Oliver Goldsmith, he cannot
explain his own poetry. None of this is true of Philosophy—
at least, not in theory; the philosopher's task is to understand,
and the poet confuses all by bringing in the unintelligible,
factors beyond human assessment, ψυχαγωγία, magic, haunting
memories and indelible.

> He with a "look you!" vents a brace of rhymes,
> And in there breaks the sudden rose herself,
> Over us, under, round us every side,
> Nay, in and out the tables and the chairs,
> Buries us with a glory, young once more,
> Pouring heaven into this shut house of life.[5]

Heaven once again; and then Aristotle comes out with the
staggering sentence that "Poetry is more philosophic, more
serious than History". Philosophic?

1 Longinus, 7, 2.   2 Longinus, 30, 1.   3 Longinus, 7, 3.
4 Plato, *Rep.* x, 607 B.   5 Browning, *Transcendentalism.*

V

"Aristotle," wrote Wordsworth in his famous preface of 1802 to *Lyrical Ballads*, "I have been told, has said, that Poetry is the most philosophic of all writing: it is so: its object is truth, not individual and local, but general, and operative; not standing upon external testimony, but carried alive into the heart by passion; truth which is its own testimony, which gives competence and confidence[1] to the tribunal to which it appeals and receives them from the same tribunal." Literature, according to Matthew Arnold, is "the interpretation of life"—a dictum disputed a good deal by some who would think rather (if they had read him) of Dionysius' evaluation of letters and syllables, who would have Poetry approximate to Music and keep up the old feud with Philosophy. But it cannot be done. Swinburne, who might have been supposed to lean this way, says outright that "Poetry divorced from moral ideas is poetry divorced from life". How is one to know life?

One of the profoundest students of Euripides says that "passionate feeling is in the last line the source of his criticism".[2] And Euripides, men said, was the philosopher on the stage, for ever quoting philosophy, attributing to his simplest characters reflexions that raise the greatest questions of all. He is the most tragic of the poets, says Aristotle. So there we have Tragedy and Philosophy in one man's heart; and why not? What is to move the heart, said Goethe, must come from the heart; and why cannot the same man feel and think? There is indeed an ancient quarrel between Poetry and Philosophy, but the fact is that the man will not be a great poet in whose heart there is no trace of that conflict. Tynnichos may write his song without it—perhaps; but we have not his song, and the greatest of British song-writers illustrates the point. Deep feeling is very near the greatest

1 In the edition of 1802 Wordsworth had "which gives strength and divinity". The words printed above he substituted thirty years later.
2 Nestle, *Euripides der Dichter der gr. Aufklärung*, p. 26.

questions, and the greatest poets are no more apt to "unpack their heart with words" on the problems of philosophy than on the problems of pain. We have to remember the words of Pascal that our Lord "handled the greatest problems so simply that you would think he had not considered them". The same is true of the great poets. When Homer described the farewells of Hector and Andromache, and the baby Astyanax showed his terror at the plume of his father's helmet and his father and mother laughed and—how simple and Wordsworthian the great poet can be!—"Hector took off his shining helmet", was there no question, no problem in Homer's heart? There has been in the heart of every reader, every human reader; and Homer waked the question.

Αἰδέομαι Τρῶας καὶ Τρῳάδας ἑλκεσιπέπλους

—and that is to balance wedded love, a wife's happiness—a conflict of duties; and you are deep in Philosophy at once.

Or take the story of Achilles. His quarrel with Agamemnon is intelligible enough; his anger, his withdrawal, his appeal to his goddess mother to secure that the Greeks suffer for their treatment of him—it is all intelligible to any passionate nature. And his anguish, when his friend is slain as a result of his withdrawal, that too is intelligible. But how do you explain the gods? Epic convention? But that will not do. Thetis or Zeus or who you will—here is the problem of prayer, of prayer granted—and if only it had not been! There is a tragic error somewhere in the story. But Homer does not moralize; so it is assumed that he did not think? that he did not realize what life and character, pain and frustration, are, because his comment is latent in his story? because he does not soliloquize like an Attic chorus, but tells the tale and leaves it to you to feel the implications, which he discovered by feeling them?

Homer had been "the education of Hellas", men told Plato—a general statement, for Sparta was little affected by him; the Spartans were dead to poetry, Pausanias said. But everywhere else Homer contributed to character.

A parallel will bring out one phase of this. The words of
Sarpedon to Glaucus are famous, and they have their place
in English history. "Friend of my soul," he says, "were it
that, once thou and I were escaped from *this* war, we should
live for ever free from age and death, neither would I myself
fight among the foremost, nor would I send thee into the
battle that gives men renown. But now—for none the less
fates of death stand over us, aye! ten thousand of them, which
mortal man may not escape nor avoid—let us go, whether
we shall yield glory to another or another to us."[1] Similar
words are spoken by Achilles, when Xanthus his horse warns
him of death—"Xanthus, why dost thou prophesy death to
me? Thou needest not. Well do I know, I myself, that it is
my fate to be slain here, far from my father and mother; but
none the less, I will not cease before I sate the Trojans with
war."[2] Ἀλλὰ καὶ ἔμπης—"for a' that an' a' that"—and now
Pericles on the Athenian character[3]—"We have this gift
beyond other peoples, so that the same men will take a risk
and calculate what it is we shall attempt, while others are
courageous from ignorance but hesitate on reflexion. They
surely would be reckoned the bravest of heart, who, with the
clearest sense both of danger and of the pleasures of life, do
not on that account shirk peril." Homer, as a modern reader
points out, is not interested in "villains"; there are heroes
in both armies at Troy, men and women who face life open-
eyed and honest-hearted in Troy and Ithaca. He shirks no
facts; there is sin and wickedness enough in the world, pain
and sadness enough; but he thinks of man as big-built and
capable of great things. "So near is grandeur to our dust"—
no, he does not say this, but he believes it and knows it and
lets us see it. The father of Niceratus was right; to have
Homer in your heart would mean greatness and truth and a
real humanity. With all that was wrong in him, Achilles was
a great pattern for a hero; and Alexander the Great so far
confirms the father of Niceratus.

Finally, a swift generalization. Men have long called

1 *Iliad*, xii, 322-8.   2 *Iliad*, xix, 420.   3 Thucydides, ii, 40, 4.

Homer "the Bible of the Greeks". "No word of the wise",
says Plato, "must be rejected; we should look into it in case
they may be saying something." Homer and the Bible are
different books, fundamentally different, in outlook, aim and
construction. Yet of each the same thing can be said—the
book built a race. For four hundred years the Bible has been
in English and in print, read and learnt by heart by countless
thousands of our people on both sides of the Atlantic. It has
shaped our speech; long controversy about translation drove
one translator and another to ever greater care. There is no
trace in the Bible's own pages of the florid elegance of the
dedication to King James. The writers of the Bible were in
deeper earnest than that committee and thought of no King
James; their endeavour was the same as John Bunyan's—"to
set down the thing as it was"; and following Tyndale more
closely than many realize, the translators caught the spirit
of the New Testament and made a simple and straight speech
for Englishmen, which has outlasted all Euphuisms and
Ciceronianisms—the speech of Bunyan and Dryden and
John Bright. The Bible, again, has given the great bulk of
English-speaking people their main literary and historical
background. It is not always realized how large a proportion
of our people have known the ancient world, the foreigner
and the heathen only through the Bible, supplemented by
missionary enthusiasts themselves inspired by the Bible.
From the Bible, directly or indirectly, from the days of Bede,
and still more since Tyndale, English men and women have
drawn their conceptions of morals, of personal and social
righteousness; and the Bible has been (one might say) our
sole source of religious ideas, whatever the influence of Plato
or Epictetus.

Now turn to Homer. We have seen how men went to him
for religious ideas, and what controversy Plato and Xenophanes and others raised about them—clear proof that Homer
did shape the religious thinking of all but the very highest
and the lowest of Greeks. Homer trained, as we have seen,
their moral sense, his lessons (as Charles Lamb put it)

"slipping into their minds while they imagined no such thing", and their hearts throbbed for Hector and Achilles and Penelope. Every man who read, read Homer, and knew that every other reading man did the same; they were on common ground, pan-Hellenic, while they stuck to Homer. So, just as the Bible has shaped the thinking of our race, Homer shaped the thinking of the Greeks, their outlook on life, their sensitiveness to beauty and right and pain, and to moral grandeur. "A love for Homer, and a reverence for him, from boyhood"—they are Plato's words and the experience of the Greek world.

TWO CENTENARIES

I Virgil   II Erasmus

I Virgil

an Appreciation[1]

ROBERT LOUIS STEVENSON was not in the stricter sense a scholar; but he had been bred at school and college in Latin, and he came to the classics as a humanist and a man of letters. His own story is full of references to his Latin authors. Who can forget the episode of the young parson fetched in a hurry at dawn to the bedside in the Davos hotel to see Stevenson, who had asked to see him, and the eager request from a very sick man as he entered the room, "For

---

[1] This was written for the Virgil Bimillenary in 1930. But was it a Bimillenary? See the following letter to *The Times*, and the Editor's rejoinder in italics—

The Birth of Horace

Sir,—I am all for celebrating the two thousandth anniversary of the birth of Horace, for celebrating every birthday of Horace, for keeping his Odes by one in shelf and heart, reading and re-reading them. *Nocturna versate manu, versate diurna.*

But this Bimillenary—however you spell it? Horace was born on 8 December, 65 B.C.; he gives us the year (*consule Manlio*), Suetonius the day. Then, say our friends—just like Humpty Dumpty and Alice—look at this:

$$\frac{\begin{array}{r} 65 \\ 1935 \end{array}}{2000}$$

It seems right, if arithmetic counts.

But, dear Sir, tell me how many years there were between 8 December, 1 B.C. and 8 December, 1 A.D. Do you add the *ones*? Might it not be just as wise to use subtraction? If it is *one* year and not two, how many years are there between 8 December 65 B.C. and 8 December, 1935? This is one of the cases where it is safer to do it on your fingers than by arithmetic. I think classical people ought to leave arithmetic alone; they are safer with their fingers. *Digito callemus*, says Horace.

Not to digress, tell me how many years you make it between 1 B.C. and 1 A.D. That is the issue.

Your obedient servant,

T. R. GLOVER.

Cambridge, 5 *April* 1935.

** *Italiam non sponte sequimur.*

God's sake, have you a Horace?" English Alcaics and
translations from Martial are found in his letters and notebooks. He was not, we learn from his biographer, and we
might have guessed it, a precise or supremely accurate
Latinist; but to understand literature and to feel it, you do
not need to be precise—perhaps you are safer there if you are
not precise. "Much have I travell'd in the realms of gold",
wrote a young man, supposed to be an apothecary's apprentice; and that was his qualification for enjoying Homer
and realizing Homer's greatness. Similarly, at some stage in
his life, Stevenson went back to his *Aeneid*, not in a translation,
however, but in the original; and in one at least of his
letters we find him calling it "one of the tops of human
achievement". The phrase is not, of course, to be taken
mathematically; it is the spontaneous phrase of one great
writer who has been enjoying another.

"And you must love him, ere to you he will seem worthy
of your love", is Wordsworth's account of the poet—not here
meaning Virgil, but the poet in general; and he is surely
right. Until you submit your mind and heart to the man of
genius, foregoing criticism, lexicography, and even history,
in sheer surrender to enjoyment, you have no chance of
reaching his secret, of capturing the supreme things which he
has to give you. This is not to renounce or denounce lexicography, metric, antiquarian research—far from it. Only,
when lexicographer and antiquary have done their utmost,
you have penetrated no further than the poet's laboratory, as
it were. Yes; he knew (right or wrong, let us concede it) all
the strange lore of old-time usage, legend, and religion that
Servius and Macrobius, in their love of him, can amass for
us; he read all the books they tell us he read and prove that
he read. But then the lexicographers and antiquaries were
equally well equipped—better equipped, perhaps—and wrote
no *Aeneids*. And, after all, as one reads the *Aeneid*, we no more
think of all that the antiquaries and their friends have been
telling us than we instinctively think of H_2O when we look at
Niagara. The torrent has somehow something that the chemist

cannot quite analyse. The poet does more, after all, with alchemy than chemistry; it is magic that he uses—"out of three sounds to frame not a fourth sound but a star"—and he himself cannot tell you how he does it. Plato knew this; the poetry of the madman, who goes, distraught and no longer master of himself, to the gates of the Muses, has something about it that the well-informed and self-possessed never achieve. Yet with the greatest poets the magic and the sheer sense forget "the ancient quarrel of poets and philosophers" and work together, like the fire and water of Aeschylus, hostile of old but now conspired.

It is the man of letters who will be most apt to recognize the great quality of the supreme poet. He is the magician's apprentice; and he knows, better than other men, how immeasurably hard it is to do the supreme things and with what miraculous ease the great man does them, and with what eternal success.

> He with a "look you!" vents a brace of rhymes,
> And in there breaks the sudden rose herself....
> Buries us with a glory, young once more,
> Pouring heaven into this shut house of life.

There never was a more industrious apprentice in the school of letters than Stevenson; and here he comes telling the scholars that the author they know so much more about than he does is out of their reckoning great.

I suppose that it was as a great piece of construction, of architecture, that the *Aeneid* impressed Stevenson. Metre and language would be more apt to touch the pure scholar so called. Tennyson has emphasized one phase of Virgil as "lord of language"—

> All the charm of all the Muses
>   often flowering in a lonely word.

The pure scholar, bred from schooldays on Latin verse, will speak with more feeling about metre. He will have at his fingers' ends the history of Latin metre from Ennius to Claudian, and he will know it not only from analysis and from counting (it may be) elisions, fourth-foot trochees, or spondaic endings, but from writing Latin verse himself, now in one style, now in another (like Stevenson's "sedulous ape"), and then realizing, more by instinct than by any analysis, that he has used here a movement which somehow, when the first throes of composition are over, seems alien to the tone or style of the master he is imitating. On reflexion he asks himself, has he seen anything quite of this type, and he is uneasy. But why has the master *not* done a thing which came so obviously? Why was that innocent pause, that quite ordinary elision, not to be found on subsequent search in the master's hundreds of lines? Why should he not have used it? Or again, to borrow a suggestion from Mr J. W. Mackail, why are verse-movements to be found in the last six books of the *Aeneid*, which, more by memory (again) than by counting, seem to the attentive reader not to have been familiar in the first six? An impossible question! Who of us is to know (we can all guess) the quiet, imperceptible changes in a poet's feeling? Did Virgil himself know or notice what Mr Mackail tells us, and tells us truly? "For variety" poets do this and that, we say bluntly. Tacitus varies phrase and grammar, has so many dozens of variants for the common note "he died". And he does it all on purpose? Does he—invariably? Well, a poet's turns of thought—and here, we had better say, of feeling—are a good deal subtler. There is a delight for the lover of Virgil, bred to verse-writing, in watching the verse-movements more closely than the poet perhaps did—consciously checking what the poet did not quite so consciously. The result may be catalogue, or may be feeling, with the student. For the reader who sits at the poet's feet (I hope this expression may be forgiven) analysis is all lost in the music; and in this as in all music, in all great creation, the enjoyment is more than the analysis—it takes you somehow further into the great man's heart.

But to return to construction. Twice lately I have read the *Aeneid* from end to end consecutively, not for class purposes, not for this commemorative essay either, but for myself, as

one would read *Don Quixote* or *As You Like It* for one's soul's
good. That play, e.g. you inevitably read as a whole, as a
unity; but I have a horrid suspicion that many scholars have,
like myself, only very seldom, if ever, the leisure to take
Odyssey or *Aeneid* as a unit and a whole. The *Odyssey* is easier,
and more of us have read it in its full completeness, and more
than once, than ever manage the same measure of justice
with Virgil. Then I bless my stars for the chances that let
me do it, and give my conclusion, never quite reached
(I think) in days when I had to do this or that book at school,
or this or that group of books with pupils in the Canadian
university, that the *Aeneid* gains immensely by being read as
Virgil conceived it, by being allowed the unity which he
planned for it and gave it. Read otherwise, one can hardly
resist the suspicion that it must inevitably drag in the second
half. How many scholars have remarked with half-surprise
that the invocation to the Muses when he comes to Italy
seems to suggest that Virgil felt somehow that he had reached
the heart of his theme? Yet the six books support one
another; the Italian half of the poem supports itself and
justifies itself, if you will drop the English use of it (for school
or college) and read it, as R. L. Stevenson read it and as Virgil
meant it to be read, as a single work, a thought-out whole.

Here I would digress a step or two. I have noticed with
great interest, in reading (alas! in examinations and prize
exercises) the work of the best undergraduate scholars of
Cambridge over a good many years, the surprising skill with
which a number of them will write Alcaics or Elegiacs and
give one somehow not only the verse- and rhythm-movements
of Horace and Ovid but will reproduce their manner of
thinking—the grace, the light touch, something of the sure
swiftness of mind that you find in their exemplars. Verse
really Virgilian I do not remember ever to have had from
them, and I ask why. Is it that the verse-movement belongs
to the massive construction and is integral with it, and that
the manner is so essentially the mind, the style so exactly the
thought, that we who are not poets on such a scale cannot

capture even the obvious and external features of the verse?
Few pieces of ancient or modern criticism have haunted me
like the saying of Longinus *On the Sublime* (ix, 2): "The great
style is the echo of the great soul" (ὕψος μεγαλοφροσύνης
ἀπήχημα); and here I think I find one of the supreme instances
and proofs of what Longinus says.

"The great soul"—I am quite clear that Longinus is right,
and I realize progressively that Virgil is a great soul. I think
of the mass of literature, Latin and Greek, that he read and
mastered in the way of poets. I cannot whole-heartedly follow
Professor Rand and Professor Tenney Frank in their recon-
structions of Virgil's earlier life from the Virgilian *Appendix*.
Much as I have enjoyed themselves and their work, I hesitate.
But one thing is clear enough. The older Virgil is a deeper,
stronger, surer nature than the young Virgil. Few things are
so hard to track as spiritual growth. Dozens of English boys
have written better at sixteen than Keats; but by twenty-one
he had had somehow an entirely different development. The
young Virgil shows the strong influence of teachers and
libraries; like the good undergraduate, he assimilates what
Siro and Parthenius teach him; he is properly Epicurean and
Alexandrian. Yet he differs from other young Romans as
well taught and as orthodox in school loyalties. He is not a
singer of Euphorion; something takes him to Theocritus—
some out-door human-hearted affinity, reinforced by admiration of Lucretius, greatest of Latins so far, and by personal
experience of danger, outrage, and bereavement. Like
Horace (whom he is not very like, far from it!) he will not
be pleased permanently by the school's Alexandrinism, nor
yet by mere Latin archaism. Each of them, like Spenser in
English, must study the great examples of the past and rethink
the native movements of his mother tongue. Horace does
not write Alcaics like Alcaeus nor Sapphics like Sappho;
Latin is not Greek; nor will Virgil write like Homer or
Apollonius, nor like Ennius or Lucretius. Some strong
native sense, some essential strength of character and of mind,
safeguards him from imitation and drives him into deeper

realization of his task, into a clearer sense of what Latin means and can do.

He gains by being an Italian, bred and born, native to his soil, no immigrant from overseas in a museum, in an alien land of *fellahin*. *Romanus Vergilius*, says the old critic. I always suppose that to most cultured people of his day Italy was a land as utterly unromantic and unlovely as the half-reclaimed Middle West of America—nothing about it Indian or Italian, as we interpret the words—a drab country of farms and ranches without a Wister's Virginian, unfamiliar as eighteenth-century Scotland, before Ossian and Cuchullin were discovered. Virgil knew better; and I need not here quote the first *Georgic* to prove it. Instead, I will digress again to personal reminiscence. The second time that I reread the *Aeneid*, I followed it up by reading the *Georgics* and after them the *Eclogues*—quite the wrong order, and yet I gained something, for it became clearer than ever how much greater the *Georgics* are than the *Eclogues*, for which, however, I had cherished for years the feeling that they are after all something more than Theocritus—an unfashionable belief. But, as I say, the *Georgics* are greater, and between them they begin the idealization of Italy.

Fluminaque antiquos subterlabentia muros.[1]

What a line! And those that follow are written in one heart at least with Ontario set for Benacus, rising with wave and voice of the sea; so true and so universal is it.

It is with his love of Italy that we link the great admiration which Virgil so obviously felt for Caesar and for Augustus. With some it is perhaps a matter of reproach to the poet, but such a judgment needs reconsideration. In spite of much written nowadays to prove that Shakespeare wrote for a practical purpose, for hire in fact, following the taste of the hour to earn his hire from his patrons, the public, it is arguable that he wrote differently from others under the same obligation to win public goodwill and wrote to please himself,

[1] *Georgics*, ii, 157.

to express what was in his own mind, to carry the approval
of the critic in his own heart. If Longinus is right in urging
that the great work comes from the great nature, let us begin
there always. What are the dominant motives with the great
nature? A quiet estimate of the purposes and of the work of
Julius and Augustus finds in them much to carry the suffrages
of all good citizens, of all lovers of Italy, and men of
peace. It is sounder criticism to interpret Augustus from
the admiration of Virgil than to start from outside and work
the other way on the presumption of motives not too high.

In the *Aeneid* the gods play a larger part than in the earlier
poems, and for two reasons. The epic modelled on Homer
obviously must have them, could not escape them; but there
is surely another and a deeper reason. Virgil had been
moving away from Epicurus for years, as we can see in
various signal passages:

> *Fortunatus et ille deos qui novit agrestis,*[1]

if not in the Silenus idyll; but above all in the philosophic
digression from the bees

> *Deum namque ire per omnes*
> *terrasque tractusque maris caelumque profundum,*[2]

where, a line above, he is willing to consider the suggestion
that the bees have something of the divine mind. In Aeneas
we have the conception of a man in close touch with the
mind of heaven. It might seem fanciful to compare the
Aeneid with the *Pilgrim's Progress*. Yet the two great works
have something in common: each is—or each carries in itself
—a certain philosophy of life, the conception of man's life
as a pilgrimage or voyage with a meaning and a purpose and,
underlying all, a divine plan shared by the human heart. No
one takes the shining ones of Bunyan as literal flesh and blood
visitants; the book is allegory, though some readers forget
this in the vividness of the character drawing. Virgil, a
former Epicurean, cannot be suspected of believing in too

1 *Georgics*, ii, 493.   2 *Georgics*, iv, 221 f.

concrete theophanies; far from it—for one of the things that
sadden his Aeneas is the fugitive nature of his contact with
heaven; his goddess mother always eludes him in spite of her
care for him:

> *Quid natum totiens, crudelis tu quoque, falsis*
> *ludis imaginibus?*[1]

Like many another man with a mission, Aeneas has his hours
of doubt and depression; his life is full of pain; *Italiam non
sponte sequor*; he has had enough of war, more than enough;
he hates the fate of Pallas and Lausus—

> *At vero ut voltum vidit morientis et ora,*
> *ora modis Anchisiades pallentia miris,*
> *ingemuit miserans graviter dextramque tetendit,*
> *et mentem patriae subiit pietatis imago.*[2]

We are reconciled in the dying Lausus to his wicked old
father, whose crimes were in the past but whose love for his
son and his horse lives till the end. No doubt there are
wavering lines in the picture. Every allegory has its gaps; the
Pilgrim's Progress and *Don Quixote* have here and there contradictions, details blurred or forgotten. Virgil had to keep
to Homer's gods, drilled to some extent after Stoic and
Roman models; but even so the actual gods were unequal to
their task. It is perhaps in this new demand made of the
gods—that they must share their purposes with men and
sustain in some real spiritual sense those who will work with
them—and in the failure of the traditional gods, that we must
look for one source at least of Sainte-Beuve's saying that for
readers of Virgil the coming of Christ "*n'a rien qui étonne*".
Virgil has never really jarred on the feelings of the church.

But whatever his readers make of his interpretation of life
in relation to the gods, there never has been any doubt that
Virgil is one of the great human poets who speak direct to the
heart and draw life as we know it at its deepest. *Sunt lacrimae
rerum et mentem mortalia tangunt.* Goethe once told Eckermann

---

1 *Aeneid*, i, 407 f.   2 *Aeneid*, x, 821-4.

that man was not born to solve the problem of this universe
but to find out wherein it consists. Few poets of antiquity or
of a later date have done more to bring home to us the
nature of that problem.

"Old Mantuan, old Mantuan! who understandeth thee not,
loves thee not." Let us borrow the precious sentence for the
greater Mantuan. How many ages have known him and loved
him, read him and reread him, had him in their hearts and
found in him the story of their hearts? How much can great
literature do for us? Not less than the utmost has Virgil done
for sixty generations, reaching, capturing, and holding the
tender hearts and the great souls. Augustine tells us how he
wept for *ipsius umbra Creusae* or *Didonem exstinctam ferroque*
ext:ema secutam. Jerome in the Catacombs could only express
what he felt with Virgil's aid:

> *Horror ubique animo, simul ipsa silentia terrent.*[1]

And to come to our own days and end, as we began, with
R. L. Stevenson, he too was haunted by the mere beauty of
a line, which to those who look back on the completed story
of his life seems a true *sors Vergiliana*:

> *Iam medio apparet fluctu nemorosa Zacynthos.*[2]

And perhaps another may be allowed a confession and tell of
two lines which have seemed to him to tell the story of life:

> *Haud equidem sine mente, reor, sine numine divum*
> *adsumus et portus delati intramus amicos.*[3]

---

1 *Aeneid*, ii, 755.   2 *Aeneid*, iii, 270. Cf. p. 30.   3 *Aeneid*, v, 56f.

II Erasmus
at Cambridge

In the course of a wandering life Erasmus paid several visits to England and made warm friends among the English, some of them significant men who were to make contributions to English thought and English education, which have never been lost and probably never will be. Colet founded or refounded St Paul's School in London; Fisher inaugurated Lady Margaret's two colleges in Cambridge; More wrote a book and made himself a name, neither of them ever forgotten. It was Fisher, it seems, who was responsible for the longest visit of Erasmus and his residence for some two years at Queens' College, Cambridge, of which Fisher had once been president.

Probably every man's story of Cambridge can be told two ways at least. The poet long ago in the *Granta* spoke of

> Our backs and bridges, bills and bells,
> Our boats and bumps, and bloods and blues,
> Our bedders, bull-dogs, and Bedells,
> Our chapels, colleges, canoes,
> Our dons and deans, and duns and dues;
> Our friends from Hayti and Siam—

and so forth. The other story is as simple: "To have struggled with work that makes everything else easy; that's what the Mathematical Tripos did for me."

Erasmus was not an undergraduate; but the two sides of his life here are pictured by Cambridge men a century later. Thomas Fuller, of Sidney Sussex, tells us how Erasmus had

his abode in Queens' College, where a study on the top of the south-west tower in the old court still retaineth his name. Here his labour in mounting so many stairs (done perchance on purpose to exercise his body and prevent corpulency) was recompensed with a pleasant prospect round about him. He often complained of the college ale, *cervisia huius loci mihi nullo modo placet* [see P. S. Allen, *Letters of Erasmus, Ep.* 226], as raw,

small, and windy; whereby it appears...Queens' College
cervisia was not *vis Cereris* but *Ceres vitiata*....The best was,
Erasmus had his *lagena* or flagon of wine (recruited weekly
from his friends at London) which he drank sometimes singly
by itself, and sometimes encouraged his faint ale with the
mixture thereof. He was public Greek professor, and first
read the grammar of Chrysoloras to a thin auditory [*Ep.* 233].

Against this view of Cambridge set some sentences of
Milton describing what was going on in those days—not
written especially with Erasmus in view; but he reminds us
of that work of Erasmus which has most influenced the
world.

When I recall to mind at last...how the bright and blissful
Reformation (by Divine Power) strook through the black and
settled Night of *Ignorance* and *Anti-christian Tyranny*, methinks
a sovereign and reviving Joy must needs rush into the Bosom
of him that reads or hears....Then was the sacred *BIBLE*
sought out of the dusty Corners where profane Falsehood and
Neglect had thrown it, the *Schools* opened, *Divine* and *Humane
Learning* rak'd out of the *Embers* of *forgotten Tongues*, the *Princes*
and *Cities* trooping apace to the new-erected Banner of
Salvation; the *Martyrs*——

But the Martyrs belong mainly to other decades, and it is
enough to refer the reader to the tractate *Of Reformation in
England*. Yet Andrew Ammonius, the sender of flagons (which
Erasmus thought might have been bigger, and better sealed),
writes (8 November 1511):

I do not wonder that the price of firewood has gone up;
every day many heretics offer us a holocaust; but more crop
up in their places; nay, the own brother of my man Thomas,
a stick more than a man, has himself started a sect and has
disciples.

Erasmus is specially vexed about the heretics and the firewood
when winter is so near (*Ep.* 240). So life is mingled, beer and
the Bible, holocausts, corks, and Greek grammar; and all of
it relevant.

Erasmus came to Cambridge at a great moment, 1511. It

was then a small town of perhaps 4000 inhabitants; there were already fifteen colleges, counting St John's, which was founded in that year but not yet built. Erasmus appears not to mention the college, but the intimate of Fisher must have heard it discussed. His own college, the College of the two Queens, was not yet very old, the second court barely fifteen years. It may, as the Master of Jesus suggests in his delightful book on the University, have reminded him of his native Holland. Brick was the common building material of both regions, while the long river-front of the college, with its walls descending abruptly into the canalized waters, would help the parallel; so too the traffic on the river, the main highway of that day; nor less, perhaps, the fen he saw from his windows, the fen still there, where in winter the fog lies thick and white. Mullinger, in his *History of Cambridge*, pictures the man we know so well from the portraits of Holbein and Dürer; the modest stature, the blue eyes and flaxen hair, "the furtive humour playing round the well-formed mouth; the quiet half-closed eyes, gleaming with the self-constrained [? self-contained] enjoyment of a shrewd observer". "The better picture", as the Greek sentence on Dürer's portrait of him reminds us, "his writings will give"; and they do—with their constant reminders of his money difficulties (though he kept a horse or two—"for lack of better exercise", says Ascham, he "wolde take his horse and ryde about the Market Hill and come agayne"), with their complaints about people and food and climate, about broken promises and "subdubious" health (he really had stone), and about nearly everything else, but also in the humour, the cleverness, the genius, evident all through the letters. *Certe ἐρασμικῶς jocaris*, says Ammonius (*Ep.* 249). And the life of the scholar, the life of the day, can be read in those letters, too.

Like some others who have been students in Cambridge, he put a lower value on the Cambs people than they do themselves—*cum summa rusticitate summam malitiam conjunxere* (*Ep.* 240). They tippled from his *lagena* on its journey and failed to deliver letters. "And some", adds Thomas Fuller,

"will say the Townsmen are no Changelings at this day."
On an earlier visit (1499) Erasmus had indeed found

the English girls divinely pretty—soft, pleasant, gentle, and
charming as the Muses; and there is besides a custom never
praised enough. When you go anywhere on a visit, they all
kiss you. They kiss you when you arrive; they kiss you when
you go; they kiss you again when you come back.... Everything full of kisses (*Ep.* 103).

The weather, too, which we in Cambridge take for granted:

Next day constant rain till dinner-time, and after dinner
lightning, thunder and showers, and my horse fell three times
on his head. Bovillus [Bullock of Queens'] has consulted the
stars and says he has found out that Jove was a little cross
(*Ep.* 225).

But it pleases him at Cambridge to "see the vestiges of
Christian poverty"; and

there is a physician here, a countryman of mine, who, by
the help of the Quintessence designs prodigious achievements,
and makes old men young and dead men live; so I have some
hope that I may recover my youth, if only I can get a taste
of Quintessence; and, if so, I sha'n't be sorry to have come.

Meanwhile the flagons of Greek wine came from time to time,
and some lines of Ammonius suggest something else; he sends
crustulum quod marsium panem vocant, with an epigram, saying
that nothing more refined or more delicious is to be found
on the tables of the pontiffs, but the eloquence of Erasmus
beats even "marchpane".

"And here—what a University," he growls; "nobody can
be found at any price who can write even moderately well"
(*Ep.* 246). Was it worth while to teach boys? He thought so.
(We must remember they were not then, as in Calverley's
days, "called emphatically men".) It was a highly honourable
task; no better service than to draw the young to Christ
(*Ep.* 237). His pupils were few; but it is worth recalling that
several scholars would have it that William Tyndale was
among them. There were people in the University (so he

"subodorates") who did not like him; there were, both then and later; Scotists then ("Why *should* you waste time, arguing with them?" asks Colet, *Ep.* 230), and later men who banned his Greek Testament. *Nosti τὴν βριταννικὴν ζηλοτυπίαν*, he writes, in his first three months (*Ep.* 250).

If he was hard up when in Cambridge, he always was, in spite of an English pension, worth to-day (in purchasing power) about £200, which should have made up a little for the lack of Fellowships and copyrights, even if it fell short of "the golden mountains of Britain he had pictured" (*Ep.* 266). He was able to go about the country a little, to London, to Canterbury and Walsingham. So we need not, perhaps, take too tragically the story told in one of his last letters from the University (*Ep.* 282):

For some months past it is just the life of a snail in its shell I have been living, shut up in doors, packed away, mugging along (*mussamus*) at my studies. There is great solitude here, most people gone from fear of plague; yet even when they are all here together, still solitude. Expenses are beyond bearing, not a farthing of profit. Take it that I swear to you by everything that is sacred, I have been here five months, no, not five; and I have spent up to sixty nobles, and had *one* from some attending my lectures, *one* and that not without much protesting and declining on my part. I am resolved in these winter months to leave no stone unturned, to throw out my sheet-anchor, as they say. If it turns out well, I shall have a nest of some sort; if not, I am resolved to fly away—I don't know whither. If all else fails, I shall in any case die somewhere. Farewell.

And fly away he did, but he did not die till 1536. It is perhaps of interest to note that, because of the plague, he withdrew at one time to Landbeach, but for want of wine returned to Cambridge—"O brave fellow-soldier of Bacchus!" wrote Ammonius, "who in the supreme peril will not desert your leader!" (*Ep.* 280). Erasmus maintained that the local *cervisia* gave him stone.

So far he was known for his *Adages* (1500), his *Manual of the Christian Soldier* (1503), *The Praise of Folly* (1509)—a scholar, a humourist, a satirist, a Grecian. His years at Cambridge were given to St Jerome and the New Testament. His Greek manuscripts were not those now esteemed, but he was a pioneer. Affinities, hardly accidental, are traced between himself and St Jerome. St Jerome, we are told, was a humanist, but a Christian humanist, whose main object was to put his scholarship at the disposal of the Church: Jerome revised the Latin version of the Bible, Erasmus was the first to publish a printed Greek Testament (1516). (The Complutensian was printed, but not yet published.) Both scholars incurred ill-will for the pains they bestowed on the sacred text. The same sort of contrast is felt between St Jerome and St Augustine as is patent between Erasmus and Luther. All along Erasmus had a keen eye for abuses in the church, and a keen pen to note them; but, when the cataclysm came, he did not like it; and neither Reformers nor anti-Reformers liked him.

Humanists, says Professor Rand in his admirable *Founders of the Middle Ages*, are "always normal", and it is well within our own experience that the mark of an educated man is that he never finally makes up his mind on any matter of first importance. Like Aeneas, when Dido sweeps in passion from him, he is "hesitating and preparing to say many things", *Porro unum est necessarium*—"For or Against"; and Erasmus will not say it—"is afraid to say it", cry some; "cannot constitutionally say it, or honestly", say others. Besides, he is looking at other things. He writes on Paul; and Luther borrows a phrase of his (or part of it)—*Paulus tonat, fulgurat, meras flammas loquitur*. But Luther understands Paul more intimately. Sin meant more to Luther than to Erasmus. Indeed no man can handle St Paul aright who has not battled with sin and who has not lived among worshippers of idols.

The types represented by Erasmus and Luther cannot understand one another; Luther's type sets the other's teeth on edge; the Erasmus type seems always to put side-issues first. "I should not have courage to risk my life for the truth...I am afraid, if tumult befel, I should imitate Peter", wrote Erasmus (Allen, *Ep*. 1218; 5 July 1521). "Erasmus", wrote Luther, "is far from the knowledge of Grace, as one who looks not at the cross, but at peace in all his writings." Peace! and who does not know to-day how useless is talk of peace when a great war is raging undecided?

Yet on the other side, too, they blamed Erasmus. His Greek Testament—the product, in large measure, of his Cambridge years, carried through by the assistance of English friends, whose money, whose ideas, whose friendship supported him—was disliked; Ignatius Loyola looked into it but complained that it spoiled his devotional emotions. It was also the text which Luther and Tyndale translated into German and English, versions which shaped nations. Erasmus' Greek Testament overturned for ever (despite councils of the church) the authority of the Latin Vulgate; and he meant it to do this. And he meant it to be translated into the "vulgar tongues".

I wish [he wrote of Gospels and Epistles] that they should be translated into all languages of all peoples, that they might be read and known, not merely by the Scots and the Irish, but even by Turks and Saracens. I wish that the husbandman may sing bits of them at his plough; that the weaver may hum them to the tune of his shuttle; that the wayfarer may with their narratives beguile the weariness of the way.

Perhaps he had a passage of Clement of Alexandria (*Protrepticus*, 100) in mind when he wrote this; perhaps, too, in his most famous sentence about the boy at the plough, Tyndale was recalling Erasmus' words. It is the succession of the saints.

Erasmus or Luther? The battle still goes on acridly as ever; the biographers bite their thumbs at one another, and write to annoy; the antithesis is never resolved; but "Wisdom is justified of all her children".

INDEX